DYNAMIC STOCK MARKET ANALYSIS WITH DOW JONES MARKET ANALYZER PLUS ™

DYNAMIC STOCK MARKET ANALYSIS WITH DOW JONES MARKET ANALYZER PLUS ™

William J. Corney

DOW JONES-IRWIN
Homewood, Illinois   60430

ISBN 0-87094-741-9

Library of Congress Catalog Card No. 86–70513

Printed in the United States of America

1 2 3 4 5 6 7 8 9 0 K 3 2 1 0 9 8 7 6

The purpose of this book is to present computerized techniques and strategies as an aid to investment decision making. The book does not promise pat answers but does provide ideas that will allow you to find your own answers. While the book makes use of sophisticated computer software and an online financial database, the reader does not have to be a computer programmer or a financial analyst to understand or to use it.

Investors contemplating the purchase of a personal computer system to aid in investment decision making will find this book useful for showing what a technical analysis software system and an information utility can do. For those investors already possessing a computer with communications capabilities and a technical stock analysis software package, this book can be put to immediate use.

The Dow Jones Market Analyzer PLUS™ and the Dow Jones News/Retrieval® financial databases are used throughout the book as the major illustrative vehicles to support the techniques and strategies presented. Standard & Poor's STOCKPAK II™ software is also used as a specialized illustrative agent for fundamental screening. Discussions of the techniques and strategies are kept as "generic" as possible, making the book useful to readers possessing a wide variety of investment software packages.

The book is divided into three parts: Introduction, Techniques, and Strategies. The introductory section discusses hardware and software requirements and presents an overview of capabilities and alternatives. The techniques section provides explanations and examples of analytical methods. The section on strategies combines the techniques explained in the previous section with online database information and applies the techniques to specific plans for investing. The techniques and strategies sections of the book are presented under the assumption that the readers have a basic working knowledge of their computer system and their technical analysis software package.

Playing the stock market is one of the most exciting activities the common man can indulge in. I hope this book will increase your pleasure by expanding your horizons while leading you toward higher annual returns from your stock market investments.

William J. Corney

CONTENTS

PART ONE

Introduction

This first section of the book provides material for readers who need information about microcomputer hardware and investment software. Chapter One provides a rationale for the use of computerized investment systems, describes the hardware components of a typical setup, and outlines important factors to consider when selecting hardware and software. The second chapter discusses types and features of investment software and information utilities. Examples are provided to show the capabilities of these investment tools.

Readers who already have a microcomputer system and relevant investment software can skip this section and proceed directly to Part Two of the book.

CHAPTER ONE

Getting Started

While most investors rank financial success as one of their most important goals, they often pursue this goal in a haphazard fashion. Few have taken the time to develop an overall plan backed by strategies that will lead them toward their objectives. Instead, they frequently make investment decisions on a piecemeal basis, without the use of consistently applied techniques.

Part of the blame for this approach to investing lies with our traditional financial information and sales system. Most information and advice that lead to investment decisions come in a predigested form from broker-salesmen, newspapers, magazines, or newsletters. This approach encourages decision making on a reactive and impulse basis. Decisions are unplanned and not necessarily part of a coherent or consistent structure that supports long-term goals. The investor assumes the role of the dependent, with "experts" giving tips on what and when to buy.

HOW A COMPUTER CAN HELP

Personal computers allow the investor to become part of the process, instead of being on the outside looking in. The system described in this book provides the means for accessing, manipulating, and analyzing a vast storehouse of financial information with a personal computer.

You will find that a computer-based information system provides more than answers; it provides an education as well.

You will learn in the best possible way: by doing. The computer also aids in structuring thought processes about investing. It will help you both develop a system for investment and establish the discipline to carry it out.

If you are a seasoned market participant with a well-defined investment strategy, the computer will save you time. This means that not only will you finish your normal tasks faster, but you will have the time to tackle the jobs that you have not previously attempted because they were too complex or took too long.

COMPONENTS OF A COMPUTER SYSTEM

You should begin to think of a computer as an entire system, not just the machine itself. Parts of a computer system can be classified into two general categories: hardware and software. The hardware category includes the physical devices that make up the equipment; software refers to the programs and data that run on the hardware. Exhibit 1.1 shows a typical hardware configuration to support investment analysis.

The system unit is the device that contains the small microchips and circuitry that form the computer itself. The unit also contains the diskette drives. Just as a record player takes information from plastic record disks, diskette drives take information from magnetic disks. (Actually, the drives act more like a tape recorder than a record player, since they are also capable of recording information.) The exhibit shows a standard two-drive configuration; the lower drive is used for the program; and the upper drive, for the data.

The display unit is a television-type tube used to provide an instantaneous visual outlet for both text and graphics. In a majority of computer applications, output is first displayed on this unit. Information that may be needed again can be transferred to the disk or printer for permanent storage.

The dot matrix printer forms characters or graphs by overlapping many small dots. Major differences among these printing devices include variations in speed, quality of character formation, noise level, size, and reliability.

The modem is the device that allows the computer to use the telephone lines to transmit data. The modem actually has

---

EXHIBIT 1.1   A Typical Hardware Configuration for Stock Market
Analysis

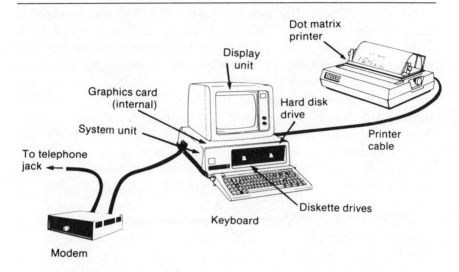

two functions. It converts computer output into a form that the
telephone lines can transmit, and it converts the input coming
back to the computer along the telephone lines into a form that
the computer can understand. Modems differ in their transmission speeds (300, 1200, and 2400 baud rates), their automatic
features (e.g., automatic dial capabilities), and their reliability.
As an option in many computers, the modem can be housed inside the system unit.

Another optional feature that is becoming more common is
the hard disk drive. With this device, considerably more data
can be stored without the burden of switching floppy disks, and
programs can be executed more rapidly.

PURCHASING COMPUTER HARDWARE

If you are thinking about purchasing a system to support your
investment analysis, what should you look for? The following
questions and comments may be of help.

Are You Considering an IBM or an IBM-Compatible System?

Like it or not, the IBM system is now the de facto standard of the industry. Almost all financial analysis software will run on IBM personal computers, and many have versions that will run on some Apple machines. For other noncompatibles, the choice of investment software is limited.

If you are contemplating an IBM compatible, you must make sure that it will run the software that you plan to buy. Just because the computer is said to be IBM compatible does not guarantee that it will run all software written for the IBM. Some IBM compatibles, for example, will not display graphics. The only sure way to know the degree of compatibility is to try it out.

The company making the compatible machine must also be assessed. What after-the-sale support does the company provide? Is the company likely to be in business next year? If the compatible is being purchased based only on its lower cost in comparison to the real thing, is the price differential great enough to cover the additional risks?

What Are the Expansion Capabilities of the Computer?

For people who buy a new computer each year, expansion capabilities are not important. However, if you plan to keep your computer for a while, you should find out if it can be adapted to new hardware developments or software requirements. Memory expansion is one important factor you should consider. General expandability in terms of the number of available expansion slots is another factor you should examine.

Would a Desktop, Transportable, or Portable Computer Be More Useful?

Some computer users who buy transportable or portable computers put them on their desks and rarely move them. For the unused portability option, they pay the price of squinting at a small or hard-to-read screen, and they may give up other useful features. Others buy full-size computers only to wish that they could move them back and forth between work and home. Computer users should very seriously consider their need or lack of need for portability before making a computer purchase commitment. This consideration should include peripheral equipment, such as printers, modems, and extra disk drives.

What Discounts Are Available for the Hardware Components?

With the fierce competition in the computer industry, almost no one pays the suggested retail price for personal computers and related equipment. Most computer stores provide discounts from the retail price, and many companies have discount programs for their employees. Moreover, if you know what you want, you may be able to obtain it from reliable mail-order firms that provide substantial price reductions. *Byte* magazine and personal references can lead you to other alternative sources for these price discounts.

PURCHASING INVESTMENT SOFTWARE

The current edition of *The Individual Investor's Microcomputer Resource Guide* (American Association of Individual Investors, Chicago, Ill., 1985) lists as currently available for purchase 54 technical analysis software packages, 11 fundamental analysis packages, 41 portfolio managers, and dozens of other software products that support specialized investment objectives. With all this software available, how can you decide which one to buy? The following comments may be helpful.

What Are Your Objectives?

In deciding on a software product you should first develop your own objectives for what the computerized investment system is to accomplish. If you want simply to chart securities, a single-function charting software package will fulfill your needs. If you want to chart and also analyze historical price and volume data, you will need technical analysis software. If you want to screen a number of stocks on fundamental factors, such as

earnings per share and dividend yield, you should have fundamental screening software. If record-keeping is a concern, you
will need portfolio management software. If you want only to
use your computer to obtain online business and investment information, you will require only a subscription to a computerized financial database retrieval service.

If you are not sure what you want to do with your system,
Part Three of this book will be helpful. This section shows
which investment software techniques and functions are required to support common investment strategies. The strategies presented include mutual fund switching, high-probability
(fundamental factor) investing, trend and cycle investing, and
stock investing in currently unattractive stocks.

As a general rule, you should consider buying a software
product that exceeds what you think are your minimum requirements. Novices in the computerized investment area often
make the mistake of buying a package with limited capability
(for example, point- and figure-charting software) then discover
that they want additional tasks (perhaps bar charting with
moving-average analysis). As time passes and you gain further
experience, you may want additional computerized functions.
But you should avoid making individual purchases to support
each new function, since a number of separate programs will
likely require different keystroke commands and may not be
able to share the same data.

Working with four or five different programs can be so cum-
bersome that you may decide to give up on the whole process or
to abandon the collection of distinct programs and repurchase
certain functions as part of an integrated system. Moreover,
the total cost of purchasing individual programs often sums to
more than the cost of buying an integrated financial software
program in the first place. The general rule is this: Unless you
are absolutely sure that you want to accomplish only a few specialized tasks with your system, think in terms of purchasing
software packages that integrate numerous techniques and
functions in the general area of your interest.

Have You Actually Used the Software?

Try the software out before you buy it. Once you have decided
on the type of software that you are interested in, you will

want to select for further consideration several products that purport to meet your requirements. Chapter Two of this book will supply you with some major alternatives for these products, and Appendix 2A provides a list of software packages that support one or more of the strategies discussed in this book. Other sources for alternatives include the previously mentioned annual publication, *The Individual Investor's Microcomputer Resource Guide,* and several financial magazines and newspapers.

Once you have selected alternatives, you should make a hands-on comparison to determine which software package or packages best suit your needs. Major software products have demonstration disks that you can purchase for a nominal fee (usually $10 or less); these demos offer an excellent way for you to become familiar with the product before you make a full commitment. You may also be able to attend seminars that discuss, compare, and allow you to try out various investment software packages. Moreover, the seminars provide you the opportunity to look over the documentation that comes with the software. This can be important, since the quality of user's manuals varies widely, ranging from excellent to unbelievably poor. As a final option, you can rent some investment software packages, and part of the rental price can be applied toward a later purchase.

Whatever prepurchase approach you take, it is important that you actually try out the package before buying. It is the surest way to avoid getting stuck with a product that doesn't quite meet your needs or that is too difficult for you to use.

What Level of Continuing Support Can Be Expected?

Company support is extremely important. If you have problems setting up or understanding the system (you probably will), is there an easy way to get help? Does the organization have a history of revising and improving its software? The software business is an extremely competitive one. Like hardware manufacturers, many software companies can be expected to experience financial difficulties and some may cease operations. What faith do you have in the future of the organization from which the product was purchased?

What Databases Are Used with the Software?

Just as a camera is useless without film, financial software is useless without data to run it on. In most cases, you can enter data manually, or you can obtain it from a financial database, either by online transmission or from disks mailed to you. It is important that you know how recent is the available data and whether it is provided daily or weekly. If a historical data set is available, the extent of past data is an obvious concern, along with the number and type of securities available for historical retrieval. The cost of the data is another important issue. Most online databases charge by actual time of usage, and some have a monthly or yearly minimum charge. It is also important that you be aware that some software is sold at a very low initial price, with later maintenance and data retrieval charges that push the total usage costs far higher than first appearances would indicate.

Unfortunately, there is not a universal format for financial data used in computer software. This means that software that can access data from Dow Jones News/Retrieval®, for example, will not work with other databases like CompuServe® or Warner, unless a conversion program either is built into the software or is externally available.

OTHER NECESSITIES

Before making use of investment software you will need both a working knowledge of your computer system and a basic understanding of the stock market. Your computer user's manual should provide the necessary basic information on computer usage. Through reading, you can quickly obtain background knowledge of the stock market. Working with investment analysis software over time will rapidly advance your sophistication. For novices in the market, I would recommend *Understanding Wall Street* by Jeffrey B. Little and Lucien Rhodes (Liberty Publishing, 1980). For those beyond the novice level, the excellent book, *Stock Market Logic* by Norman D. Fosback, is a must (Institute of Econometric Research, 1985). An encyclopedic overview of technical analysis can be obtained from *Technical Analysis Explained,* (2nd ed., by Martin J. Pring,

McGraw-Hill, 1985). Other important sources that relate to specific topics discussed in this book are listed at the end of each chapter.

THE SOFTWARE–HARDWARE CONFIGURATION USED IN THIS BOOK

Stock market techniques and strategies discussed in this book are illustrated using the Dow Jones Market Analyzer PLUS™ for technical analysis; The Dow Jones News/Retrieval databases for supplying price, volume, and fundamental data; and Standard & Poor's STOCKPAK II™ software system for fundamental screening. An IBM PC was used to run the programs, with a 1200 baud Hayes modem for communications and an Epson MX-100 dot matrix printer to create all graphical exhibits.

This software-hardware configuration, while typical of what a serious individual investor might use, is not the only one capable of producing the results discussed in the book. Chapter Two will discuss some of the more important alternatives that relate to the techniques and strategies discussed. Hopefully, investors with a wide variety of computer-based configurations will find this book useful.

Alternatives and Capabilities

There are two distinct approaches to analysis in the stock market. *Technical analysis* is the study of supply and demand for stocks, primarily through the study of changes in price and volume. *Fundamental analysis* is the study of factors related to stock value, including such measures as profits, sales, dividends, inflation, and interest rates. It has been said that fundamental analysis can best answer the question of *what* to buy and sell, while technical analysis can best indicate *when* to buy and sell.

Accomplishing a comprehensive technical analysis requires a considerable amount of mathematical manipulation on relatively limited types of data (in most cases, just price and volume). Fundamental analysis, on the other hand, typically involves using a few, simple mathematical techniques on a large and comprehensive set of financial data.

The makeup of software used to accomplish technical and fundamental analysis reflects these basic differences. Technical analysis software is technique oriented, with its programs processing numerous individual formulas and methodologies, each of which provides insight into a stock's current status. Fundamental analysis software, on the other hand, is oriented to the data instead of to the techniques. It offers easy access to a vast storehouse of important fundamental data and provides a search mechanism for finding stocks that satisfy desired fundamental criteria.

TECHNICAL ANALYSIS SOFTWARE

To make a comprehensive technical analysis, computer software must support techniques that can assess trends, determine the importance of cycles, measure the relative performance of stocks and indexes, make an analysis of volume, and determine support and resistance levels.

Accomplishing these tasks requires a basic set of techniques which include; (1) price and volume charts; (2) moving averages which can be both varied in length and offset; (3) trendlines; (4) price, volume, and moving-average oscillators; (5) relative-strength charts; (6) price-volume relationship charts; and (7) support and resistance lines. Moreover, the software must have access to current price and volume data for a wide range of securities.

Many software packages that perform graphing and that provide a comprehensive technical analysis have a similar basic core of techniques. These techniques are the focus of Part Two of this book. Specific software packages will differ in terms of numbers and types of technical indicators, ease of use, automatic functions, keystroke patterns, types of data used for analysis, special features, and cost.

Exhibit 2.1 compares a number of popular technical software packages and shows how they relate to the techniques discussed in this book. The exhibit is not exhaustive, but it provides a representative sample of the more popular technical software packages that support a wide range of technical functions. Appendix 2A provides a more comprehensive listing of both IBM and Apple software products that purport to be useful in technical analysis. Many of these provide limited analytical capability or limited support of specialized technical functions. You can obtain specifics on these packages from the addresses provided in the exhibit. Your choice of a specific software package, of course, will depend on your objectives and requirements.

FUNDAMENTAL ANALYSIS SOFTWARE

The major functions of fundamental analysis software are to provide access to a wide range of timely and accurate data and to perform user-selected screening of the available information.

EXHIBIT 2.1 Comparisons of Popular Technical Software Packages

Chapter and Topic	Major Techniques Discussed and Illustrated in this Book with the Dow Jones Market Analyzer Plus	N-Squared Stock Analyzer (N-Squared Computing)	The Technical Investor (Savant Corp.)	Telescan Analyzer (Telescan, Inc.)	Trendline II (Standard & Poor's)	Wall Street Window (R&D Software)	Winning on Wall Street (Summa Software)
Chapter Three: Trends and trend reversals	Simple moving average	x	x	x	x	x	x
	Weighted moving average	—	x	—	x	x	x
	Exponential moving average	x	x	x	x	x	x
	User-defined oscillators	x	x	x	x	x	x
	Technical factor screening	—	—	—	—	—	—
	Trendlines	x	x	x	x	x	x
	Regression	x	x	—	—	—	x
	Range volatility	—	—	—	—	—	—
	Directional movement indicators	—	—	—	—	—	—
Chapter Four: Cycle analysis	Simple moving averages	x	x	On-screen sine wave for cycle analysis	x	x	x
	Moving average trading bands	x	x		x	x	x
	Centered moving averages	x	x		x	x	x
Chapter Five: Relative performance	Relative strength charting	x	x	x	x	x	x
	Custom index creation	—	—	—	—	—	—
	RSI	x	x	—	—	—	—
	Relative strength filtering	—	—	—	—	—	—
	Comparison charting	x	x	—	x	x	x

Feature						
Chapter Six:						
Volume						
Volume bar charting	x	x	x	x	x	x
Volume filtering	—	—	—	—	—	—
Negative volume	—	x	—	x	x	x
Positive volume	x	x	—	x	x	x
On-balance volume	—	x	x	x	x	x
Price-volume trend	x	x	—	x	x	—
Accumulation/Distribution indicator	—	x	—	x	—	x
Daily volume indicator	x	x	—	—	x	x
Chapter Seven:						
Support, resistance, and price patterns						
Speed resistance lines	x	x	x	x	x	x
Horizontal lines	x	x	—	—	x	x
Point and figure charting	x	x	—	—	—	x
Other Features						
Semilog charts	x	(Spreadsheet)	x	x	x	—
Portfolio management	(Spreadsheet)	x	—	—	x	x
Link to spreadsheet	x	x	—	—	—	—
Autorun feature	x	x	—	x	x	x
Special features	Considerable user flexibility	Integrated with other products	Graphs of fundamental data	Scrolling up to four years of data	Outstanding graphics	Strategy optimization
Major databases	Dow Jones / Warner / CompuServe / Manual	Dow Jones / Warner / Hale / Manual	Limited to the Telescan database	Warner / Manual	Dow Jones / Warner / Dataspeed / Manual	Dow Jones / Hale / Manual

Data for this exhibit was obtained from sources believed to be reliable. Because software is continually being revised, it is essential to obtain current information before making a purchase decision.

Screening refers to the process of searching through a large group of data to find a subset that has desired attributes. As an example, a group of airline industry stocks could be searched to find all of those which have price to earnings ratios of 14 to 1 or less *and* which show at least a 10 percent increase in sales from the previous year.

The objective of the fundamental screening effort is to answer the question, "What specific stocks, from a large set of stocks, should I consider buying (or selling)?" Four popular software packages for handling the tasks of fundamental analysis are STOCKPAK II, Micro PMS, the Dow Jones Market Microscope™, and Value/Screen.

STOCKPAK II

STOCKPAK II (Standard & Poor's Corporation, 25 Broadway, New York, N.Y. 10004) provides fundamental data and allows screening on up to 4,500 stocks. Ninety-one data items are provided for each stock and are coded on four floppy disks. The disks are updated and sent out monthly on a subscription basis. The user has the option of receiving data for New York Stock Exchange (NYSE) issues, American Stock Exchange (ASE) issues, over-the-counter (OTC) stocks, all issues, or a composite of assorted stocks from all three markets. Both IBM and Apple computers are supported. This system provides the most comprehensive screening analysis currently available to the individual investor for use on a personal computer. It is used as the illustrative vehicle for screening in Chapter Ten of this book.

Micro PMS

Micro PMS (The Boston Company, 1 Boston Place, Boston, Mass. 02106) offers the ability to screen up to 2,000 stocks using IBM hardware. Fifty fundamental data indicators are provided for each stock on diskettes updated monthly. The program also provides portfolio management and price charting.

Dow Jones Market Microscope

Market Microscope (Dow Jones & Company, Inc., Box 300, Princeton, N.J. 08540) accesses data and permits screening for up to 3,150 companies and 170 industry groups. Data are obtained from the Dow Jones News/Retrieval online databases for the stocks of interest. Both IBM and Apple systems are supported. Because data on stocks to be screened are not obtained from diskettes but must be selectively downloaded, this program finds primary application in screening among a prechosen group of stocks (for example, automobile manufacturers) instead of from a large universe of securities.

Value/Screen

Value/Screen (Value Line, Inc., 711 Third Avenue, New York, N.Y. 10017) provides screening capability on up to 1,650 stocks with data available on diskettes by monthly or quarterly subscription. Thirty-two indicators are provided for the stocks, including the popular Value Line stock rankings. IBM and Apple are supported.

DATABASES

As we have seen, computerized databases exist in both online and diskette form. Because of data incompatibility between many software programs, the databases you use will depend on the software you have purchased. Exhibit 2.1 indicates which databases are accessible for data manipulation by the software packages presented. As the exhibit shows, manual data entry is also possible for most software.

The online financial information service used in this book is Dow Jones News/Retrieval (P.O. Box 300, Princeton, N.J. 08540). This database can be accessed automatically by the Dow Jones Market Analyzer PLUS program to provide price and volume updates and a wide range of other information useful to an investor. A summary of the available financial information from Dow Jones News/Retrieval is shown in Exhibit 2.2.

The exhibit indicates a wealth of information that goes beyond price, volume, and raw fundamental data. The information available through the service is accessible by any computer with communications capabilities and a password from Dow Jones & Company, Inc.

The Warner Computer Services databases (Warner Computer Services, Inc., 605 Third Avenue, New York, N.Y. 10158)

EXHIBIT 2.2 Dow Jones News/Retrieval Financial Databases

THE DATABASES

BUSINESS AND INVESTOR SERVICES

//CQE	**Enhanced Current Quotes** • Delayed quotes on common and preferred stocks and bonds, mutual funds, options and U.S. Treasury issues • Quotes feature a news alert identifying companies on which current-day news has run on the Dow Jones News Service
//DJA	**Historical Dow Jones Averages** • Daily high, low, close and volume for the last trading year • Historical data for industrials, transportation, utilities and 64 stock composites • By specific date or 12-day period
//FUTURES	**Dow Jones Futures Quotes** • Commodity quotes from the major North American exchanges • Delayed prices on more than 80 commodities • Includes daily open, high, low, last and settlement price; lifetime high and low; volume and open interest and current-day ticks
//HQ	**Dow Jones Historical Quotes** • Daily volume, high, low and close for stock quotes and composites • Monthly summaries to 1979 • Quarterly summaries to 1978
//RTQ	**Real-Time Quotes** • Quotes with no delay for stocks trading on the New York, American, Pacific and Midwest stock exchanges • Features a news alert to identify companies on which news has run for the current day on the Dow Jones News Service
//TRACK	**Dow Jones Tracking Service** • Create and track up to 5 profiles of as many as 25 companies each • Quotes feature a news alert identifying companies on which current-day news has run on the Dow Jones News Service
//DJNEWS	**Dow Jones News** • News from The Wall Street Journal, Barron's and the Dow Jones News Service (the Broadtape) • Stories 90 seconds to 90 days old
//TEXT	**Text-Search: The Dow Jones News Archive** • Selected articles from The Wall Street Journal, Barron's and Dow Jones News Service (the Broadtape) as they appeared in the Dow Jones News database • Search back to June 1979 using special commands combining words, dates and symbols
//TEXT	**Text-Search: The Wall Street Journal** • Every news article that has appeared or has been scheduled for publication in The Wall Street Journal since January 1984 • Online publication of The Journal at 6 a.m. every business day
//TEXT	**Text-Search: The Washington Post Online** • Every news article from the daily and Sunday editions of the Washington Post since January 1984 • New editions available approximately 48 hours after print publication
//UPDATE	**Weekly Economic Update** • A review of the week's top economic events and a glimpse of the month ahead • Analysis of the week's top economic news

//WSJ	**The Wall Street Journal Highlights Online** • Headlines and summaries of major stories • Includes front-page news, front- and back-page features, market pages, editorial columns and commentary
//DEFINE	**The Words of Wall Street** • A comprehensive lexicon of investment terminology • More than 2,000 words and phrases defined
//DSCLO	**Disclosure II** • 10-K extracts, company profiles and detailed data on more than 10,000 companies • From SEC filings • Includes detailed stock ownership information, quarterly balance sheets and financial ratios
//EARN	**Corporate Earnings Estimator** • Latest earnings-per-share forecasts by top Wall Street analysts • Covers 3,000 widely followed companies
//INVEST	**Investext** • Full texts of company and industry research reports from leading American and Canadian investment banking firms • Current, forecasted and historical marketing and financial information • More than 13,000 reports released over the last year on more than 3,000 companies and 50 industries
//KYODO	**Japan Economic Daily** • Same-day coverage of major business, economic and political news from Japan • Includes daily Japanese financial market wrap-up
//MEDGEN	**Media General Financial Services** • Detailed corporate financial information on 4,300 companies and 180 industries • Major categories include revenue, earnings, dividends, volume, ratios and price changes
//MMS	**Economic and Foreign Exchange Survey** • Weekly survey of economists and money market dealers at 50 leading financial institutions in the U.S. • Includes median forecasts of domestic monetary and economic indicators • Weekly consensus analysis and forecasts of foreign exchange rates by 30 foreign-exchange dealers
//SP	**Standard & Poor's Online** • Financial profiles of more than 4,600 companies • Major categories include financial overview, projected earnings, dividends and company operations
//WSW	**Wall $treet Week Online** • Transcripts of the Wall Street Week television program hosted by Louis Rukeyser • Four most recent programs available
//FIDELITY	**Fidelity Investor's Express** • Electronic brokerage service • Orders for stocks and options placed online • Portfolio management and recordkeeping • Message service to Fidelity

are a useful supplement to the Dow Jones News/Retrieval service. While the Dow Jones database provides daily historical data that extend back one year, the Warner database provides data extending back as far as 10 years. The Warner service also provides historical pricing information on mutual funds and specialized stock indexes. At the time of the writing of this book, an inexpensive Warner connector program disk was being prepared by Warner Computer Services for use by owners of the Dow Jones Market Analyzer PLUS and other software packages that read the RTR (Market Analyzer PLUS) format. This will enable historical data to be downloaded directly to a data disk in the format necessary for use by these software packages.

Some other popular computerized financial database services include The Source (1616 Anderson Road, McLean, Va. 22102), CompuServe (5000 Arlington Centre Boulevard, Columbus, Ohio 43220), Nightline (1929 N. Harlem Avenue, Chicago, Ill. 60635), and Hale Systems (1044 Northern Boulevard, Roslyn, N.Y. 11576). A comprehensive listing of computerized database services is presented in *The Individual Investor's Microcomputer Resource Guide.* The *Dow Jones-Irwin Guide to Online Investing* (Dow Jones-Irwin, Homewood, Ill., 1986) is a useful source for detailed information on major database services.

ADDITIONAL SOFTWARE

Economic and General Market Analysis Software

Several available software products are dedicated to the analysis of economic and general market data. The N-Squared Market Analyzer™ (5318 Forest Ridge Road, Silverton, Oreg. 97318), for example, is designed to manipulate and graphically display economic and general-market data that can be used for predicting the stock market. The database consists of Barron's Market Laboratory data along with an economic-indicators database containing over 130 items pertaining to employment, production, consumption, capital investment, prices, money and credit, inventories, personal income, national income, price movements, labor, defense, foreign stock market composites, and others.

The Technician (Computer Asset Management, P.O. Box 26743, Salt Lake City, Utah 84126) is another technical analysis program dedicated to forecasting the market as a whole. It utilizes an online database with over 70 market and economic indicators, such as the T-bill rate, short interest data, and odd-lot information.

Spreadsheet Software

In addition to the specialized investment software, mentioned previously, you can also use generalized spreadsheet software to provide a valuable supplementary aid. You can use a spreadsheet to support a wide variety of customized applications, without having knowledge of computer programming.

You can get an idea of what a spreadsheet is if you visualize a blackboard that has many horizontal and vertical lines drawn on it. Assume the horizontal lines form rows marked 1 through 20, and the vertical lines form columns marked A through Z. The blackboard divided into such columns and rows would represent a large matrix of boxes, with each box having a unique address (for example, column E, row 12). Each box can contain information, such as letters, numbers, mathematical symbols, or formulas.

A spreadsheet program in a computer has the same type of structure, with the user deciding what the computerized boxes should contain. Once the matrix structure is set up, the computer can rapidly fill the appropriate boxes with data and make

---

EXHIBIT 2.3 Spreadsheet Example

READY

	A STOCK	B V-LAST	C V-BID	D SHARES	E CURRENT VALUE	F PURCHASE PRICE	G CHANGE	H % CHANGE
1								
2								
3								
4	---
5	V-TAN	65	63	400	26,000	14,000	12,000	85.71%
6	V-IBM	110	109	200	22,000	16,600	5,400	32.53%
7	V-AHP	50	50	500	25,000	11,000	14,000	127.27%
8	V-GE	105	105	100	10,500	10,000	500	5.00%
9	V-DJ	60	58	700	42,000	20,000	22,000	110.00%
10								
11								
12								
13	TOTAL				125,500	71,600	53,900	75.28%
14								
15								
16								
17								
18								
19								
20								

manipulations as prescribed by the user. Exhibit 2.3 provides an example of output from this extremely flexible software.

Many spreadsheet software products exist, including Lotus 1–2–3®, SuperCalc3, Multiplan, and CalcStar.® Common investment applications for spreadsheets include portfolio management and composite-index construction. Exhibit 2.1 indicates which of the technical software packages allow data to be converted into a form for use in spreadsheets.

APPENDIX 2A: TECHNICAL ANALYSIS SOFTWARE (IBM, APPLE, AND COMPATIBLES)

Software Name	Source
Active Investor Series (IBM)	Interactive Data Corp. 486 Totten Pond Rd. Waltham, Mass. 02254-9113

A comprehensive set of programs combining technical price-volume tools with fundamental analysis and portfolio management.

Advanced Chart Trader Plus (IBM, Apple)	Investor's Toolkit, Ltd. 7441 W. Archer Avenue Summit, Ill. 60501

A technical program with some hard-to-find indicators, including fibonacci projections,a swing wave day counter, and Gann's square of nine, along with numerous other, more common techniques.

Auto Trader II (IBM)	AVINCO Corporation P.O. Box 189 Sharpsburg, Md. 21782

Price charting, moving averages, file maintenance.

Compu-Trac (IBM, Apple)	Compu-Track 1021 9th Street New Orleans, La. 70115

Comprehensive technical analysis software featuring major indicators and techniques.

Computer Investor Software Series (Apple)	Microcomputing Research 29 Estancia Marana, Ariz. 85238

A portfolio-based series of integrated programs that create bar graphs and allow some basic technical analysis on the data.

DSG/Insight (IBM)	Decision Support Group 66 Pearl Street, 207 New York, N.Y. 10004

An integrated technical analysis package featuring easy data manipulation to support a variety of user-specified indicators.

Forecast Plus (IBM)	Walonick Associates 5624 Girard Ave., South Minneapolis, Minn. 55419

A sophisticated forecasting package using moving averages and numerous statistical techniques.

Fundgraf (IBM)	Parson's Software 118 Woodshire Drive Parkersburg, W.V. 26101

Creates graphs with moving averages for generating buy and sell signals and makes selected numeric comparisons.

High-Tech	MicroVest
(IBM, Apple)	P.O. Box 272
	Macomb, Il. 61455

A comprehensive technical analysis package offering major tools, graphically displayed.

M.A.G.I.C.	$Ware Tools for Investors
(IBM, Apple)	P.O. Box 645
	San Luis Rey, Calif. 92068

A software package that specializes in moving average and moving-average oscillator constructions and their relation to buy and sell strategies.

Market Analyst	Anidata
(IBM, Apple)	7200 Westfield Ave.
	Pennsauken, N.J. 08100

A fully integrated system of technical analysis and portfolio management. Many graphically displayed technical indicators are supported.

Market Analyzer PLUS	Dow Jones & Company, Inc.
(IBM)	P.O. Box 300
	Princeton, N.J. 08540

This book uses the Market Analyzer PLUS to illustrate the techniques and strategies presented.

Market Charter II	RTR Software, Inc.
(Apple)	444 Executive Center Blvd., Suite 225
	El Paso, Tex. 79902

Created by the same organization that developed the Market Analyzer Plus, this package has many of the basic functions of technical analysis.

Market Eas-alyzer	Wall Street Graphics
(Apple)	P.O. Box 562
	Wall Street Station
	New York, N.Y. 10268

A comprehensive technical analysis software package encompassing charting, numerous technical indicators, and data maintenance.

Market Illustrator	N-Squared Computing
(Apple)	5318 Forest Ridge Rd.
	Silverton, Oreg. 97381

A charting program that also permits the use of basic technical indicators.

Profit Stalker II	Button Down Software
(Apple)	P.O. Box 19493
	San Diego, Calif. 92119

An analysis package for the Apple Macintosh that charts and has most all the major tools of technical analysis.

Stock Analyzer	N-Squared Computing
(IBM, Apple)	5318 Forest Ridge Rd.
	Silverton, Oreg. 97381

See Exhibit 2.1

StockChart II
(IBM)

Micro Investment Software
9621 Bowie Way
Stockton, Calif. 95203

This software performs a wide range of technical analysis including charting, moving averages, volume analysis, and trendlines.

Stock Charting
(IBM)

Diamond Head Software
841 Bishop St., Suite 1618
Honolulu, Hawaii 96813

Price, volume, and moving-average charting.

Stockcraft
(Apple)

Decision Economics
14 Old Farm Road
Cedar Knolls, N.J. 07927

An integrated package consisting of technical analysis, portfolio management, and trading optimization. Moving averages are generated and are used as the basis for buy and sell signals.

Stock-Folio
(Apple)

Micro Program Designs
5440 Crestline Road
Wilmington, Del. 19808

Software to aid in portfolio management and to create moving averages and relative strength calculations.

Stock Momentum Studies
(Apple)

Troy-Folan Productions
29 Miller Road
Wayne, N.J. 07470

A technical analysis package making use of moving averages and related techniques.

Stockplot
(IBM)

Cook Compusystems
309 Lincolnshire
Irving, Tex. 75061

Charting and moving-average average analysis.

Telescan Analyzer
(BM)

Telescan, Inc.
11011 Richmond Ave, Suite 600
Houston, Tex. 77042

See Exhibit 2.1.

The Stox/C
(IBM)

Sydney Development Corporation
600 1385 West 8th Ave.
Vancouver, B.C. Canada V6H 3V9

Price charting, moving averages, and other basic tools of technical analysis.

The Technical Investor
(IBM)

Savant Corporation
P.O. Box 440278
Houston, Tex. 77244

See Exhibit 2.1.

Trendline II
(IBM)

Standard & Poor's Corp.
25 Broadway
New York, N.Y. 10004

See Exhibit 2.1.

Wall Street Plotter
(Apple)

Dickens Data Systems
6065 Atlantic Blvd.
Norcross, Ga. 30071

A price and volume-charting package incorporating moving averages.

Wall Street Techniques
(IBM, Apple)

Smith Micro Software
P.O. Box 7137
Huntington Beach, Calif. 92615

A technical analysis package having most of the standard indicators along with user-defined functions.

Wall Street Window
(IBM)

R&D Software Associates
2210 Burgee Court
Reston, Va. 22090

See Exhibit 2.1.

Window on Wall Street
(IBM)

Bristol Financial Systems
23 Bristol Place
Wilton, Conn. 06897

An integrated system of charting, technical analysis, and portfolio management.

Winning on Wall Street
(IBM, Apple)

Summa Software Corporation
P.O. Box 2046
Beaverton, Oreg. 97075

See Exhibit 2.1.

PART TWO

Techniques

The purpose of this section is to present the major tools of technical stock market analysis. The primary objective of this type of analysis is to provide timing evidence for the purchase and sale of securities. For most of the examples provided, daily stock prices are used for illustrative purposes. Many of the techniques presented here will be applied to other data in later parts of this book.

Developing skills with technical tools is like learning to play the piano. You can read about playing the piano and you can listen to others play, but if you want to become a good piano player you must spend considerable time practicing on your own. The best way to use this part of the book is to quickly read over each chapter, then sit down in front of your keyboard (computer, not piano) and practice. Fortunately, technical analysis is quite easy to master, and before long you will be doing naturally what seemed difficult at first.

The first chapter in this part of the book (Chapter Three), Identifying Trends and Trend Reversals, shows how to define stock price movements and become aware of excesses that may lead to reversals. Chapter Four, Cycle Analysis, demonstrates the techniques that can be used to make sense of time cycles and business-related cycles. Chapter Five, Relative Performance, explains the variety of approaches that can be used to measure the performance of one stock or index against another or against itself over time. Chapter Six, Volume Analysis, shows how volume and price-volume relationships can be used to add to the understanding of price movements. Chapter Seven, Support, Resistance, and Price Patterns, indicates how to set goals for current and future trend movements. It also discusses and illustrates historical chart patterns.

The majority of exhibits in this section will provide the output from the analysis along with the Dow Jones Market Analyzer PLUS keystrokes used to create the output. Readers who have other software that can produce similar results should refer to their user's manual to obtain the proper methodology.

It is important to remember that none of the techniques presented is intended to be used in isolation. It is essential to develop an overall investment strategy and to support that strategy with a complex of techniques and evidence. The objective of Part Three is to accomplish these tasks. Only through a well-defined and comprehensive investment approach can you hope to put the odds for success in your favor.

CHAPTER THREE

Identifying Trends and Trend Reversals

"The trend is your friend," is one of the oldest sayings on Wall Street. When trends persist over time, they give investors a chance to ride with the movement and to prepare themselves for opportunities that come with trend changes.

Exhibit 3.1 shows a daily price history of Chrysler Corporation. If viewed from a short-term perspective, the price appears to be moving up and down rapidly on a day-to-day basis, across the entire time span covered by the chart. Looking at the chart with a longer-term view, the price undergoes a general downward movement followed by a general upward movement. Taking still another look, this time from an intermediate-term perspective, you can see the price history tracing a rather consistent pattern of successive peaks and valleys. Since a trend is simply a price movement in a single direction, each of these three movements can be viewed as tracing price trends on the chart.

If you are a long-term investor, you may dismiss as "noise" those movements that intermediate- and short-term investors see as significant. On the other hand, if you are a short-term trader, your buy-and-sell decision criteria may not incorporate information concerning the long-term trend. Meaningful trend analysis requires a customized approach that supports the time frame and strategy of the individual investor. The computer, with its power of rapid calculation and limitless display of analytical results, can provide the information that supports your exact needs.

EXHIBIT 3.1 Chrysler Corporation Price History

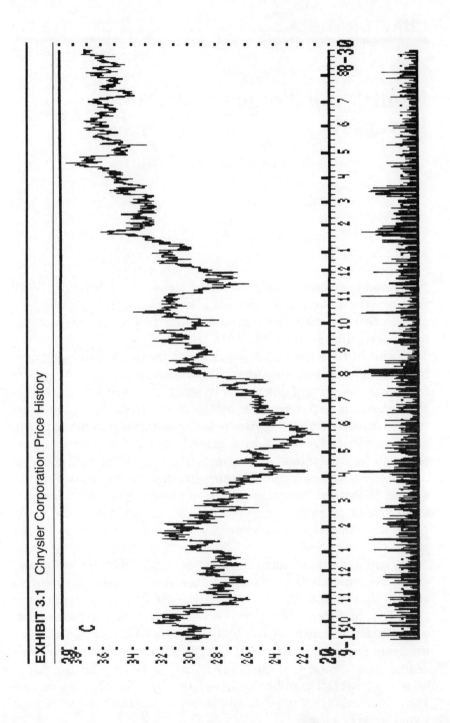

The objectives of trend analysis are to identify the particular movements of interest and to determine changes of direction. While these are difficult tasks, many techniques are available to aid in their accomplishment.

MOVING AVERAGES AND TREND ANALYSIS

Moving averages are mathematical tools that can be used to smooth and decompose fluctuating time series data. Like a wrench that allows a mechanic to take apart a piece of machinery, moving averages can disassemble time series data by suppressing, isolating, and displaying various components of historical prices for further analysis.

At one time, the two greatest drawbacks to using moving averages were excessive calculation time and chance of error. These risks have been eliminated with the use of computers to accomplish with precision and in seconds those tasks that used to require hours of hand calculations. The market analyst is now free to concentrate on the application of moving averages rather than on their construction.

There are three basic types of moving averages: the simple, the weighted, and the exponential. Each moving average type has its own features which make it more (or less) desirable in certain situations. If you are not familiar with moving averages, an overview of their structure and characteristics can be found in many books dealing with technical analysis. The previously mentioned book, *Technical Analysis Explained,* by Martin J. Pring, is a good source.

Many chart services provide moving averages superimposed on their price charts. For all charts presented, simple moving averages of fixed lengths and predetermined leads are typically used. Unfortunately, the moving averages provided may not be appropriate to your data, your investment horizon, or the analysis that you want to make. As we will see, only with a computer and technical market software can you make full use of moving average techniques.

Trend Identification

> *Is the stock in an uptrend or a downtrend?*

To reveal trends, moving averages must remove unwanted fluctuations from data. Exhibit 3.2 shows a 139-day simple moving
average made from the same Chrysler Corporation closing
prices displayed in Exhibit 3.1. Comparing the 139-day moving
average to the price history, you can see that the short-term
rapid movements and the intermediate-term fluctuations have
been eliminated, making the long-term trend clearly visible. In
fact, if the daily price data were not shown, it would appear
that no intermediate- or short-term fluctuations existed at all!

The length of the moving average is critical for revealing
the trend of interest. In general, short-term trends are displayed by moving averages from days to weeks in length,
intermediate-term trends from weeks to months in length, and
long-term trends from months to years in length. While the
best length to use depends on both your objectives and the variability inherent in the data itself, approximations to the short-,
intermediate-, and long-term trends can be made with 12-day,
55-day, and 150-day moving averages.

In choosing the right length, you should understand that
moving averages remove or attenuate all fluctuations within
frequencies shorter than the length of the moving average. To
use a simple moving average as a trend identifier, you first find
the longest peak-to-peak (or bottom-to-bottom) fluctuation that
you view as nonsignificant in terms of your investment horizon
and strategy. The length of the moving average is then set to
this value, thus insuring that all fluctuations less than or
equal to this size will be eliminated or reduced by the moving
average. The trend of importance will then be displayed. Exhibit 3.3 offers an example of how this is accomplished.

Assume that you would like to identify the overall up-and-
down trends of General Motors stock displayed in Exhibit 3.3.
You would like to construct a simple moving average that
would eliminate the day-to-day fluctuations and the intermediate-term movements appearing on the chart. Let's say, for this
example, that the longest peak-to-peak fluctuation that you

EXHIBIT 3.2 Simple Moving Average Trend Identifier

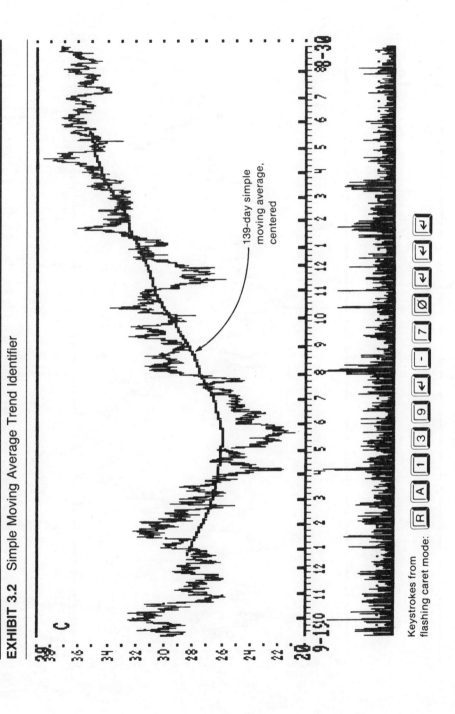

139-day simple
moving average,
centered

Keystrokes from
flashing caret mode:

R A 1 3 9 ↵ - 7 Ø ↵ ↵ ↵

EXHIBIT 3.3 Length Determination of Simple Moving Average

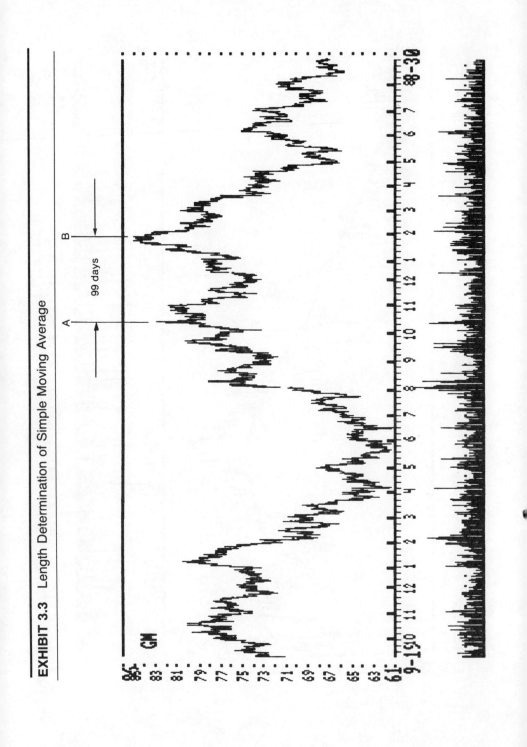

would like ignored by the trend identifier is from Point *A* to Point *B* on the chart. A count reveals 99 trading days between the peaks. Setting a moving average length to this number provides the best fit to your requirements.

Exhibit 3.4 shows a simple moving average of 99 days plotted with the price data. You can see how the fluctuations deemed unimportant are eliminated by the moving average. The high parts of the nonsignificant price movements have been averaged with the low parts, resulting in a moving average that cuts through the center of the longer of these movements and ignores the shorter ones. The desired trend is thereby revealed.

Another method for revealing the trend of interest is to initially create a moving average with an approximate length to fit your needs; then assess the result and, if necessary, adjust the length and try again. For short-term trends, 12 days (the default value on the Dow Jones Market Analyzer PLUS) usually provides a good result. For the intermediate-term trend you can first try a length of 55 days; and for the long-term trend, 150 days. With practice you will become quite proficient at rapidly finding the moving average length that will eliminate the unwanted fluctuations and will display the trend most important to you. Before the advent of the computer and technical analysis software, this approach would have been infeasible because of the calculation time required.

When using weighted or exponential moving averages to display the trend, the trial-and-error method just described is preferred. This is because the front-weighted moving averages give more emphasis to the latest price values, making the counting method ineffective in "canceling" the high and low fluctuations.

In most cases, once you have found an appropriate moving average, it will be usable for a considerable length of time in the future. Occasionally, however, a stock's volatility and frequency of fluctuations may change in a major way. (This can happen, for example, when an OTC stock moves to a major exchange.) When important changes occur, the moving-average length will also need to be changed. By choosing a moving-average length with one of the procedures indicated, you can always find a proper representation of the current trend.

EXHIBIT 3.4 99-Day Trend Identifier for General Motors

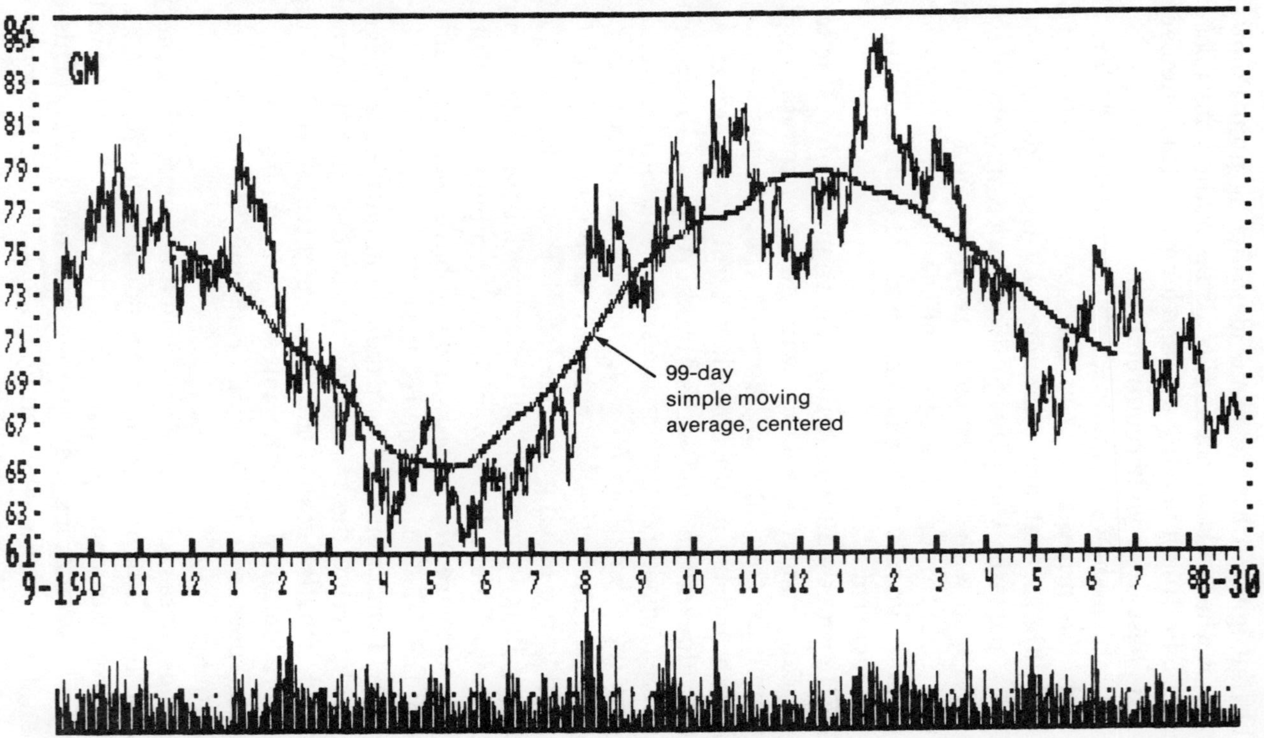

99-day
simple moving
average, centered

GM

Keystrokes from flashing
caret mode to create moving average: R A 9 9 ↵ - 5 ⌀ 9 9 ↵ ↵

Once the appropriate moving average is constructed, the interpretation is straightforward. The direction of the moving average represents the direction of the trend, and the slope of the moving average represents the force (or strength) of the trend.

The charts used up to this point have illustrated simple moving averages. Later examples will show how weighted and exponential moving averages can be used to support specialized objectives.

Moving Averages and Changes in Trend

> *Has the trend changed direction?*

The dream of every investor is to be able to determine the exact tops and the exact bottoms of price movements. A more realistic approach for these investors, however, might be to catch the major part of the important moves for a particular time horizon, instead of trying to capture the entire price rise. (Such an optimistic investor can be compared to the golfer who continually expects a hole in one.) The trend-change identification methods explained here, when combined with other evidence, provide an opportunity to attain the more modest and reasonable objective.

Three moving average techniques that you can use as an aid in determining changes in trend are (1) the moving average crossings approach, (2) the three-step reversal technique, and (3) the percentage change method. As with other price-based techniques discussed in this book, the moving average trend change methods do not predict future price movements; they merely identify the current situation. As we will see, knowing what the present trend is and recognizing when it has changed direction will often benefit the astute investor.

Moving Average Crossings. To use this approach, two moving averages of different lengths are constructed. Trend-change signals are given when the shorter-length moving average crosses above or below the longer one. The longer moving average portrays the trend that you are interested in. The shorter moving average, which acts as a trigger, is set to remove the noise or unimportant fluctuations in the data. Exhibit 3.5 provides an example of how this system is used to give intermediate trend turnaround points.

The oscillator shown below the price chart is used to facilitate the identification of trend-change signals. It displays the difference between the two moving averages plotted above it on the price chart. When the zero line (the dark horizontal line) is crossed, the moving averages in the price chart have also crossed, indicating a defined trend reversal.

Crossing from below the horizontal line to above the horizontal line indicates a defined trend reversal to the upside. This occurs at points labeled 2 and 4. Crossing from above the horizontal line to below the horizontal line occurs at points 1 and 3. These penetrations signal defined trend reversals to the downside.

The lengths of the moving averages required for this technique are found using the trial-and-error or the counting methods described in the trend identification section. The exponential moving average seems to work best with this sytem because of its responsiveness to change coupled with its stability during periods of sideways movement. This combination allows for an early identification of trend changes while it reduces the chance of whipsaws.

To identify long-term trend reversals with the two-moving average system, a long-term moving average and an intermediate-term moving average are used to provide the defined reversal points. As before, trial and error can be used to find the best lengths.

Of all the moving average trend-change identification systems, the moving average crossings approach has the widest applicability. It is the work horse of this class of techniques and should be high on your priority list for mastery.

Some stock market technicians use a single moving average in combination with a closing price to define trend changes. This approach is extremely sensitive to short-term price changes and often results in an excessive number of trend-change signals. These whipsaws can be especially troublesome when determining short- to intermediate-term trends in vola-

EXHIBIT 3.5 Defined Trend Changes: Moving Average Crossings

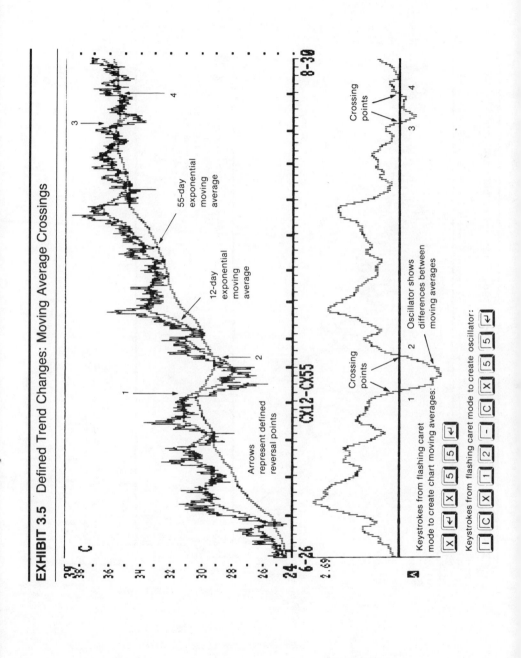

EXHIBIT 3.6 The Single Moving Average Trend-Change Identifier and the Whipsaw Problem

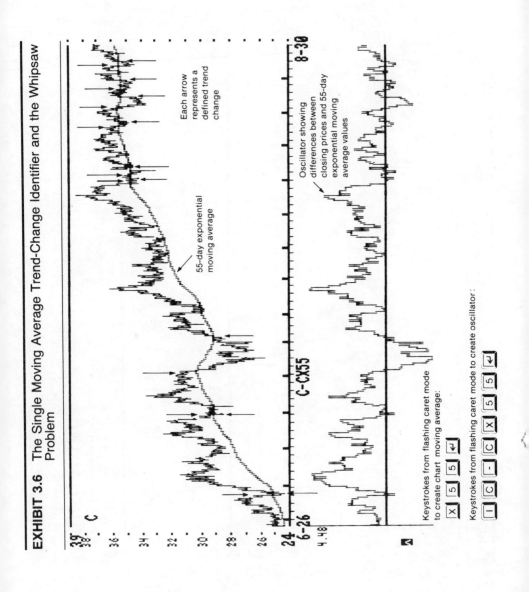

Each arrow represents a defined trend change

55-day exponential moving average

Oscillator showing differences between closing prices and 55-day exponential moving average values

Keystrokes from flashing caret mode to create chart moving average:

X 5 5 ↵

Keystrokes from flashing caret mode to create oscillator:

1 C - C X 5 5 ↵

tile stocks. Exhibit 3.6 shows how this can happen, using the same stock (for comparative purposes) as shown in Exhibit 3.5.

As you can see, the exhibit shows a large number of defined trend changes. While this number can be reduced by trying moving averages of different lengths, whipsaws will always remain a major problem. For this reason, you should use the popular price-crossing method with special care.

One useful and appropriate application for this price-crossing method is as a screening device when large numbers of stocks are being tracked. In place of the time-consuming task of graphing each stock, the list can be filtered to find only those stocks currently above their moving average. From this reduced list an individualized trend analysis can be made. Exhibit 3.7 shows how the filtering is done, using the View Summary report on the Dow Jones Market Analyzer PLUS.

The exhibit shows that 17 of the 27 stocks on the data disk are above their short-term (12-day) moving average. Combining this information with the percent change and price change data in the columns to the left of the c/adc (close over the average daily close) column, you can make an identification of rapidly rising stocks within an uptrend. You would then further analyze these stocks using other trend techniques discussed in this chapter.

The View Summary report form is quite flexible, since the length of the moving average and the change period can be chosen at will. You can also order the stocks on your data disk from prices far above their moving average (high c/adc) to prices far below their moving average (low c/adc). This provides a rapid comparative view of stocks in uptrends and in downtrends.

Percentage Change Method.   This method signals trend changes when closing prices have gone beyond the moving average by an amount that exceeds a fixed percentage. Smoothed prices are typically used as the trigger mechanism, and the choice of moving average length depends on the degree of sensitivity desired. Exhibit 3.8 shows a typical configuration with a 3 percent offset around a 55-day exponential moving average.

Defined trend changes to the upside occur when the smoothed closing price penetrates the *upper* offset. Defined

EXHIBIT 3.7 Price over Moving Average Filter

date: 01-01-1980

stock	close	1 day change change	% ch	Closing price over the 12-day moving average 12 day average c/adc	v/adv	14 day volatility vlty	posn	rstr
AXP	44.50	0.25	0.6	1.04	0.65	1.74	97	65
BA	47.00	1.62	3.6	1.05	1.37	2.83	94	58
KO	71.25	0.12	0.2	1.01	0.38	0.92	94	62
DAL	39.63	-0.62	-1.5	1.01	0.89	1.87	70	41
DOW	36.63	-0.12	-0.3	1.04	1.47	2.14	89	64
XON	53.88	0.13	0.2	1.01	0.76	1.56	89	62
KM	33.88	0.63	1.9	1.04	1.98	1.82	88	68
MMC	74.25	-0.25	-0.3	1.05	1.23	1.65	94	71
GE	59.50	-0.38	-0.6	1.00	0.70	1.86	57	53
INTC	24.00	1.25	5.5	1.04	0.98	3.35	82	50
IBM	130.50	1.37	1.1	1.03	1.52	1.33	95	65
MCIC	9.25	0.25	2.8	1.03	1.12	2.83	67	61
MRK	112.50	-0.50	-0.4	1.01	1.05	1.19	77	58
MMM	77.63	0.13	0.2	1.00	1.09	1.16	60	55
PAC	73.00	0.50	0.7	1.03	1.09	1.17	95	63
MOT	32.63	0.63	2.0	1.02	1.35	3.72	78	48

63.0% (17/27) satisfied C/ADC greater than or equal to 1.0

Percent satisfying filter

<FgDn>   <R> Re-Filter   <Esc> Menu

Keystrokes from main menu: [↵] [D] [ESC] [F] [3] [1] [1] [.] [∅] [↵]

[O] (view summary)

EXHIBIT 3.8 Overview of the Percentage Change Method

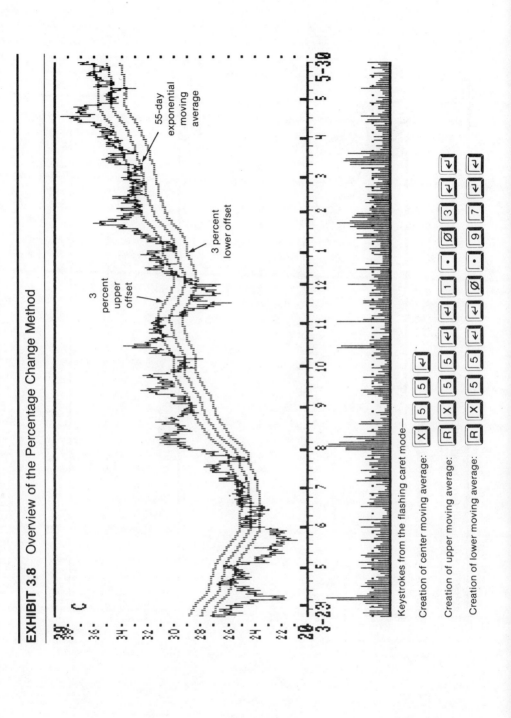

Keystrokes from the flashing caret mode—

Creation of center moving average:

Creation of upper moving average:

Creation of lower moving average:

EXHIBIT 3.9 Defined Trend Changes: Example Showing the Percentage Change Method

Chart A: Defined downtrend points

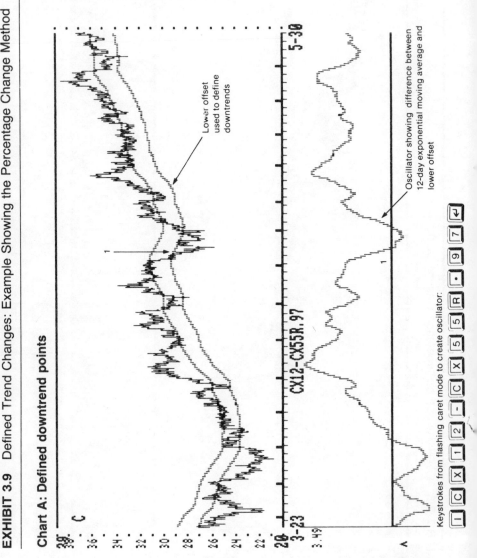

Lower offset used to define downtrends

Oscillator showing difference between 12-day exponential moving average and lower offset

CX12–CX55R.97

Keystrokes from flashing caret mode to create oscillator:

1 C X 1 2 - C X 5 5 R . 9 7 ↵

Chart B: Defined uptrend points

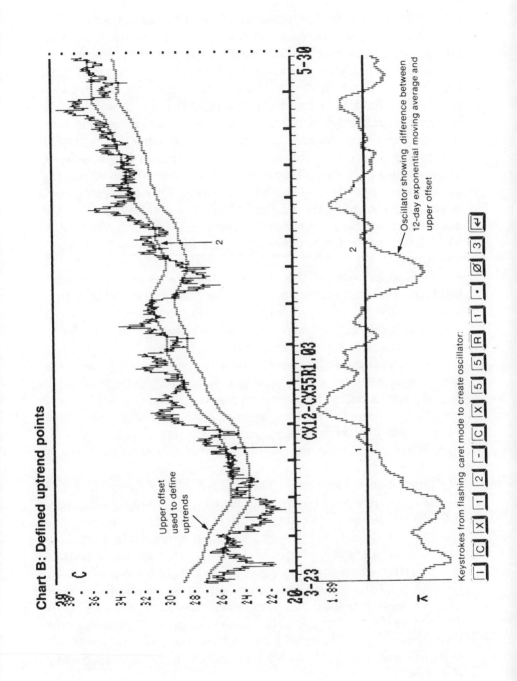

Upper offset used to define uptrends

2

1

CX12-CX55R1.03

C

38.
38-
36-
34-
32-
30-
28-
26-
24-
22-
20-
3-23

5-30

Oscillator showing difference between 12-day exponential moving average and upper offset

2

1

1.89

K

Keystrokes from flashing caret mode to create oscillator:

1 C X 1 2 - C X 5 5 R 1 . Ø 3 ↵

trend changes to the downside occur when the smoothed closing price crosses below the *lower* offset. The exact points of defined trend change can be clarified through the use of oscillators.

Exhibit 3.9, Chart A, shows a defined downtrend point, and Exhibit 3.9, Chart B, shows defined uptrend points using oscillators with data for Chrysler Corporation. Point 1 in Chart A indicates a defined downtrend, as the oscillator crosses the zero line and goes downward at that point. In Chart B, uptrend points are defined by the zero line crossings to the upside at Points 1 and 2. Note that an upside signal remains in effect until a down signal is given, and vice versa. Other crossings between these signals are ignored. Also notice that the example does not show the center moving average shown in Exhibit 3.8. This moving average is not used to generate signals, so it is not required.

The offset around the moving average is found through trial and error on historical data, based on previous volatility. As with other moving average methods, you should carefully choose the moving average that reflects the trend of interest, using methods previously discussed.

The percentage change approach is particularly useful for stocks that have been in consolidation for long periods of time. In this situation, other trend-change identifiers would likely provide numerous whipsaws because of the prolonged sideways action. Many distressed and out-of-favor stocks fit this category. This application will be discussed in Chapter Twelve.

Three-Step Reversal Technique. This form of trend identification requires a simple counting of moving-average increases or decreases. If the trend is upwards or sideways, a change to a downtrend is signaled when three declines are observed from a previous high. Conversely, an uptrend is defined as occurring when three increases are seen following a bottom. Exhibit 3.10 shows how this approach works in practice.

The theory behind the three-step approach is that, while one or two changes may be due to chance or to other nonpersistent causes, three changes indicate that the reversal represents a significant move. The trend is therefore defined as having changed.

The weighted moving average is most frequently used for

EXHIBIT 3.10   Defined Trend Changes: Three-Step Reversal
Technique

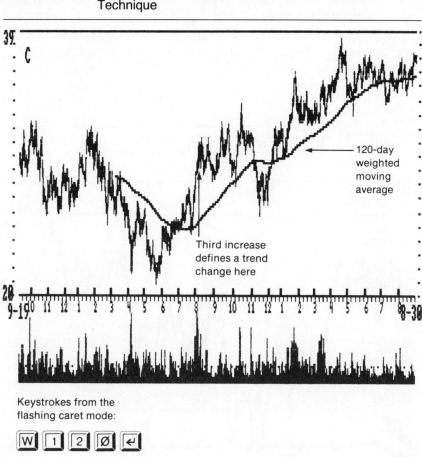

120-day
weighted
moving
average

Third increase
defines a trend
change here

Keystrokes from the
flashing caret mode:

this technique, followed in frequency of use by the exponential
moving average. Simple moving averages are not used because
they place equal weights on all historical values making up the
average. This means that an increase or decrease in the moving average could just as likely be due to old data being dropped out of the averaging process as it is due to current data
being added. This uncertainty increases the odds that false signals could be generated.

A major advantage of this trend-change identification technique is that false trend-change signals are minimized during

sideways price movements that take place over extended periods of time. In these trendless cases, many other techniques become badly whipsawed.

For clarity, you may sometimes want to plot the moving average below the price chart. Exhibit 3.11 shows how this is done, using the Dow Jones Industrial Average as an example. To further ensure that three changes have been made, you can

---

EXHIBIT 3.11   Defined Reversal on Dow Jones Industrial Average
Using the Three-Step Reversal Technique

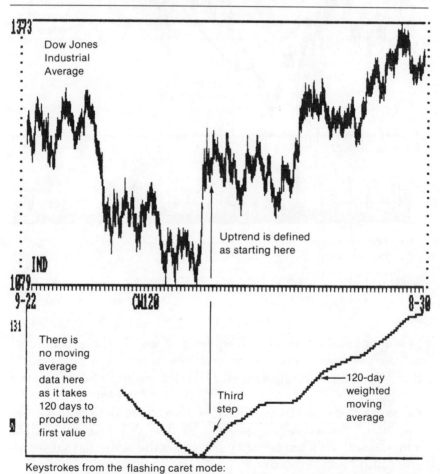

Keystrokes from the flashing caret mode:

display the data values along the left side of the chart by pressing **Q** while in the flashing caret mode.

This trend-definition technique is frequently used to reveal the primary trend in stock prices. Once this trend has been established, specific tactics can be employed within the trend until a reversal becomes evident. For example, "Only be a buyer of stocks during a primary uptrend" is an old stock market rule that can be supported by this system. Looking again at Exhibit 3.11, you can see that a time zone for stock purchases under this rule would start from the point shown on the chart and would continue for three downward steps from the point that a subsequent high took place.

Another area of application is the establishment of secular trends for economic data, such as the value of the dollar or industrial production.

When using the three-step method, and all other moving average techniques, you must be careful to choose the proper moving-average length to meet your needs.

Trend Overextension Oscillators

Has the current trend overextended itself?

The theory behind the trend overextension oscillator indicates that extreme values from a trend are essentially temporary in nature. Prices are often driven up by overenthusiasm and driven down by excessive despair. When departure from the trend is "too far—too fast," a return to more normal levels can be expected. The farther the price moves away from what could be considered a normal level, the greater is the probability that the difference cannot be sustained. Rapid price advances, for example, are like an exhausted sprinter who must either rest or collapse.

There are two major approaches to constructing moving average overextended price oscillators. The first approach uses the difference between the current price and a trend-revealing moving average. The second approach takes the difference between current and historical trend-revealing moving average values.

Price Minus Moving Average Oscillator. This oscillator displays the price, with the trend-revealing moving average values subtracted out. The result is a graph of leftovers that represent all movements about the trend. Exhibits 3.12, 3.13, and 3.14 offer examples.

Looking first at the short-term oscillator in Exhibit 3.12, you can see price peaks that extend beyond upper and lower levels that are marked *unsustainable*. Prices that exceed these levels have little chance of continuation. Consequently, you can expect to see either a pause or a reversal in the price movement shown on the chart above the oscillator. Arrows on the chart illustrate the points at which the oscillator peaked in unsustainable territory. As you can see, most short-term reversals were identified.

For this method to work properly, you must choose limits above and below the oscillator zero line to signal the extreme levels of departure from what is normal. You can do this after creating an oscillator by pressing **L** for a horizontal line. After some effort and experimentation you will find the lines that chop off the peaks on either side of the zero line. Once you have found these lines you can save their magnitude as part of a customized Auto Run (see your user's manual for instructions). While past price dynamics do not guarantee future behavior, the chaos appearing in rapid price movements tends to be relatively stable over time, providing generally good results for this technique.

As previously mentioned, the arrows in Exhibit 3.12 (and also Exhibits 3.13 and 3.14) identify those prices that peaked at some point beyond the unsustainable lines. In practice it is impossible to consistently find the point at which the price makes its exact high or low. One way of dealing with this limitation is to combine this approach with the three-step reversal technique discussed earlier. After the oscillator has entered unsustainable territory, wait until three declines from the peak have occurred before assuming that a reversal has taken place. Another approach is to regard the entire period beyond the unsustainable level as "overbought" or "oversold." Still another approach is to wait until the indicator has changed direction and has returned to the region lying within the unsustainable lines before you define a reversal from overextended territory.

EXHIBIT 3.12 Short-Term Trend Overextension: Price Minus Moving Average Oscillator

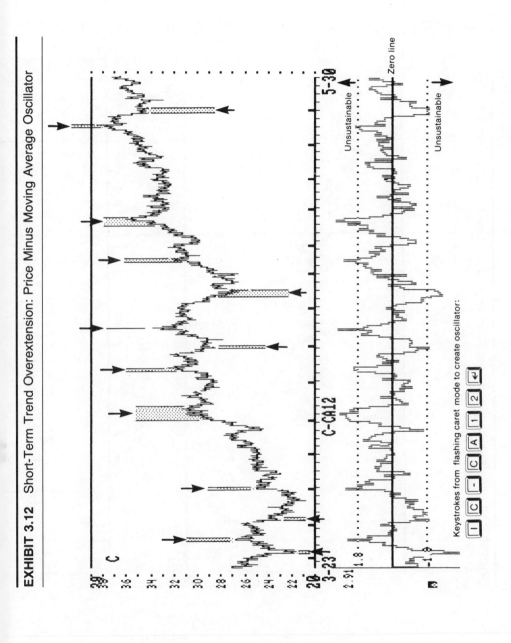

EXHIBIT 3.13 Intermediate-Term Trend Overextension: Price Minus Moving Average Oscillator

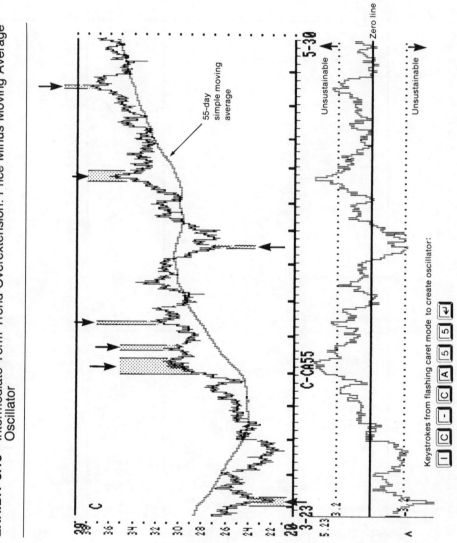

55-day simple moving average

Unsustainable

Zero line

Unsustainable

Keystrokes from flashing caret mode to create oscillator:

I C - C A 5 5 ↵

EXHIBIT 3.14 Long-Term Trend Overextension: Price Minus Moving Average Oscillator

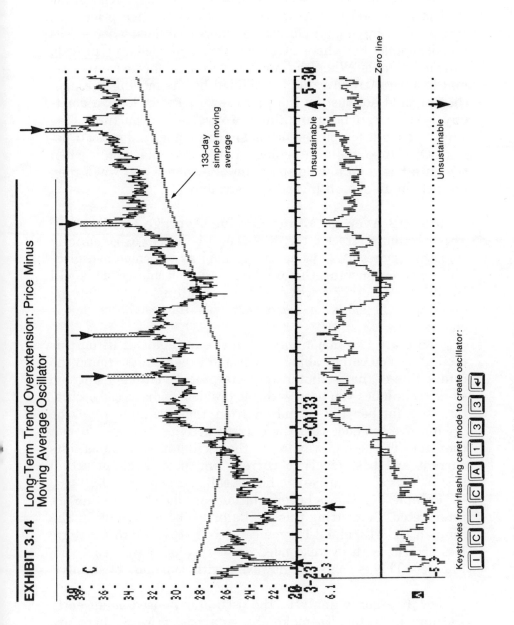

133-day simple moving average

C-CA133

Unsustainable

Zero line

Unsustainable

5-30

Keystrokes from flashing caret mode to create oscillator:

`/` `C` `-` `C` `A` `1` `3` `3` `↵`

The overextension oscillator can be used by adventurous traders as an aid to selling (or selling short) when prices are rising, or for buying (or closing out short positions) when prices are dropping. For the rest of us, this approach can provide warning signals. When the current price is so far above its normal historical trend value (as defined by the moving average) that it could not sustain that high level for very long, a don't-buy posture can be maintained. Conversely, departures of a similar magnitude on the downside can signal a don't-sell period. Of course, definite actions should take place only when they are based on a wide spectrum of evidence and when they are part of an overall investment strategy.

Moving Average Minus Moving Average Oscillator. This oscillator tracks the difference between exponentially smoothed prices 12 days apart. As long as the smoothed price difference is constant, the oscillator will not change. This will be the case whether prices are rising or falling. Only when the difference increases or decreases will the oscillator levels change.

There are two major ways to make an analysis using this oscillator. You can establish upper and lower limits around the center line of the oscillator and interpret deviations using the same techniques you used with the previously discussed oscillator. The farther the deviation from the oscillator line, the greater are the odds that the current activity in price will not continue. The second way to use the oscillator is to compare its current and past levels to current and past levels of actual prices. This comparative method is called *divergence analysis.*

Exhibit 3.15 shows how deviations around the zero line are interpreted. Comparing this oscillator to the oscillators in Exhibits 3.12, 3.13, and 3.14, you can see that the movements are less erratic, with overextended areas (peaks) more clearly delineated. This is achieved, however, with some loss of sensitivity.

For divergence analysis, the oscillator is used as an early warning indicator. To make this analysis, price changes are compared to oscillator changes. Whenever prices rise higher than their most recent previous high, or fall lower than their most recent previous low, comparisons are made to level

EXHIBIT 3.15 Overextension Oscillator: Moving Average Minus Moving Average (peaking approach)

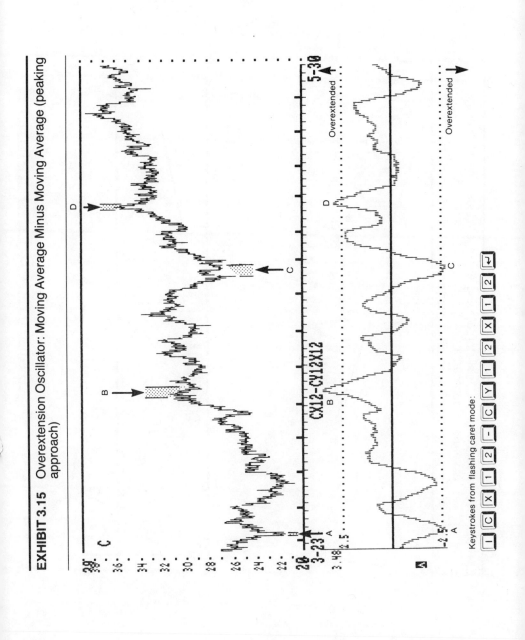

Keystrokes from flashing caret mode:

EXHIBIT 3.16 Overextension Oscillator: Moving Average Minus Moving Average (divergence approach)

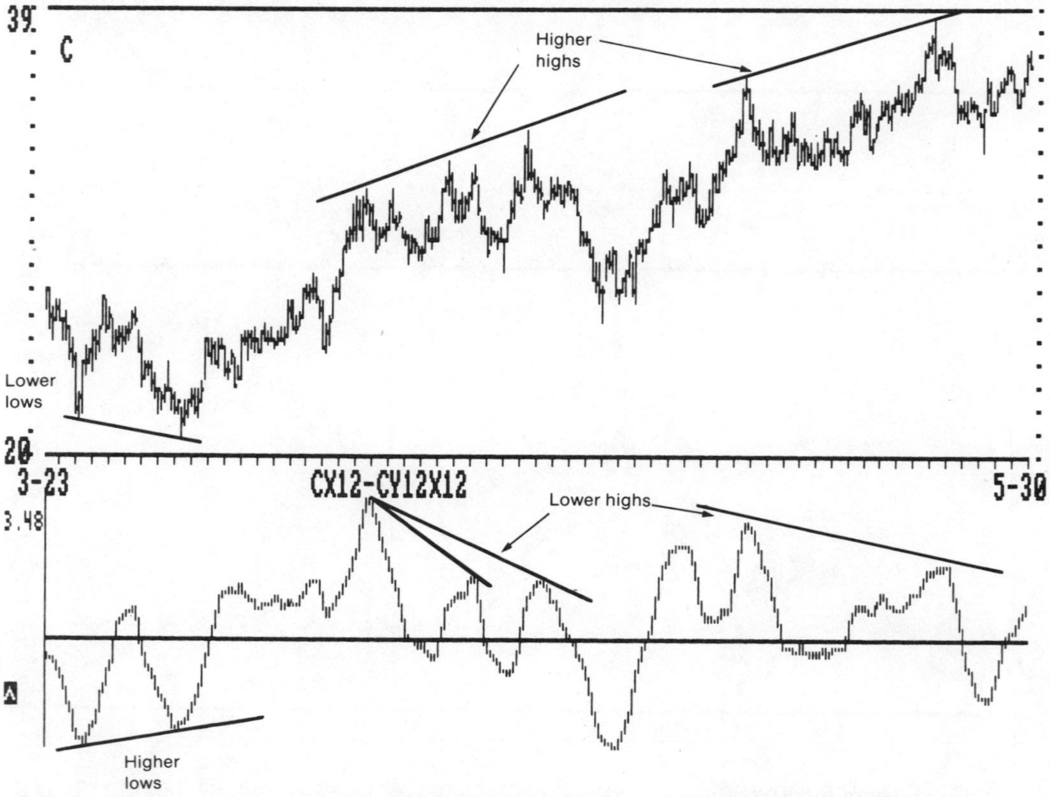

Keystrokes from flashing caret mode: ⊣ 2 1 X 2 ↵ Y C - 2 1 X 1 X C 1

changes shown in the oscillator. The key to the analysis is to look for divergencies between the two.

When a stock is declining, lower lows are compared to corresponding lows in the oscillator. If they are higher, instead of lower than their most recent previous level, the oscillator indicates possible stalling of price-change dynamics to the downside (see Exhibit 3.16). Conversely, when a stock is advancing, if higher highs are matched by lower lows in the oscillator, stalling may again be taking place, this time to the upside (again see Exhibit 3.16).

The oscillators shown in Exhibits 3.15 and 3.16 make use of 12-day exponential moving averages. While this moving average type and length appear to work well for a wide variety of stocks, you should make tests to determine if they are appropriate in each particular application.

As with other methods discussed in this part of the book, it is important for you to understand that the strict interpretation of these oscillators does not include the forecasting of future price levels. It simply provides information about the current state of affairs with reference to past or other performance information.

OTHER TECHNIQUES FOR TREND ANALYSIS

Besides moving averages, you can use a number of other methods for trend analysis. These methods are based on certain characteristics of historical price patterns. Like the moving average techniques, their primary purpose is to increase your understanding of the current situation.

Trend Lines

Is the current trend intact?

Price movements often occur with a series of ascending bottoms during uptrends and descending tops during downtrends. Trend lines can be established by connecting the lower prices of a rising stock movement and the higher prices of a falling stock

EXHIBIT 3.17   Trendline Construction Procedure

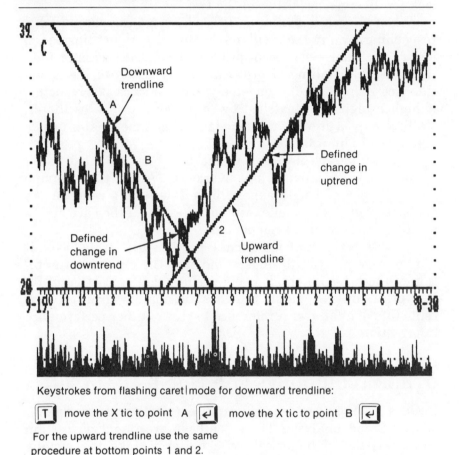

Keystrokes from flashing caret | mode for downward trendline:

[T]   move the X tic to point   A   [↵]   move the X tic to point   B   [↵]

For the upward trendline use the same
procedure at bottom points 1 and 2.

movement. Exhibit 3.17 shows downward- and upward-sloping
trendlines and the defined trend-change points.

The general interpretation is that as long as prices do not
penetrate the current trendline, the trend is defined as being
intact.

To represent price action properly, the semilog scale instead
of the arithmetic scale should be used for charting. For small-
percentage price movements the difference is negligible, and either chart can be used. The choice of scales becomes critical,
however, when prices undergo large percentage changes.

Exhibit 3.18 shows identical trendlines drawn on semilog and arithmetic charts. As you can see, the results are quite different. The arithmetic-scaled chart shows a gap between prices and the trendline at the right side of the chart, while the semilog display shows prices on the trendline. The trendline on the upper (percentage) chart is a better model of the trend and therefore should be used, since it eliminates scaling distortions at higher price levels.

Sample size plays a major role in the degree of confidence you can have in a trendline. The longer the trendline has been in force (number of days) and the more times the price bottoms have touched the trendline and then reversed, then the more comfortable you can feel about using the trendline as a valid model of the price movement.

EXHIBIT 3.18   The Effect of Scaling on Trendline Display

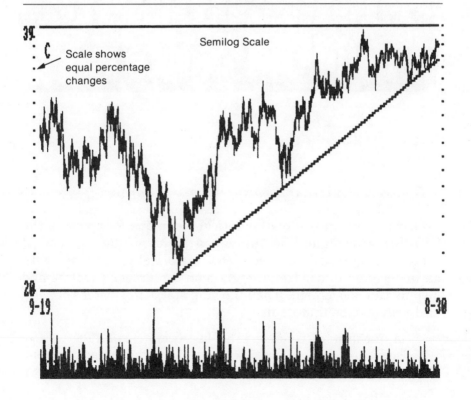

EXHIBIT 3.18   *(concluded)*

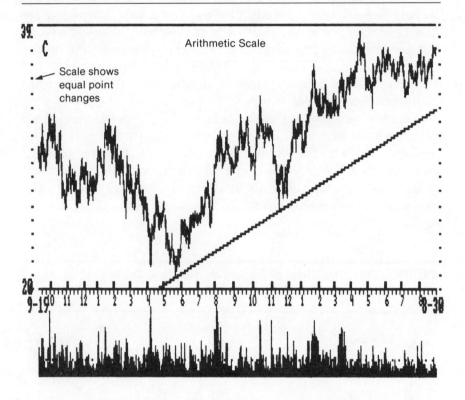

Linear Regression

Is there a significant departure from a linear trend?

Linear regression is a mathematical technique for creating the best-fitting straight line through a series of data points. If there is some reason to believe that historical prices move with an underlying linear trend, regression can properly isolate and display this movement. The following story illustrates the general principle behind its use.

A problem of training. The instructors in a flight school adopted a policy of consistent positive reinforcement recommended by psychologists. They verbally reinforced each successful execution of a flight maneuver. After some experience with this training approach, the instructors claimed that contrary to psychological doctrine, high praise for good execution of complex maneuvers typically results in a decrement of performance on the next try. What should the psychologist say in response?

Regression is inevitable in flight maneuvers because performance is not perfectly reliable and progress between successive maneuvers is slow. Hence, pilots who did exceptionally well on one trial are likely to deteriorate on the next, regardless of the instructors' reaction to the initial success. The experienced flight instructors actually discovered the regression but attributed it to the detrimental effect of positive reinforcement.[1]

Just as the pilots experienced a regression back to their mean level of performance, so may stock prices regress back to their intrinsic rate of increase or decrease as represented by the regression line.

Deviations from the regression line are viewed in a probabilistic sense. The larger the deviation, the smaller the probability that it will persist over time.

As a stock price increases, it becomes psychologically more appealing. This appeal may initiate additional purchases and may drive the price further from the mean. Eventually the price may reach an unsustainable point from where it regresses back toward the mean value. The opposite may occur when a stock is doing poorly.

Constructing a regression line with hand calculations is a formidable mathematical task. With a computer, however, regression-line construction becomes more practical, but this is both an advantage and a disadvantage. The computer makes the task so easy that users may be tempted to use the concept for situations that are not quite applicable.

When you create a regression line, it is extremely important that you have evidence of linear movement. While a regression line can be drawn through any data, it will be of value only if the overall thrust of movement is linear (i.e., in a straight line).

One way to aid in this determination is to look for linear

---

[1]Daniel Kahneman and Amos Tversky, "On the Psychology of Prediction," *Psychological Review* 80, no. 4 (July 1973), pp.237–51.

underpinnings of the price. This typically involves a history of linear earnings and cash-flow or dividend trends. If evidence of linearity cannot be found, *this technique should be avoided.*

Exhibit 3.19 shows examples of stocks with a long-term linear increase in earnings and dividends. These stocks are viable candidates for long-term regression analysis while the underlying linear trends continue.

You should note that regression analysis does not predict that the price, earnings, dividends, or other measures of performance will continue to move in a linear fashion. It simply provides probabilistic expectations that current prices can be sustained based on the *assumption* of continued underlying linear trends.

Exhibit 3.20 provides an example of a regression line superimposed on a linear price trend. In Chapter Six we will see how regression analysis can be used to support other objectives.

Range Volatility

Does range volatility indicate a reversal in trend?

Market technician J. Welles Wilder, Jr., defined the "true range" in prices as the largest of the following price differences: (1) today's low to today's high, (2) yesterday's close to today's high, or (3) yesterday's close to today's low.[2] This range measure is related to price volatility; the greater the true range, the greater the volatility. By making a moving average of range values, a smoothed volatility indicator, called the *trend range,* can be created and used to define trend reversals.

The Daily Reports Program of the Dow Jones Market Analyzer PLUS (**P**-View Trend from the Main Menu) provides this trend range indicator. A multiple of the trend range is used to provide limit points for defining trend reversals. The limit points are placed under the prices during rising trends and are placed above the prices during declining trends. Trend rever-

---

[2]J. Welles Wilder, Jr., *New Concepts in Technical Trading Systems* (Greensboro, N.C.: Trend Research, 1978).

EXHIBIT 3.19 Candidates for Regression Analysis

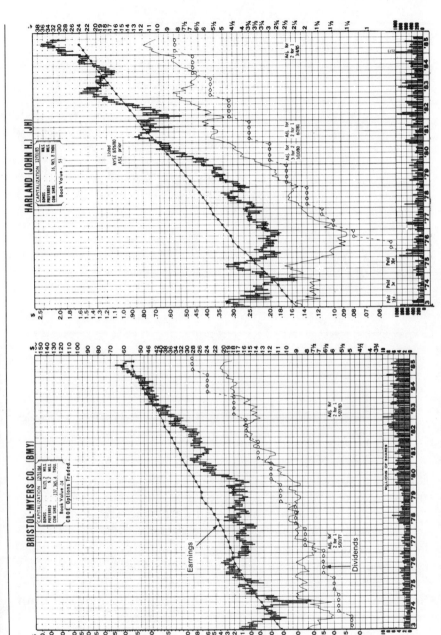

Charts courtesy of Securities Research Co., 208 Newbury St., Boston, Mass. 02116.

EXHIBIT 3.20 Regression Analysis

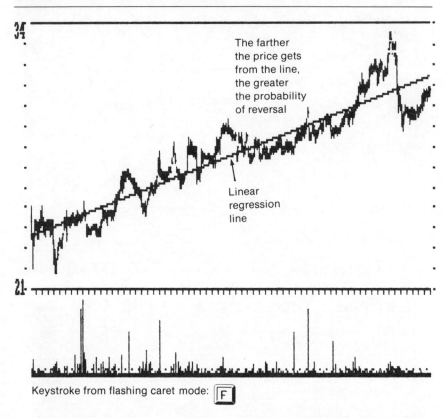

Keystroke from flashing caret mode: F

sals take place when the price reverses and closes below (in rising periods) or above (in falling periods) the limit points.

Exhibit 3.21 shows View Trend data with trend range figures and stop point magnitude calculations. New trend range data are made available each day, as new high, low, and close data are downloaded and the View Trend program is run. Each day's limit point magnitude is calculated by simply multiplying the given trend range by 3.0. Exhibit 3.22 shows how the limit point magnitude can define a reversal in trend.

Let's suppose, for example, that you shorted the stock at some time in the past. As long as the price keeps dropping, you're happy. What you are worried about is a reversal in price to the upside. The small circles that arbitrarily start at point A on the diagram represent an upper limit for each day, such

EXHIBIT 3.21 View Trend Data and Stop Point Magnitude Calculation

stock	close	trend range	% up trend	% down trend	strength of trend	trend index	trend rating	action index
C	32.88	0.91	24.60	19.75	10.93	22.60	25.36	173

Limit
point
magnitude
= .91 × 3.0 = 2.73

Trend   Constant
range

EXHIBIT 3.22 Range Volatility Trend Identification

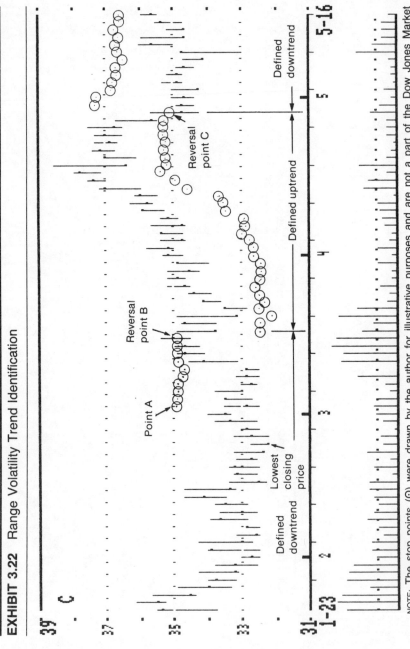

NOTE: The stop points (⊙) were drawn by the author for illustrative purposes and are not a part of the Dow Jones Market Analyzer Plus program.

that, if the price should close above the limit, the short position would be covered. This is seen occurring at point B.

The limit points from point A in the chart to point B are found by adding the daily limit point magnitude figure to the best closing price you've seen since you shorted the stock. This price level is shown on the chart, and each of the little circle limit points have been created by adding the respective day's limit point magnitude figure to that level.

With the close above the limit at point B, the trend is defined as having changed. Now let's assume that you have covered your short and that you have gone long. Now you are worried about the stock falling in price, so you will put your limits below the daily prices. How far below? Each day's limit point magnitude is subtracted from the best closing price that you've seen since you bought the stock. As the price rises in the chart, this best closing price also rises. Finally, at point C, the limit is broken as the prices fall. The trend is therefore defined as having changed again, this time to the downside.

When a stock is volatile, this trend-defining technique will back off the limit, giving the price additional room to swing without triggering a reversal. Conversely, when the price is less volatile, the limit will close in. Parameters of this technique can easily be adjusted to meet the requirements of individual stock movements. Exhibit 3.22 uses a constant value of 3.0 and a moving average of seven days for calculating the trend range. Experimentation will provide the best parameters across different stocks. To use the technique you do not have to plot the limits as shown in the exhibit. You can simply multiply the current day's trend range by your constant value and add it to the best close for the current trend. As long as you have not exceeded the limit, you can assume that the trend is intact.

Trend Ranking Indicators

How do my stocks rank with respect to the direction and strength of trend?

If you are following a large number of stocks, it is important that you have a relative measure for trend comparison between them. Indicators in the Dow Jones Market Analyzer PLUS View Trend report provide this information, both for the direction and the strength of the trend. Moreover, this report allows you to rank (order) from high to low or to filter (establish cutoff points) for any of the indicators.

Exhibit 3.23 provides an example of the Trend Report for 25 stocks, using data over a 14-day period. The trend range indicator was explained in the preceding section, so the present discussion will relate to the other indicators shown in the exhibit.

Looking first at the % up trend and % down trend columns, these percentage figures represent the portion of movement, over the number of days specified, that can be classified as up movement or down movement. These percentages are based on the system developed by J. Welles Wilder, Jr., to define what he calls "directional movement" (+ DI and − DI in his symbology).

The strength of trend is the numeric difference between the % up trend and % down trend divided by their sum (Wilder's DX indicator). The result is given in a percentage form that allows for an easy numeric trend comparison between stocks. If a stock is not in a clear uptrend or downtrend over the period specified, the % up trend and % down trend numbers will be about equal, making their difference very small. A small difference will result in a small strength of trend reading. This can be seen with BankAmerica (BA), Exxon (XON), and Intel (INTC) stock trend data. Conversely, a large difference will result in a large strength of trend reading, as shown by Marsh & McLennan (MMC) and Goodyear (GT). You should note that the strength of trend figures does not show the direction of trend movement.

The trend index (based on Wilder's ADX) represents the current value of a simple moving average of the strength of trend. As the strength of trend rises over time, the trend index will also rise. The trend index will lag behind the strength of trend, however, since all moving averages lag behind the data used to create them. As the strength of trend loses steam and starts to fall, it will cross the trend index. Like all moving average systems, the crossing points and the extreme differences yield important information.

The trend rating (based on Wilder's ADXR) is a smoothed

EXHIBIT 3.23 Example of the View Trend Daily Report for Stocks

14 day trend report

stock	close	trend range	% up trend	% down trend	strength of trend	trend index	trend rating	action index
AA	32.13	0.57	18.74	29.94	23.01	28.52	26.27	231
AXP	44.50	0.87	33.79	16.06	35.55	18.57	17.17	461
T	20.63	0.45	10.25	22.09	36.59	16.98	13.90	359
BA	47.00	1.25	27.17	29.50	4.12	22.41	19.77	75
KO	71.25	0.65	25.83	15.31	25.58	17.41	17.28	198
DAL	39.63	0.80	19.22	29.86	21.67	45.18	48.87	274
DOW	36.63	0.75	28.66	17.28	24.77	12.27	12.44	306
XON	53.88	0.83	29.03	25.37	6.73	10.32	14.98	76
KM	33.88	0.65	40.72	19.51	35.20	23.63	24.38	393
KMB	61.00	0.78	35.67	24.11	19.28	21.69	16.42	194
MMC	74.25	1.16	46.84	14.73	52.16	24.34	18.49	703
BAC	13.88	0.45	16.40	24.21	19.23	27.54	34.53	232
GE	59.50	0.97	29.42	19.45	20.39	23.56	24.47	256
GM	66.38	1.22	16.68	30.40	29.15	14.50	15.07	437
GT	26.13	0.45	14.19	36.71	44.23	28.77	22.83	391
INTC	24.00	0.72	40.74	40.96	0.27	16.01	14.51	4
IBM	130.50	1.73	34.87	15.13	39.48	20.78	18.45	596
EK	42.63	0.76	10.08	19.44	31.71	20.06	19.73	370
MCIC	9.25	0.23	37.79	25.01	20.35	21.48	20.15	154
MRK	112.50	1.28	31.03	23.32	14.17	26.86	35.43	172
MER	27.75	0.81	17.57	29.18	24.83	29.63	32.94	381
MMM	77.63	0.90	23.64	12.93	29.31	24.80	26.20	299
MO	74.00	1.24	22.08	28.99	13.53	27.39	32.57	195
PAC	73.00	0.90	32.84	20.37	23.45	27.67	34.97	246
MOT	32.63	1.07	21.38	29.75	16.37	23.32	18.71	306

Keystrokes from main menu:

[P] View trend [↵] [D]

To order or filter:

[ESC] Follow prompts

trend index, with the smoothing based on a two-value average. The current trend index and its value 14 days ago are added and divided by two. This number provides a benchmark for the trend index, indicating present position compared with past position.

The last column provides the action index. This index combines current strength of trend data with potential volatility based on price level.

How are these measures used to indicate which stocks from a large set are worth a closer look? The following represents some possibilities.

1. Order all stocks from highest % up trend to lowest, and consider those stocks with % up trends larger then their % down trends as potential purchase candidates. Ignore all others or view them as possible short candidates. Further analysis would be made on the group of identified stocks.

2. Order stocks based on strength of trend, and compare this value to the trend index and trend rating. Those stocks that have a large strength of trend and that are also above their trend index and trend ratings values would be candidates for overbought/oversold analysis.

3. Search the % up trend and % down trend columns for equivalent or near-equivalent values (crossing points). When a downtrend reverses to an uptrend or an uptrend reverses to a downtrend these two measures will become equal at or near the time of reversal. Screening stocks for equivalencies provides a rapid way to identify turnaround candidates for further analysis.

4. Scan the strength of trend and trend index columns for equivalent or near-equivalent values on the same stock. When these two measures are the same, this means the strength of trend is crossing its simple moving average (the trend index). A change in trend is therefore possible, so a further analysis is appropriate. The odds of a meaningful trend reversal occurring are increased if the two values are high (over 70) or if they are low (under 30).

5. Filter the stocks for trend ratings of 25 or less, and, until these ratings improve, carefully avoid using any of the trend-following techniques discussed in this chapter. These direction-

less stocks will typically generate whipsaws as long as their trend rating is low. Techniques, including divergence analysis and relative strength, are more appropriate to these stocks.

6. Flag all stocks with a trend index that is numerically larger than either the % up trend or % down trend, and track the index over time. When the index begins turning downward, a further analysis is signaled as a reversal in price may be occurring.

7. Order all stocks by the action index, and trade only those stocks that are high on the list. Those aggressive traders using trend-following techniques will be interested in knowing that this indicator shows where the most action is likely to be.

A nice feature of the Trend Report is that it can make a comparative graphical analysis of stocks. This is extremely valuable for a second level of analysis. For example, Exhibit 3.24 shows stocks ordered on the basis of the action index. As you can see, the number one stock is Beatrice (BRY).

This stock looks interesting, but how does it rank in comparison with different stocks on the other measures? The

---

EXHIBIT 3.24 Trend Report Ordered by Action Index

14 day trend report

stock	close	trend range	% up trend	% down trend	strength of trend	trend index	trend rating	action index
BRY	44.13	1.68	37.04	14.64	43.35	50.51	46.56	1095
TRN	690.70	12.20	18.96	12.19	21.73	20.09	22.21	1009
CAW	16.50	0.57	31.14	9.82	32.06	32.65	30.41	735
IND	1334.00	16.67	15.39	11.23	15.63	18.88	21.92	714
AD	105.00	5.43	55.71	44.29	11.43	12.49	15.05	605
AZA	24.25	0.61	44.12	20.50	36.56	11.69	11.73	455
MHP	44.13	0.97	18.46	34.99	30.92	31.22	27.13	452
HON	61.63	0.99	15.01	28.07	30.30	20.97	26.75	384
DIS	89.00	1.07	34.46	17.98	31.43	76.31	20.22	357
UTL	159.70	2.10	14.69	11.46	12.34	24.49	36.26	205
C	37.13	0.64	29.02	22.18	13.35	12.37	13.62	140
DD	57.75	0.69	20.25	26.61	13.56	22.41	20.11	123
GM	67.38	0.98	21.38	26.25	10.21	17.81	16.58	121
MKY	12.38	0.42	19.10	23.16	9.62	25.26	33.11	115
PRD	31.63	0.60	23.93	28.17	8.15	14.60	17.44	88
NVP	30.75	0.54	17.93	15.48	7.33	20.98	29.05	71
DOW	35.88	0.50	24.39	20.72	8.13	16.90	22.25	68
PLN	15.75	0.42	17.77	16.01	5.22	19.24	26.04	55
F	44.00	0.60	19.14	21.09	4.87	7.36	8.41	44
AUTO	127.21	1.91	19.32	18.39	2.47	10.33	13.85	42
IBM	126.63	1.43	25.22	26.37	2.23	10.62	14.14	28

Keystrokes from main menu:

 (view trend)

EXHIBIT 3.25 Graphical Representation of Trend Report with BRY Highlighted

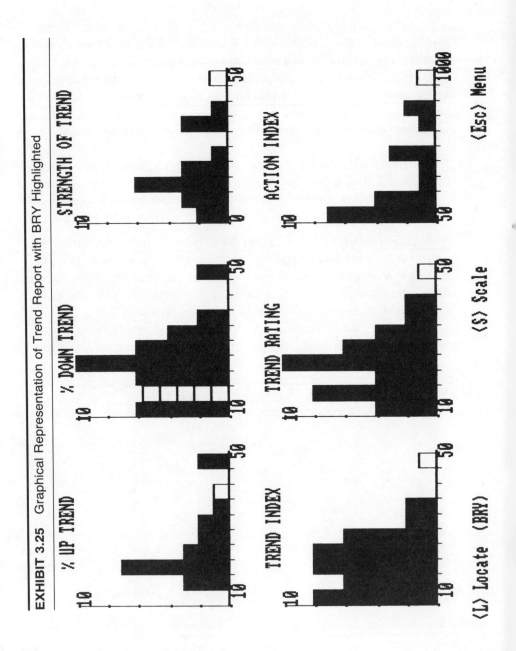

graphical representation (Exhibit 3.25) readily shows this comparative ranking.

The Trend Report is provided with a default value of 14 days. This time period supports short- to intermediate-term traders. To support longer-term trends, the period length can be increased. Through experimentation you can determine the best length for your investment objectives.

SELECTED REFERENCES

APPEL, GERALD, and W. F. HITSCHLER. *Stock Market Trading Systems.* Homewood, Ill.: Dow Jones-Irwin, 1980.

HURST, J. M. *The Profit Magic of Stock Transaction Timing.* Englewood Cliffs, N.J.: Prentice-Hall, 1970.

JAIN, C. L. "Decomposition: What Is It? What Does It Do? How Is It Used?" *The Journal of Business Forecasting,* Winter 1984–1985, pp.22–28.

MAKRIDAKIS, S.; S. C. WHEELWRIGHT; and V. E. McGEE. *Forecasting: Methods and Applications.* 2nd ed. New York: John Wiley & Sons, 1983.

SCHEINMAN, WILLIAM X. *Why Most Investors Are Mostly Wrong Most of the Time.* New York: Lancer Books, 1970.

WILDER, J. WELLES, JR. *New Concepts in Technical Trading Systems.* Greensboro, N.C.: Trend Research, 1978.

CHAPTER FOUR

Cycle Analysis

There are two major classes of cycles in the field of investments: time cycles and business cycles. Each cycle type requires its own form of technical analysis.

Time cycles are financial reoccurrences that happen with relatively constant frequency. Stock market technicians have identified 5-day, 6-week, 18-week, 4-year, 18-year, 54-year cycles and many others. While many time cycles are not linked to known causes, some are said to be related to time-based events like sunspots, phases of the moon, or presidential elections. As you may imagine, many of the proposed cycles are controversial.

The other type of cycles, business cycles, are directly associated with changing economic conditions. Certain events in our economy are cyclic; they happen again and again, with major differences in frequency and amplitude distinguishing each new cyclic occurrence from the previous one. In simple terms, our economy goes through repeated periods of expansion and contraction. While this is happening, a host of financial variables—including interest rates, the money supply, inflation, stock prices, metal prices, bond prices, and others—undergo their own cyclic changes within the context of the overall economic cycle.

TIME CYCLES

The unique characteristic of time cycles is that repeated fluctuations occur within constant (or nearly constant) time periods. Time periods that are linked to calendar time can be analyzed simply by charting historical data and marking the points where cycle bottoms and tops are supposed to occur. If the cycle exists, projections can be made into the future.

One of the most widely touted calendar cycles is the presidential election cycle. It is also one of the few cycles that has a logical underpinning. Prior to election time the incumbent party would like to have a strong economy, or at minimum, to have the public perceive that a strong economy is to come. To accomplish this the incumbent party may resort to tactics ranging from "jawboning," to increasing spending (with the help of Congress), to increasing the money supply (with the help of the Federal Reserve Board).

Exhibit 4.1 shows the monthly closing prices of the Standard & Poor's 500 Average back to January 1948. (The data were obtained from *Barron's* and were manually entered.) Arrows pointing downward display times of presidential elections; arrows pointing upward indicate times of off-year congressional elections.

As the exhibit shows, the historical results for this cycle are excellent. If the market average or its equivalent had been purchased at a time corresponding to a congressional election and had been sold at a time corresponding to the following presidential election, profits would have accrued for every cycle shown in the exhibit.

The analysis for other calendar-based cycles, including end-of-month, holiday, and seasonal cycles, is the same; simply chart and mark historical data. If the cycle existed in the past, it can provide useful input to future investment decision making.

Some proposed time cycles are said to exist independently of calendar time. A stock, for example, may reach a new bottom approximately every 20 trading days. What is the appropriate method for analyzing this type of time cycle?

The basic approach is to create a simple moving average with a length equal to the cycle length. The moving average

EXHIBIT 4.1 The Election Cycle

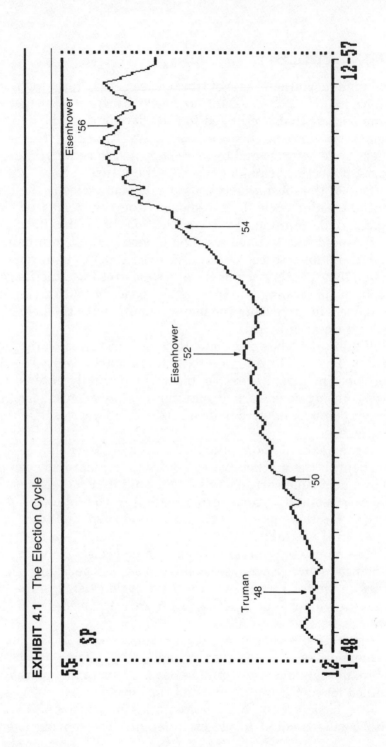

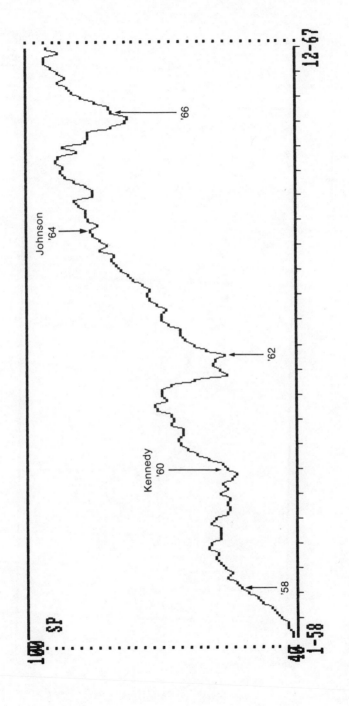

EXHIBIT 4.1 *(concluded)*

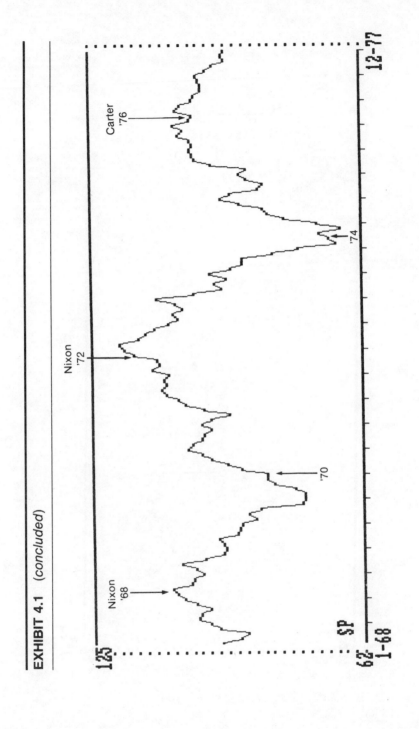

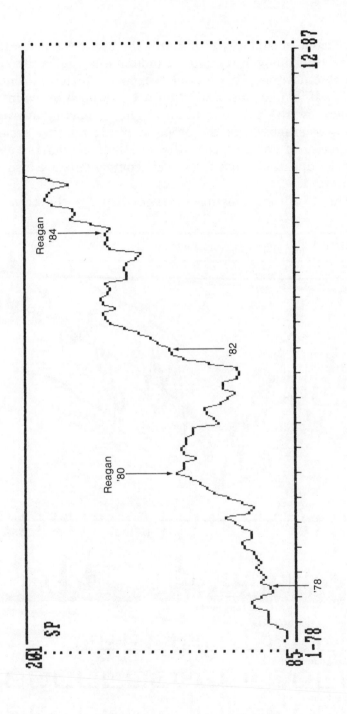

constructed in this way eliminates the cyclic component, while it simultaneously attenuates randomness and other shorter-term fluctuations. This occurs because a full cycle contains a "high half" and a "low half" that are averaged into a mid-level position by the full-length unweighted moving average. As moving averages have the property of attenuating cycles that are shorter in duration than the length of the moving average, the brief duration (high-frequency) components are also largely eliminated.

The resultant moving average displays the trend about

EXHIBIT 4.2   Simple Moving Average Cyclic Envelope

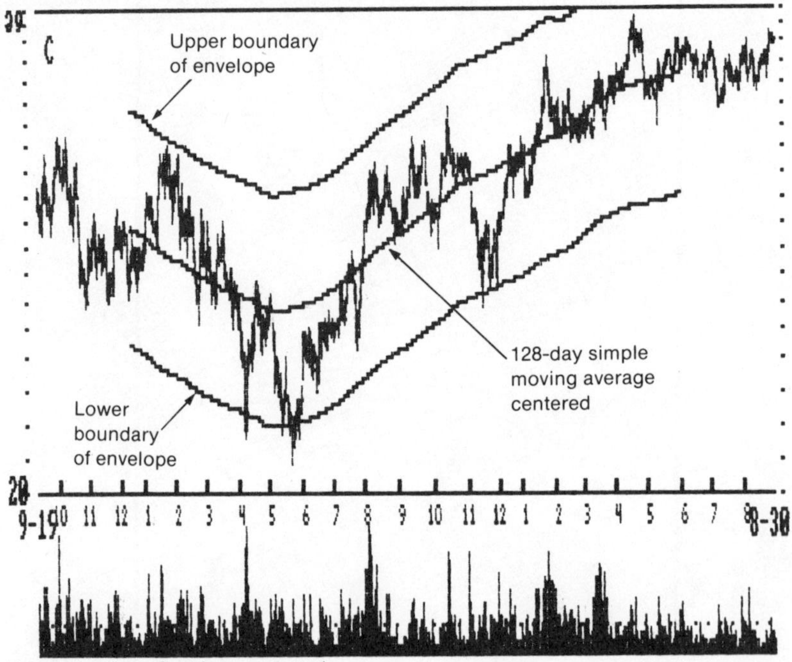

Keystrokes from flashing caret mode
Center moving average—

[R] [A] [1] [2] [8] [↵] [-] [6] [4] [↵] [↵] [↵]

Upper boundary—

[R] [A] [1] [2] [8] [↵] [-] [6] [4] [↵] [1] [.] [1] [5] [↵] [↵]

Lower boundary—

[R] [A] [1] [2] [8] [↵] [-] [6] [4] [↵] [Ø] [.] [8] [5] [↵] [↵]

which the prices are cycling. By offsetting this moving average above and below its normal position, it is possible for you to create an envelope within which the prices will cycle. The time cycle is thereby displayed within the envelope. Exhibit 4.2 shows what the cycle envelope looks like.

If the cycle length is known beforehand, the length of the simple moving average can be set to that value. If the cycle length is not known, you will have to estimate it from historical data. Exhibit 4.3 illustrates this procedure.

EXHIBIT 4.3 Cyclic Period Determination

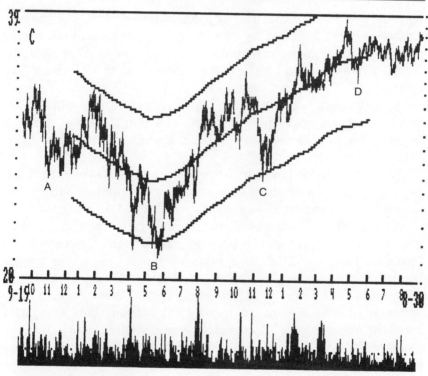

A to B 139 trading days

B to C 128 trading days

C to D 117 trading days

$$\text{Average} = \frac{139 + 128 + 117}{3} = 128$$

Those points that appear to be cyclic bottoms are identified. Counts are made of the number of trading days that have occurred from one bottom to the next, and an average is taken for all periods identified. For the example shown, the average is 128 days. A simple moving average, center plotted, is made using this length. Through trial and error, moving average offsets are created to complete the cyclic envelope.

As you can see, there is a subjective element inherent in the procedure. You may have to guess when identifying some of the cycle lengths; for that reason, a different individual may identify different cycle lengths. However, differences will tend to be minimized by the averaging process, if a large enough sample size is used.

You should note that the upper and lower bounds of the envelope are not touched by the changing price on each cyclic move. This is because randomness and (possibly) other shorter-period cycles are "riding" on the prices within the identified cycle.

Either short-, intermediate-, or long-term cycles can be isolated using the envelope approach. The length chosen for use depends on your investment horizon and characteristics of the data.

It may also be possible for you to identify cycles that lie within cycles. To analyze this situation, envelopes within envelopes are constructed as shown in Exhibit 4.4.

The exhibit illustrates a short-term cyclic envelope within the longer-term envelope previously constructed. This envelope contains a cycle of 26 days, a length found by using the counting method shown in Exhibit 4.3.

Besides empirically determining cycles through counting, you may also be able to use theoretical cycle periods as a basis for creating envelopes. As previously mentioned, many time cycles are thought to exist in the market. With the approach just shown, you can test the trading significance of any of these cycles. You merely have to construct a simple moving average with a length equal to the length of the proposed cycle, then center plot it and build an enclosing envelope. You can visually inspect the enclosed fluctuations to determine if they are sufficient in amplitude and regularity to allow for profitable trading.

EXHIBIT 4.4   Cyclic Envelope within an Envelope

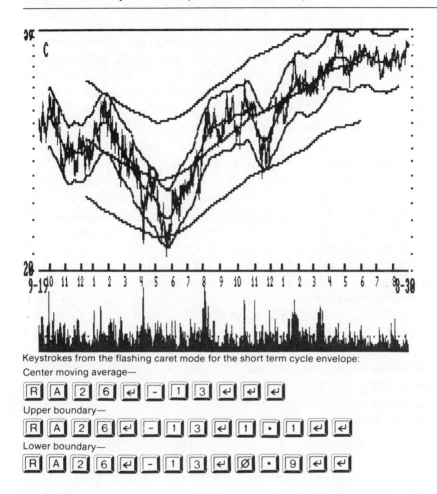

Keystrokes from the flashing caret mode for the short term cycle envelope:

Center moving average—

R A 2 6 ↵ - 1 3 ↵ ↵ ↵

Upper boundary—

R A 2 6 ↵ - 1 3 ↵ 1 . 1 ↵ ↵

Lower boundary—

R A 2 6 ↵ - 1 3 ↵ Ø . 9 ↵ ↵

PROBLEMS AND LIMITATIONS OF TIME–CYCLE ANALYSIS

The major issue you should consider when using time cycles is whether these cycles will extend into the future. Establishing historical validity will help you to find candidates that are likely to have subsequent value.

Using a large enough sample of past cycles can aid you in your analysis. The smaller your sample number, the less confidence you can have in your result. If possible, 20 or more past cycles should be used for establishing historical cycle periodicity.

If the daily cycle that is under investigation includes weekends and holidays, it is important that you take these nontrading days into account. To reflect the days without data, you may have to shorten somewhat the length of the simple moving average. A 14 calendar-day cycle, for example, would have only 10 trading days associated with it, since there are two weekends in the period. Occasional trading holidays do not introduce a significant error into the analysis and generally can be ignored. For those cycles that can be characterized in periods that are greater than a few days in length (i.e., weeks, months, or years), and for which weekly, monthly, or yearly data are available, nontrading days do not pose a problem because each unit of time has data associated with it.

In the entire field of price analysis there is probably no area more prone to analyst abuse than time cycles. Prices do fluctuate, and it is easy to "see" recurring time cycles among the fluctuations. This is especially true if the analyst (1) believes cycles are there and is determined to find them, (2) is not willing to use a moving-average decomposition technique to verify the cycle's past existence and trading potential, and (3) is willing to accept loose verification rules for explaining nonconfirming price action.

It is important that you do not fall into the alluring cycle trap that allows otherwise rational people to offer endless excuses when their predictions based on time cycles do not work out. For example, the following statements have recently been made: "The cycle called it perfectly, the market just reversed itself by 180 degrees from that expected"; "This time the cycle period doubled itself"; and "The market would have gone down as predicted by the cycle, but it was going up so strongly that the cyclic downturn was totally dominated by the upturn."

Confidence in time-cycle analysis is enhanced if the cycle in question is based on some identifiable factor (other than simple price action) that makes sense on a cause-and-effect basis. If you observe an apparent cyclic effect, yet you cannot find even a hint of what the cause of that cycle might be (or if the causal connection makes you feel uncomfortable because it appears to be something like sunspots or moon phases), you may want to avoid time-cycle analysis and use other techniques on which to base your decisions.

Some analysts believe that time-cyclic price action is more useful for investment decision making when it is cast into other analytical frameworks. One approach is to use trend overextension analysis; the other is to use the clear backward look technique on the rising and falling prices.

Trend overextension was covered in Chapter Three. With this interpretation, instead of using the cyclic action to anticipate price changes through repeating time periods, you will use the amplitude-only part of each cycle to generate buy-and-sell opportunities, based on deviations from the average. The often-fickle timing of the cycles then becomes unimportant for decision purposes.

The clear backward look technique uses cyclic behavior to establish analytical trigger points. These points tell you when you should get serious enough about the downphase in the cycle to make further technical analysis. For this technique to be applicable, a stock must be in a declining phase from a peak. After a preestablished period of time has elapsed from the time of the peak, you take a backward look from the closing price. If the look is "clear" to the time of the high, the trigger is set. If not, the trigger is delayed until a new closing low is established. If the stock does not make a new low but rises back up to the old high, then the backward look is called off until a new declining phase begins. Exhibit 4.5 illustrates how this technique works.

As the chart shows, intraday price fluctuations are removed by using only closing prices. With a trigger period of 13 days, clear backward looks from peaks are seen occurring at the three points indicated. The trigger points are not buy points but are used to "trigger" a further analysis. They indicate that, based on past cyclic action, the stock has fallen for a long enough time period such that a reversal may occur soon. You can now be interested in the stock to the point of using other techniques (Chapters Three through Seven) for making a full-blown bottom analysis.

This technique guarantees purchases at discounts from peak prices, although it does not guarantee that you will buy at

EXHIBIT 4.5 The Clear Backward Look Trigger

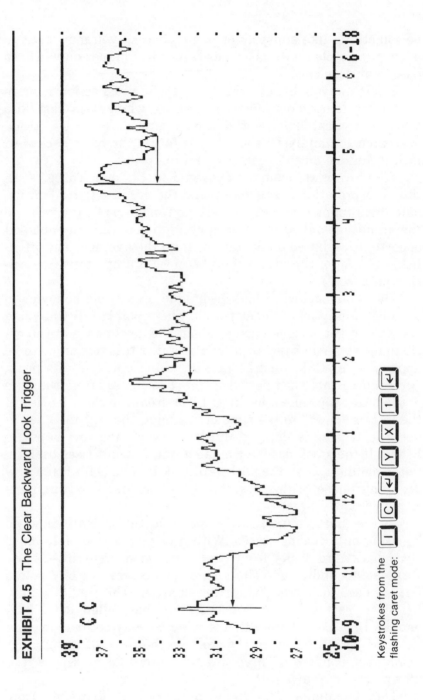

Keystrokes from the
flashing caret mode: I C ↵ Y X 1 ↵

a favorable time. The trigger period is typically set from one third to one half the period length of previous cycles, with the exact value derived from experimentation on past data. This approach is also applicable for triggering an analysis for short selling on rising prices. For an example of how this technique is used as part of an investment strategy, turn to Chapter Nine, High Probability Investing.

BUSINESS CYCLES

Business cycles do not lend themselves to the same type of analysis used on time cycles. This is because the period of recurring changes of business-cycle data varies significantly from cycle to cycle, making it impossible to specify a cycle length.

The approach used for business-cycle analysis is to view the cyclic movements as recurring up and down trends. This permits trend-analysis techniques to be used. Moving averages, for example, can be applied to the data to remove short-term fluctuations, display the up and down trends of interest, and establish defined change-of-direction points.

Interest rates are one of the most important factors in the business cycle and will be used here to demonstrate methods. Because interest rates represent the cost of money, a rate increase can slow the economy, and a rate decrease can have the opposite effect.

Exhibit 4.6 shows a weekly plot of corporate bond rates (*Barron's* "Best Bond" data) with a moving average crossing system used to identify defined trend-change points. The key to creating a workable system is choosing the proper lengths for the moving averages. If the system is too sensitive, numerous false signals will be given; if the system is too insensitive, major changes will have already have taken place before a signal is given.

As shown in Exhibit 4.6, a 12-week exponential moving average is used to filter short-term fluctuations and to trigger the defined direction change points. A 40-week exponential moving average is used to reveal the intermediate-term trend. When the 12-week exponential moving average crosses the 40-week average, a defined change of direction is said to occur. The arrows in the exhibit show past changes.

EXHIBIT 4.6 Corporate Bond Interest Rate Trend Identifier

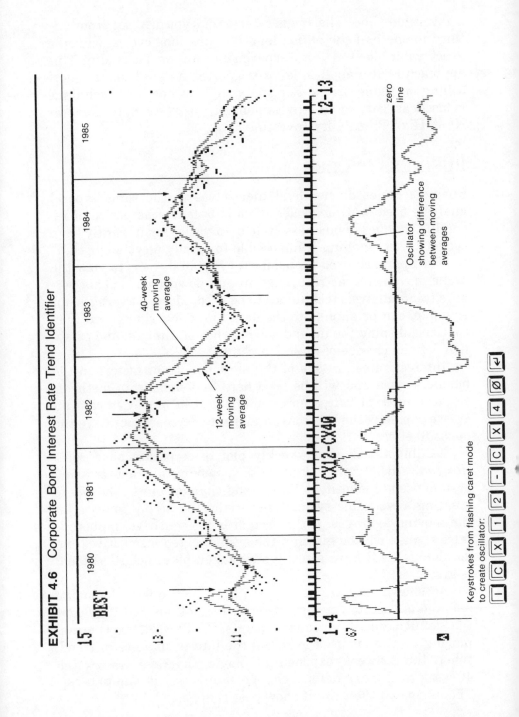

Moving-average lengths are found using trial and error as discussed in Chapter Three. The crossings indicate a change in direction as defined by the system. It is important to understand that the crossings provide no information regarding the expected duration of the trend in interest rates, nor of the future level of the trend.

When dealing with other economic-based cycle data that does not have a constant period, the principles used in the interest rate example can be applied. The cyclic movements are treated as trends, and trend-identification methods are used for analysis. Besides the moving averages crossing method used here, other approaches (e.g., the percentage change or three-step reversal methods) may also be used. The choice is based on the current situation, the effectiveness of the techniques on the specific historical data, and the personal preference of the investor.

SELECTED REFERENCES

ALLVINE, F. C. "Presidential Elections and the Stock Market: Will the Cycle Hold?" *AAII Journal,* June 1984, pp. 9–12.

APPEL, GERALD, and W. F. HITSSCHLER, *Stock Market Trading Systems.* Homewood, Ill.: Dow Jones-Irwin, 1980.

CORNEY, WILLIAM J. "Moving Averages and Cycle Analysis." *Dowline,* September–October, 1985, pp. 36–37.

HAYES, MICHAEL. *The Dow Jones-Irwin Guide to Stock Market Cycles.* Homewood, Ill.: Dow Jones-Irwin, 1977.

HURST, J. M. *The Magic of Stock Transaction Timing.* Englewood Cliffs, N.J.: Prentice-Hall, 1970.

CHAPTER FIVE

Relative Performance

When making judgments on quality, it is natural for you to make comparisons. If you are in the market for a car, a television, or some other consumer good, you may find that a useful approach is to check the performance of different brands and models against each other to find the one that's best for you.

With stocks, you can take the same basic approach. For example, you can compare an individual stock with other stocks, with groups of stocks, or even with itself over time for the purpose of increasing the chance of finding a good deal.

Two basic approaches are available to help you make relative performance comparisons. The first, called *relative strength,* is a ratio measure of the relative percentage price change over time in two stocks or other quantities of interest. The second, called *comparison charting,* is the simultaneous plotting from a base line of two or more issues on a single percentage change chart. Each of these approaches will be explained in turn.

RELATIVE STRENGTH

The Dow Jones Market Analyzer PLUS has two built-in relative strength measures—the relative strength ratio indicator and the Welles Wilder relative strength measure.

The relative strength ratio indicator is accessed from the main menu by selecting X (Relative Strength). This indicator chart displays the ratio of two selected stocks or averages across their common data history. If the two histories change by the same percentage amount, the ratio remains unchanged and the relative strength chart displays a straight line. This line will be traced independent of the direction the compared values are moving, so long as they are moving in tandem with the same percentage change.

If the percentage changes differ, the relative strength line will move up or down based on the differing percent change relationships. The change will take place even if both price histories are falling (or rising) together, so long as the changes are occurring at different percentage rates. For example, if Stock A declines by 20 percent while Stock B is declining by 50 percent, the relative strength chart of Stock A against Stock B (i.e., B as the base for the ratio) will show a rise, since Stock A is performing better, relative to Stock B.

There are a number of ways to use this relative strength measurement and charting technique. Some ideas follow.

How does the stock's performance compare to the overall market?

During a rising market, a portfolio of stocks that are strong relative to the market will tend to perform better than a portfolio of stocks that are weak relative to the market. Relative strength can therefore be used as an important part of a selection criteria during bull markets.

Conversely, during bear markets, stocks that are weak relative to the market often produce larger-percentage short-term gains than those evident in the overall market when a turnaround arrives. Reversals from major sell-offs offer the best opportunity for taking advantage of this situation.

Exhibit 5.1 shows price movements of the Chrysler Corporation, the Dow Jones Industrial Average, and the relative price movements of Chrysler versus the Dow.

The charts illustrate the relative strength phenomenon just mentioned. The drop in the Dow from January 1984 to June 1984 (16 percent) was accompanied by a worse performance, on a percentage basis, by Chrysler Corporation (33 percent). This disparity is shown by the downtrending line in the relative strength chart.

EXHIBIT 5.1 Relative Strength: Chrysler to the Dow Jones Industrial Average

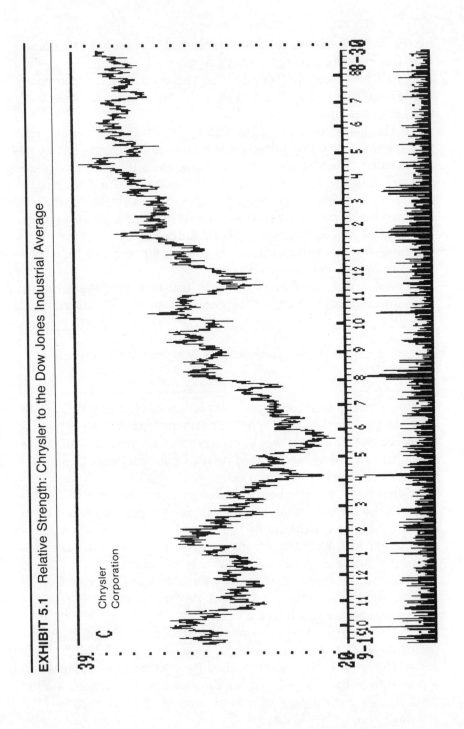

Chrysler
Corporation

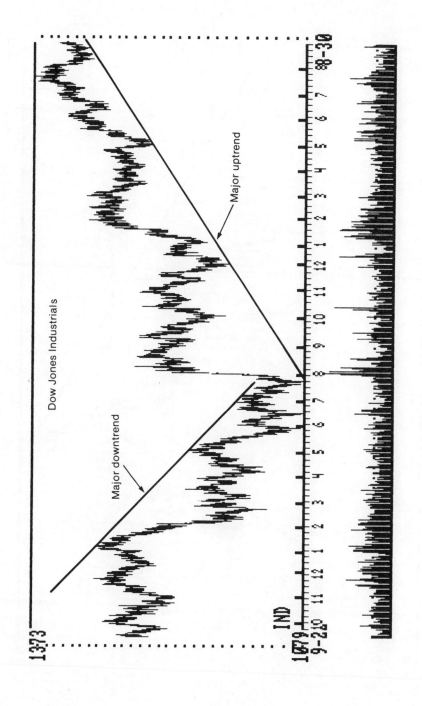

EXHIBIT 5.1 *(concluded)*

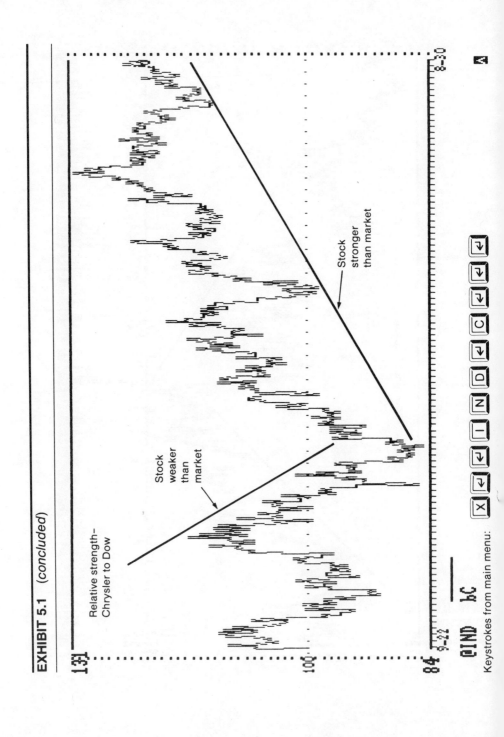

Relative strength–
Chrysler to Dow

Stock
weaker
than
market

Stock
stronger
than market

Keystrokes from main menu:

When the Dow subsequently reversed direction, its initial thrust produced a rise of about 4 percent, while Chrysler rose about 50 percent! The stock, which was much weaker than the market, became much stronger than the market on the turn-around.

> *How does the stock's performance compare with its industry group?*

The stock market can be thought of as being composed of numerous industry groups, each having its own price-change behavior. For example, utility companies may be doing quite well while the steel industry is in a decline and the high-technology stocks are in the doldrums. With this in mind, a rational strategy for stock selection may include choosing the better-acting industry groups first, then confining stock purchases to the best-acting stocks in those groups.

Relative strength charting allows you to compare the performance of industry groups to each other, and of individual stocks against their respective industry group averages. Stocks with poor relative strength in a strong industry group would be avoided, while stocks with good relative strength would be candidates for purchase. It is important to remember the fact that just because a stock is rising does not imply that its relative strength is favorable. What we are looking for are stocks that are rising faster, on a percentage basis, than their industry-group average is rising.

Exhibit 5.2 provides an example of how a stock-to-industry-group relative-strength analysis is made. The first chart shows General Motors stock; the second chart, a group average for the automobile industry; and the last chart, a tracing of the relative strength of General Motors against the automobile group index.

The industry group shows an early rising trend followed by a rather flat price movement. General Motor's relative strength indicates a weak comparative performance early on, followed by very poor relative price movement for the last half of the time period shown. Note that GM stock was rising while the industry-group average was rising. Its relative strength, how-

EXHIBIT 5.2 Relative Strength: GM to Automotive Average

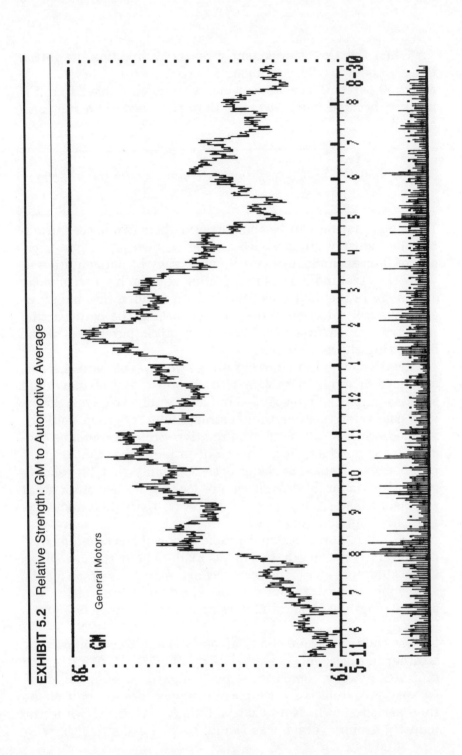

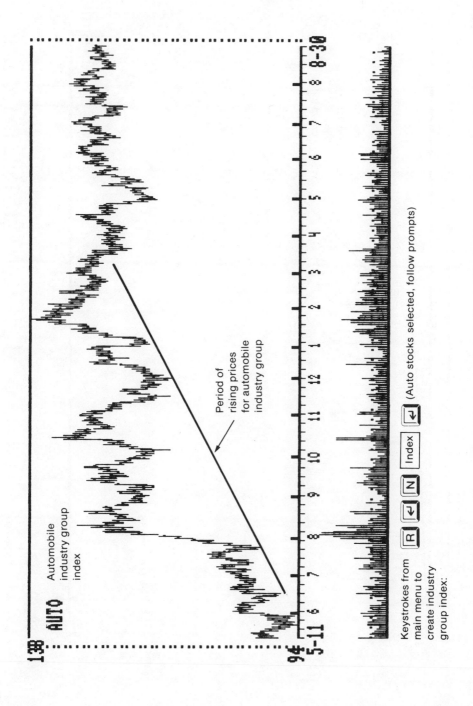

AUTO

Automobile industry group index

Period of rising prices for automobile industry group

1.38

94 5-11 6 7 8 9 10 11 12 1 2 3 4 5 6 7 8 8-30

Keystrokes from main menu to create industry group index:

R ↵ N Index ↵ (Auto stocks selected, follow prompts)

EXHIBIT 5.2 *(concluded)*

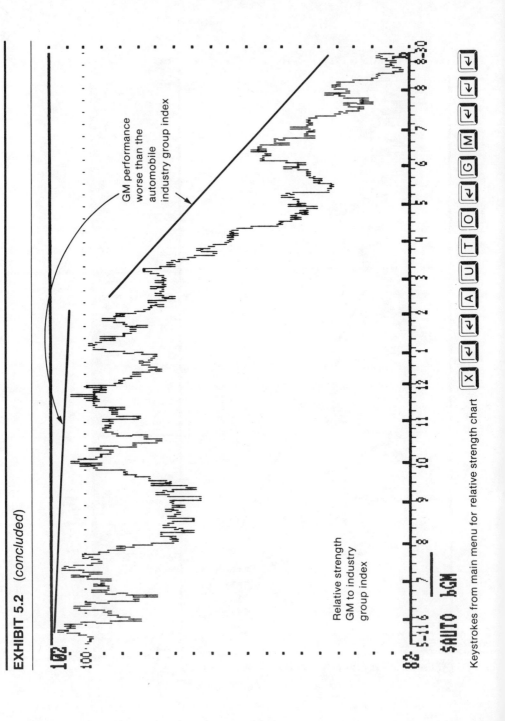

GM performance worse than the automobile industry group index

Relative strength GM to industry group index

$AUTO bGM

82

5-11 6

Keystrokes from main menu for relative strength chart

X ↵ ↵ A U T O ↵ G M ↵ ↵ ↵

ever, was showing an overall decline in trend. An investor contemplating participation in the automobile industry group during the period shown on the chart should have considered alternative stocks.

The automobile industry group index shown in Exhibit 5.2 was made by the Dow Jones Market Analyzer PLUS from individual automobile stock data histories. The keystrokes used in its creation are shown in the exhibit.

The ability to create your own average can be very useful, as we will see in the strategy section of this book. You are no longer confined to looking at the widely publicized industry groups, but you are free to analyze any group you have an interest in.

How does one stock's price performance compare with another?

The stock selection process often involves choosing between a number of stocks that have been culled from a larger group. An aid to making the final decision can come from relative strength comparisons between the stocks. For example, if an investor wants to purchase one of two stocks that look equally attractive, a relative strength chart would show which of the two possess a stronger price performance.

Simple trendline analysis (explained in Chapter Three) made on the relative strength chart is usually sufficient to show the prevailing trend. As long as a rising trendline between major bottoms is unbroken, a rising trend is defined as being in progress. Conversely, as long as a falling major-peak trendline is unbroken, a declining relative strength trend is defined as occurring. Exhibit 5.3 illustrates this comparison between the Ford Motor Company and General Motors. Uptrends indicate Ford has a stronger relative strength than does GM; downtrends favor GM over Ford.

EXHIBIT 5.3   Relative Strength: Ford to GM

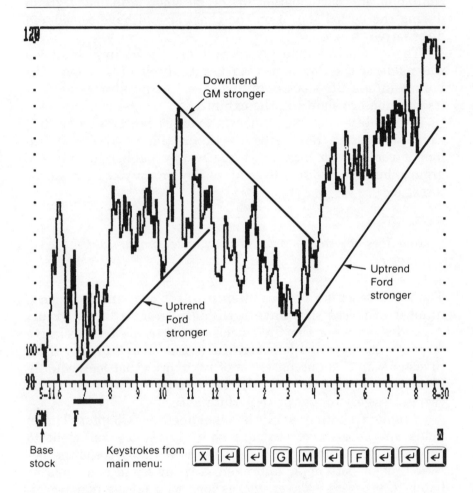

Does the stock price movement appear to be gaining or losing strength?

A popular measure of a stock's *internal* relative strength is the Welles Wilder relative strength index. This index gives the percent of total price change over a chosen number of periods represented by price increases. If, for example, prices rose one point each day for four days, then dropped two points on the fifth day, the relative strength reading would be 4/6 (four points of price increases divided by six total points of price changes).

There are two ways of using this indicator. One way is to compare its changing levels with changing stock price levels through divergence analysis. The second way is to assess extremes in the indicator's value.

Exhibit 5.4 shows how this indicator can be used to provide evidence of loss of trend strength by means of divergence analysis. Rising highs in price that are not confirmed by rising relative strength indicate a deteriorating situation. Conversely, prices that reach lower lows while the relative strength measure reaches higher lows indicates an improving situation.

The number of periods used to create this index can vary based on the time horizon of the investor. The chart shown displays a 55-day range for intermediate- to long-term analysis. Shorter periods can be used for more sensitive readings. Exhibit 5.5 shows the same chart but with a 14-day relative strength range. This is the range that Welles Wilder uses to produce his RSI readings.

Assessing high and low levels of internal relative strength is a fairly reliable method for finding unsustainable price moves. When the relative strength measure exceeds 70, the price can be thought of as entering a region in which a stalling of the price rise or a reversal to the downside can be expected. Conversely, when the measure is less than 30, a stalling of the price decline or a reversal to the upside can be expected. Of course, this indicator does not indicate the exact timing of a reversal or the extent of a price move. Exhibit 5.6 illustrates the 30 and 70 RSI levels.

If you track a number of stocks, you can rapidly screen them on RSI using the Dow Jones Market Analyzer PLUS without charting each one individually. The View Summary report not only calculates the Welles Wilder relative strength but also allows you to establish the extreme cutoff points just discussed for filtering purposes. Exhibit 5.7 shows how one issue with a relative strength reading greater than or equal to 70 was flagged from a group of seven issues. This report can just as easily be used to filter stocks for relative strengths of 30 or less.

EXHIBIT 5.4 Fifty-Five-Day Internal Relative Strength: Chrysler Corporation

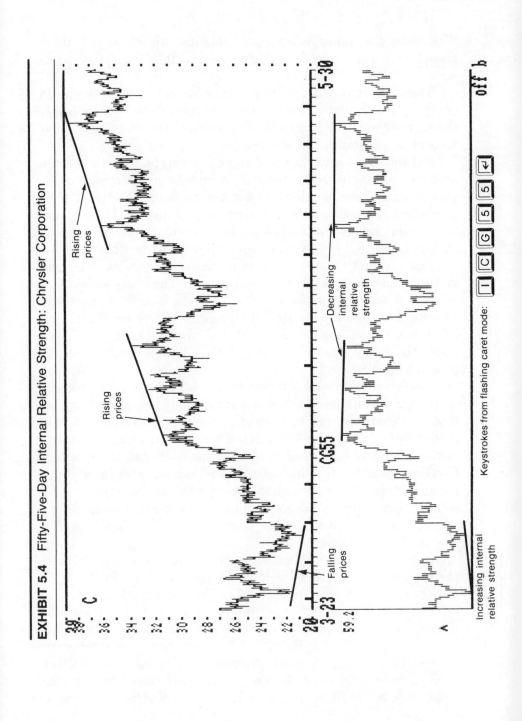

EXHIBIT 5.5 Fourteen-Day Internal Relative Strength: Chrysler Corporation

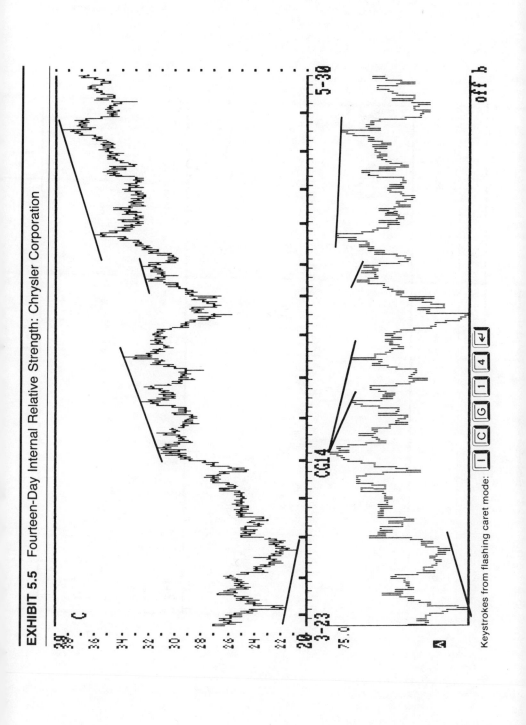

Keystrokes from flashing caret mode:

EXHIBIT 5.6 Extreme Values in Internal Relative Strength

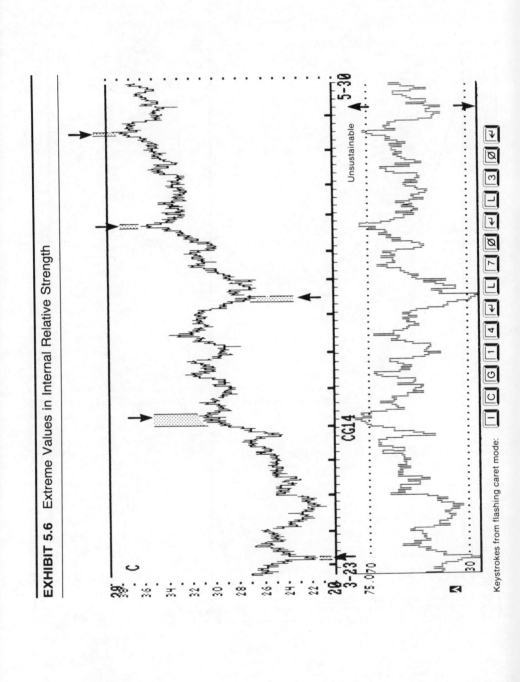

Keystrokes from flashing caret mode:

EXHIBIT 5.7   Relative Strength Filter for Extreme Values

---

stock	close	1 day change		12 day average			14 day volatility	
		change	% ch	c/adc	v/adv	vlty	posn	rstr
DEF	13.55	-0.04	-0.3	1.01	1.03	1.00	77	73

14.3% (1/7) satisfied RELATIVE STRENGTH greater than or equal to 70

<R> Re-Filter   <Esc> Menu

Percent
meeting
established
standard

Keystrokes from main menu:

O (view summary)   ↵ D ESC F 7 1 7 Ø ↵

Does the relative strength of the Utility average indicate a possible coming upmove in the Industrials?

Movements in the Dow Jones Utility Average have long been used as a portent of the major direction of the Dow Jones Industrial Average. Why might this be true?

As a group, utility stocks are very sensitive to interest rate changes and to beliefs concerning possible future changes in these rates. As interest rates rise, these heavy-debt-laden organizations are faced with increased costs; as rates fall, their costs also fall. Falling rates (or expectations thereof) often result in rising utility stock prices, with rising rates (or their expectation) yielding falling prices.

While interest rate changes also affect costs for other companies, the impact tends to be less dramatic and less immediate than it is for utilities, since the debt burden for these companies is usually less than that of the utilities. The result for stock market activity is often an immediate price adjustment to

EXHIBIT 5.8 Relative Strength: Utilities to Dow Industrials

Chart A

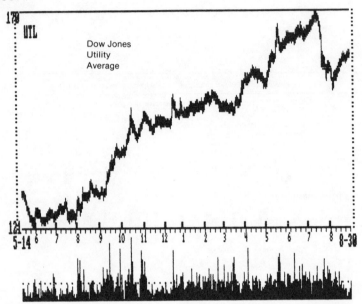

Dow Jones Utility Average

Chart B

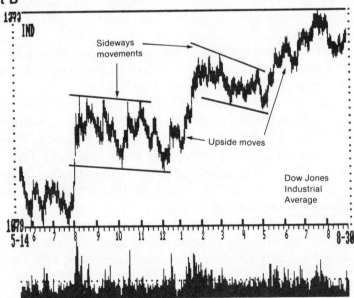

Sideways movements

Upside moves

Dow Jones Industrial Average

Chart C

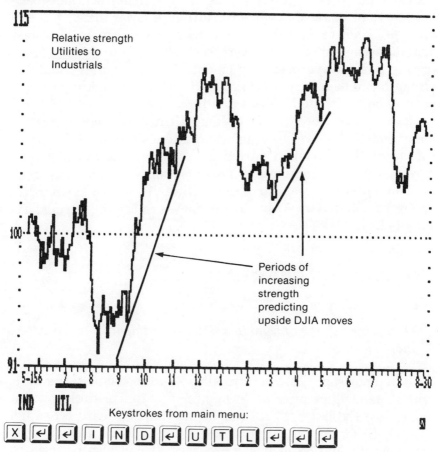

Relative strength
Utilities to
Industrials

Periods of
increasing
strength
predicting
upside DJIA moves

Keystrokes from main menu:

interest rate changes (or their forecasts) for the utilities, followed later by share price changes in the industrials.

Unfortunately, the preceding scenario does not always work
out as planned. Other factors are often viewed as more important than are interest rate changes in moving the market up or
down. As an example, during periods of mildly rising interest
rates, investors may look beyond the current situation to lower
rates later, or they may value stocks based on earnings more
than on the interest rate environment.

In general, falling rates (resulting in higher utility share prices) tend to be a better predictor of a rising overall stock market than increasing rates (resulting in lower utility prices) are a predictor of a falling stock market. Furthermore, the predictive mechanism tends to work best when the stock market is tracing a sideways price movement. At these times, relative strength can be a very useful analytical tool for making a comparison between the Utilities and Industrials.

Exhibit 5.8 shows the Dow Jones Utility Average, the Dow Jones Industrial Average, and the relative strength of the Utilities to the Industrials. Chart B shows two periods of sideways movements of the Industrials. These periods were characterized by strong relative strength of the Utilities, as shown in Chart C and were followed by strong upside moves in the Industrials, as expected.

COMPARISON CHARTING

> *Over time, what happens to a $100 investment in two or more stocks?*

The Comparison Chart feature allows you to compare the individual percentage price performance of up to five stocks on one chart (see Exhibit 5.9). Although this charting feature has little benefit for analytical purposes, it does provide a quick comparative evaluation of past purchases. It can also be used to play "what if" games on past data. (For example, What if I bought Ford instead of GM on April 12 and sold on May 19 instead of on June 2?)

SELECTED REFERENCES

COPPOCK, E. S. C. "Practical Relative Strength Charting." In *The Encyclopedia of Stock Market Techniques.* Larchmont, N.Y.: Investors Intelligence, 1985, pp. 7-1–7-45.

FOSBACK, NORMAN G. *Stock Market Logic.* Fort Lauderdale, Fla.: The Institute for Economic Research, 1985.

EXHIBIT 5.9 Comparison Chart: GM and Ford

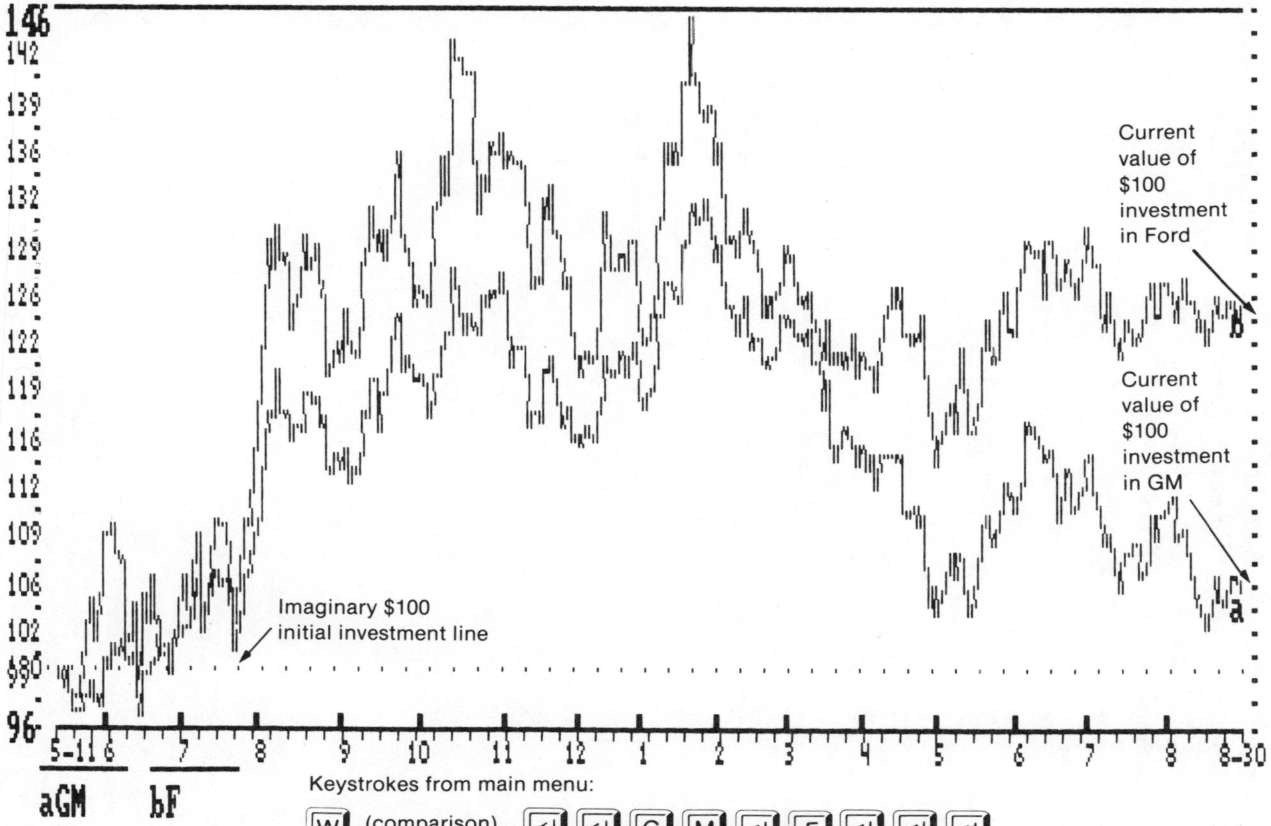
146
142
139
136
132
129
126
122
119
116
112
109
106
102
99
96
5-11 6 7 8 9 10 11 12 1 2 3 4 5 6 7 8 8-30
aGM
bF
Imaginary $100 initial investment line
Current value of $100 investment in Ford
Current value of $100 investment in GM
b
a

Keystrokes from main menu:

W (comparison) ↵ ↵ G M ↵ F ↵ ↵ ↵

A

MERKLE, DANIEL R. *Relative Strength and Stock Market Timing.* Alton, Ill.: Traders Research, 1967.

WILDER, WELLS J. *New Concepts in Technical Trading Systems.* Greensboro, N.C.: Trend Research, 1978.

CHAPTER SIX

Volume

There are numerous ways to use trading volume for stock analysis. The most elemental approach involves plotting volume and comparing its changing magnitude with price action. More sophisticated methods involve either partitioning total volume into components or developing price-volume functions.

The Dow Jones Market Analyzer PLUS automatically creates and plots six volume indicators and allows you to custom build many others. Each of the six indicators will be discussed in this chapter, along with ideas for other volume analysis techniques.

TOTAL VOLUME LINE CHARTS

What are current total volume changes saying about price action?

In general, volume demonstrates conviction of price change. You can think of high volume as a shout, low volume as a whisper. In human communications, shouts and whispers are usually very important for helping us to understand just how much someone really means what they are saying. Unfortunately, we are often fooled by loud or quiet words from someone whose real motives are obscure. The stock market acts in similar fashion.

EXHIBIT 6.1 High-Volume Price Reversal from a Support Level

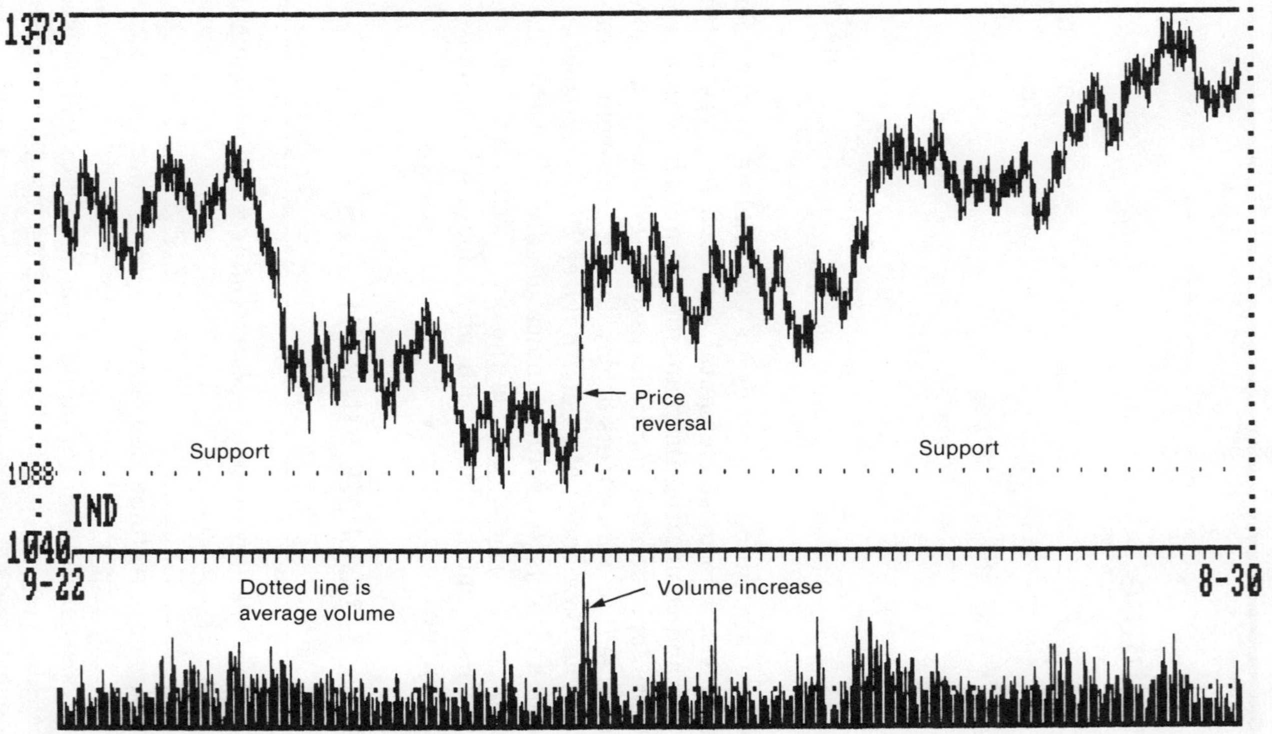

Four basic generalizations help us understand the meaning of stock volume. Like all generalizations, these are far from absolute. They can, however, offer valuable clues to what is really happening in the market.

Generalization 1.   When price breaks out on high volume from a support or a resistance zone, or from a widely followed chart pattern, the increasing volume lends conviction to the move in price. On an upmove, sharp volume is the investors' shout. "I think this upmove is for real!" On a drop in price, the volume increase is like the yell: "Get out! We think prices are going lower!" Exhibit 6.1 shows an example of a major reversal from a support level on high volume.

The term *high volume* for this and other generalizations refers to volume spikes that are well above the average volume (dotted line on the chart) and that clearly stand out when compared to nearby volume peaks.

Generalization 2.   After a substantial rally has taken place, if a volume increase appears on a further price rise it is often a warning signal that a near-term top or "blow-off" is at hand. "It's all over but for the shouting," is an apt description of this situation. Exhibit 6.2 shows examples of this phenomenon.

Generalization 3.   When prices fall at an accelerating rate accompanied by increasing volume, an unsustainable condition, sometimes called a *wash-out* or *selling climax,* is occurring. This condition will likely result in a sharp price reversal, and it is the investors' scream of panic. During this panic state, it may seem to an investor that there is no end to the depths that prices will fall. From a psychological standpoint, this is the most difficult time for investors to buy, since emotions are then a dominant factor in investment decision making. Exhibit 6.3 shows a volume peak with the point of resolution at A.

As an aid to using this generalization, as well as Generalizations 1 and 2, a volume "limit line" can be constructed using past data. This line is used as an alert to the possibility of a volume message. When the limit line is exceeded, the three vol-

EXHIBIT 6.2 Near-Term Topping or Blow-Off Action

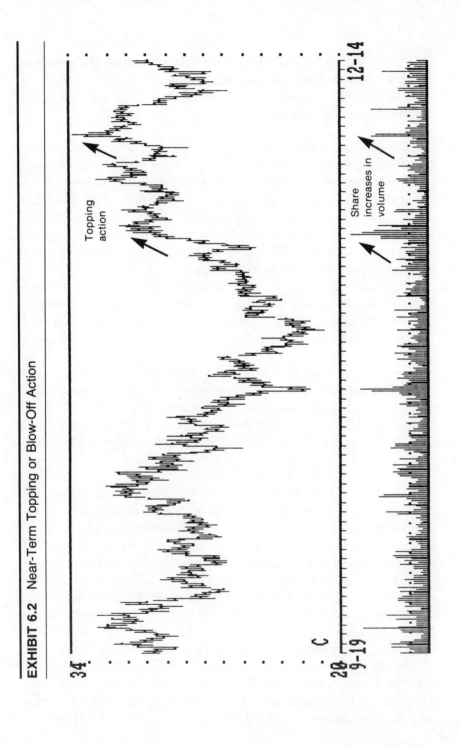

EXHIBIT 6.3 The Selling Climax

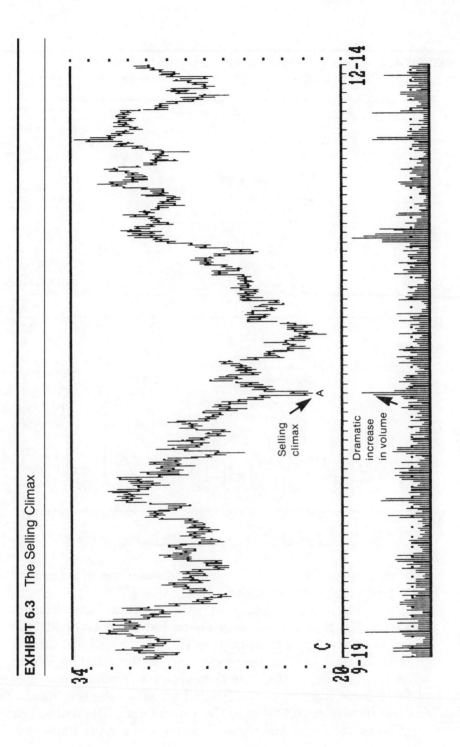

EXHIBIT 6.4   The Regression Limit Line and High-Volume Alerts

---

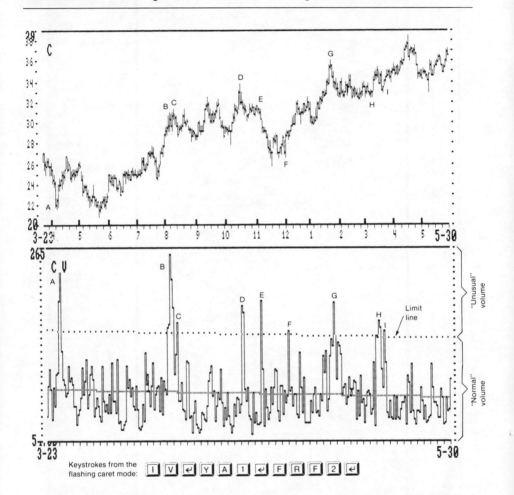

Keystrokes from the flashing caret mode: Ⅰ Ⅴ ↵ Ⅴ Ⅰ Ⅰ ↵ Ⅰ Ⅰ Ⅰ ↵

ume generalizations can be reviewed to see if one of them may
be appropriate to the situation.

The limit line is constructed with the Dow Jones Market
Analyzer PLUS on an indicator chart. Exhibit 6.4 provides an
example of how this can be accomplished.

The vertical bars in the lower part of the chart represent
daily volume. The dotted line that appears through the center
of the volume is a regression line, which offers the best mathematical fit of a straight line to the volume data. The dotted line
parallel to and above the regression line is an upper limit line.

The regression line is used to represent an average level of volume. Volume at or near this line can be thought of as "normal" in magnitude. Volume that departs greatly from this line (as shown by the freestanding spikes on the diagram) are considered atypical or abnormal. Unusual volume is defined precisely by those spikes (marked A through I) extending above the limit line.

The limit line is constructed using the statistician's measure of unusualness: the standard deviation. A two–standard deviation limit above the regression line is used to specify an unusually high level of volume. This is a commonly used standard that generally provides good results.

You should monitor volume using the limit line to see if it exceeds the two–standard deviation limit. If so, something unusual is happening, signaling the importance of taking a closer look at the stock from the standpoint of the volume messages previously discussed.

If you have many stocks to follow, the Dow Jones Market Analyzer PLUS View Summary report provides a time-saving alternative to making a graphical analysis of each stock. In place of limit line construction, the report provides a listing of stocks that exceed a percentage of volume above an average

---

EXHIBIT 6.5   View Summary Volume Filter

| stock | close | 1 day change | | 12 day average | | 14 day volatility | |
		change	% ch	c/adc.	v/adv	vlty	posn	rstr
KM	33.88	0.63	1.9	1.04	1.98	1.82	88	68
IBM	130.50	1.37	1.1	1.03	1.52	1.33	95	65

7.4% (2/27) satisfied V/ADV greater than or equal to 1.5

↑
Percent
satisfying
requirement

<R> Re-Filter   <Esc> Menu

Keystrokes from main menu:

|O| (view summary) |↵| |D| |ESC| |F| |4| |1| |1| |.| |5| |↵|

EXHIBIT 6.6 Low Volume on Sideways Price Movement during Uptrend

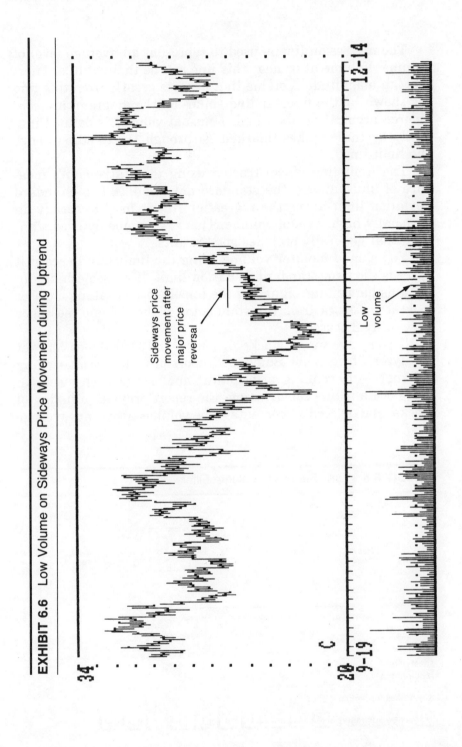

Sideways price movement after major price reversal

Low volume

34.

20.
9-19   12-14

level. The report is quite flexible, allowing you to change both the time period and the percentage to be exceeded. As an example, Exhibit 6.5 shows the results of a 27-stock filter for a volume of 50 percent or more above the average of the past 12 days. These stocks can then be the subject of further analysis.

Generalization 4.   After a major price reversal to the upside, low-volume periods (sometimes called volume *holes*) often occur during sideways movements as price consolidation takes place. It's like a calm before the upward storm of stock prices resumes. Many traders find these periods to be favorable times in which to make purchases, when other evidence confirms the purchase decision. Exhibit 6.6 provides an example.

NEGATIVE VOLUME INDICATOR

> *Does it appear that the price rise is topping?*

The negative volume indicator (NVI) provides a representation of price trends when volume is decreasing. The *only* time this indicator changes in value is when volume is dropping on a period-to-period basis. If prices fall while volume is decreasing, the negative volume indicator will also fall. If prices rise while volume is decreasing, the negative volume indicator will also rise. For all other price-volume situations, the negative volume indicator remains constant.

Because it is common for prices to fall on decreasing volume, a falling negative volume indicator represents typical behavior. A rising negative volume indicator (prices rising on decreasing volume) may be evidence that something "unusual" is going on.

If prices rise sharply after a substantial decline, and the negative volume indicator also rises, you should view the rally with suspicion, because prices are rising on decreasing volume. Increasing monetary commitment in the form of rising numbers of shares is not powering the upmove. This makes the increase in prices difficult to sustain (see Exhibit 6.7). These false price moves are sometimes called *technical rallies* or *bear traps*.

EXHIBIT 6.7 Unsustainable Price Reversal during Downtrend

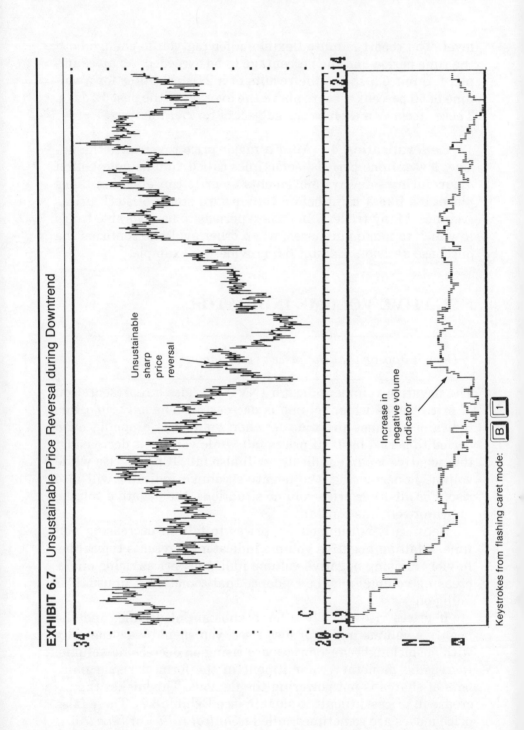

Unsustainable sharp price reversal

Increase in negative volume indicator

Keystrokes from flashing caret mode: B 1

Moreover, if prices are in a well-defined uptrend and the negative volume indicator begins to rise, a topping out of prices may be occurring. This decreasing volume may represent a declining interest in the stock or a transfer of stock from "strong hands" to "weak hands" as the unsophisticated small investors step in to make purchases.

Exhibit 6.8, Chart A, uses shaded areas to show rising prices that are accompanied by well-defined increases in the negative volume indicator. You should note that this analysis always proceeds from the price to the indicator, and not the other way around. As rising prices begin to appear, you should check the indicator to see if it is increasing (volume decreasing with the price rise). If so, the permanency of the rise is suspect. If the indicator is *not* rising, then *no* information is furnished. The indicator does not confirm price advances.

Exhibit 6.8, Chart B, shows another example of this indicator during both rising and falling price trends. You can see that no hint was given of the major price peak, although valuable information was provided on some other price rises. This points out the selective nature of this indicator and reaffirms its major area of application: pinpointing times of price increase without volume support. All the other reasons for lack of price-rise follow-through (and there are many) are ignored by this indicator. It provides but one symptom of illness.

To aid you in interpreting the indicator, you may find it helpful to smooth out the short-term fluctuations using a three-day moving average. Exhibit 6.9 illustrates both how this is accomplished and how it should be interpreted.

Norman Fosback, author of *Stock Market Logic,* has found another way to use the negative volume indicator. By taking a simple one-year moving average of the indicator on a weekly basis for the Dow Jones Industrial Average and comparing the current value of the indicator to the average, he assesses the odds of being in a bull market. Based on 35 years of data, Fosback has found that when the negative volume indicator is above its one-year moving average, the odds are better than 95 in 100 in favor of a bull market. Fosback feels that this is one of the best bull market prediction indicators available.

EXHIBIT 6.8 Rising Prices Accompanied by Rising Negative Volume Indicator

Chart A

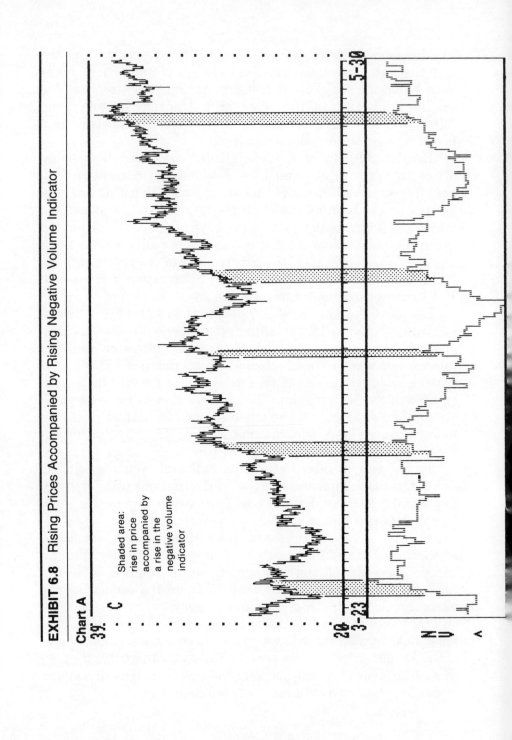

Shaded area: rise in price accompanied by a rise in the negative volume indicator

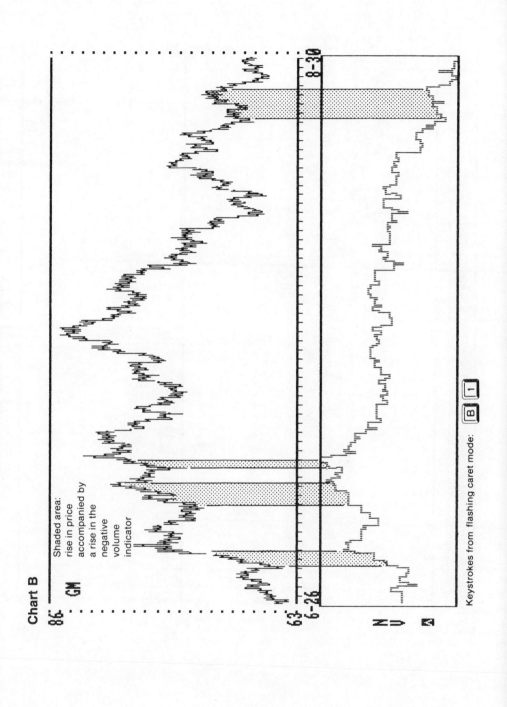

Chart B

GM

Shaded area:
rise in price
accompanied by
a rise in the
negative
volume
indicator

86

63
6-26

8-30

N

↓

◢

Keystrokes from flashing caret mode: B 1

EXHIBIT 6.9 Smoothed Representation of Negative Volume Indicator

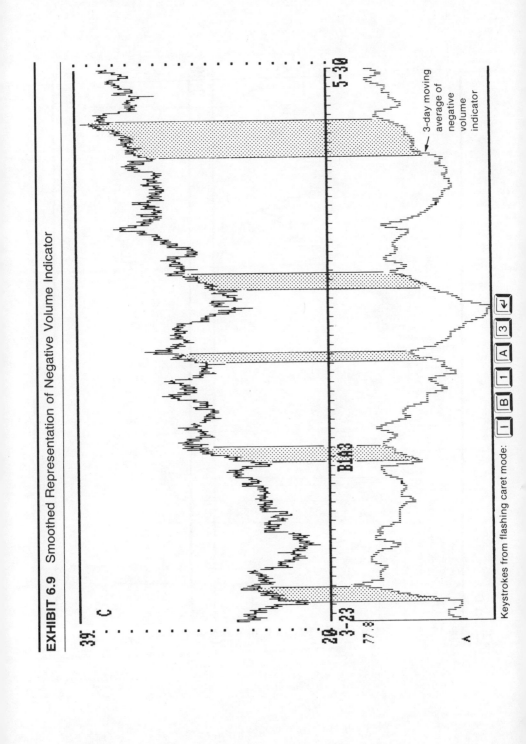

3-day moving average of negative volume indicator

Keystrokes from flashing caret mode: 1 B 1 A 3 ↵

POSITIVE VOLUME INDICATOR

Does it appear that an uptrend in prices has commenced?

The positive volume indicator (PVI) measures the trend of prices during periods of advancing volume. It displays for advancing volume the same type of information that the negative volume indicator portrays for declining volume. While the negative volume indicator is primarily used to indicate price topping, the positive volume indicator is used to indicate price bottom reversals.

The only time the positive volume indicator changes in numeric value is when volume is increasing on a period-to-period basis. When the positive volume indicator rises, this means volume is increasing as prices are rising. When the positive volume indicator falls, this means that volume is increasing as prices are dropping.

Increasing volume on rising prices is typical behavior for stocks. As long as a stock is in an uptrend, the positive volume indicator should be expected to display a rising trend. Since minor price corrections are not usually accompanied by heavy volume, the positive volume indicator will tend to maintain an upward trend until the price has actually reversed direction. At that time, volume tends to pick up on declining prices, driving the indicator down.

Trend identification for the positive volume indicator is used primarily as an aid for confirming reversals from price bottoms. It provides especially useful evidence for identifying an upturn in price after a substantial decline has taken place. Exhibit 6.10 shows a 50-day intermediate-term simple moving average of the positive volume indicator to yield intermediate trend-reversal signals to the upside. Note that the only signals of value with this indicator are rises through the moving average; downward breaks are ignored. Like all moving average techniques, sideways movements may result in numerous whipsaws.

EXHIBIT 6.10 Positive Volume Indicator for Identifying the Start of Uptrends

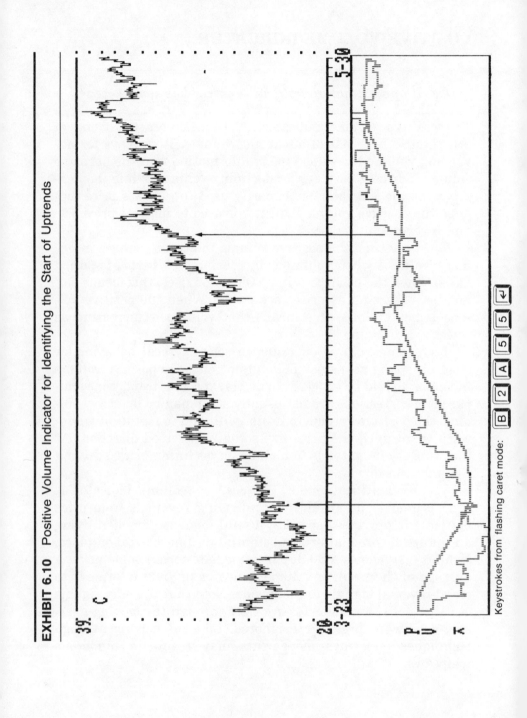

Keystrokes from flashing caret mode: B 2 A 5 5 ↵

INDICATORS OF ACCUMULATION AND DISTRIBUTION

> *Does the stock appear to be under accumulation or distribution?*

The cumulative volume indicator (CVI), price volume trend (PVT), and accumulation/distribution indicator (ADI) all purport to accomplish the same task: to measure the accumulation or distribution of stock. Stock accumulation refers to the purchase accumulation of stock by the more sophisticated investors in anticipation of a rise in prices. The opposite situation prevails during periods of distribution, since stock is said to move from the knowledgeable to the uninformed.

The cumulative volume indicator, also known as on-balance volume, was developed by Joseph E. Granville.[1] This indicator is a running total of volume, with each day's figure added to or subtracted from the total based on whether the closing price is up or down for the day. On-balance volume represents the approximate cumulative difference between volume that is making prices rise and volume that is making prices decline. It should be noted that the construction of the indicator requires the entire volume for the day to be added to or subtracted from the total, irrespective of the magnitude of the price change.

The cumulative volume indicator is used by noting significant peak-to-peak and bottom-to-bottom divergencies between its action and price action of the stock. Exhibit 6.11 illustrates how this analysis is made.

Looking at the price chart, Points A and B are compared to Points 1 and 2 on the cumulative volume indicator chart. The lines drawn on the two charts are used to show divergencies. The cumulative volume indicator shows a stronger reading at Point 2 than it shows at Point 1, while the price at B is not correspondingly higher than it is at A. Although the price went down, the up volume, on balance, has increased. This is viewed

---

[1]Joseph E. Granville, *Granville's New Key to Stock Market Profits* (Prentice-Hall, 1963).

EXHIBIT 6.11 Divergence Analysis on the Cumulative Volume Indicator

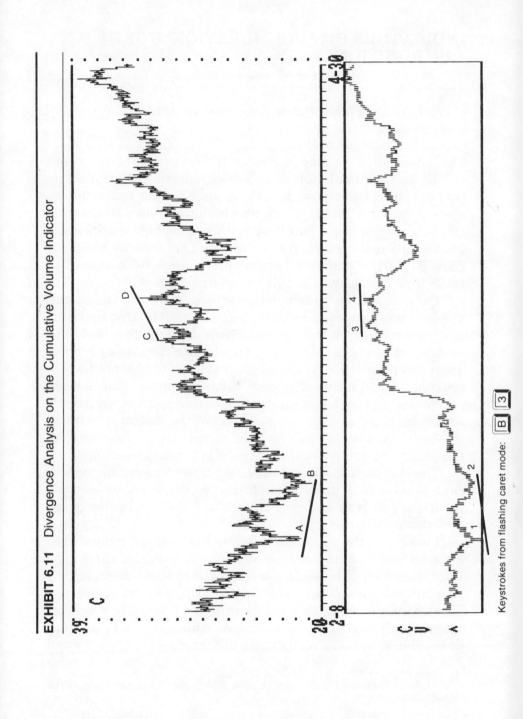

Keystrokes from flashing caret mode: [B] [3]

as reflecting a bullish accumulation of stock from Point A to Point B.

The same type of analysis can be made when a stock or market average is reaching new highs. Distribution is indicated if the high reached by the cumulative volume indicator does not correspond with the high attained by price.

One criticism that has been made against this volume indicator is that the magnitude of daily price change is irrelevant in its calculation. By assigning a plus or minus sign to each day's volume, only the direction of price change matters, not the amount. Further, it is assumed that if the price is up for the day, all the volume throughout the day is up volume. On down days, the assumption is that all the volume is down volume.

Advocates of this technique believe that, despite its simplistic construction, the cumulative volume indicator can help investors recognize major periods of accumulation and distribution. Advocates say that the technique works best when it is used in conjunction with chart patterns, such as the type to be discussed in Chapter Seven.

An indicator that is closely allied with the cumulative volume indicator is the price-volume trend. This indicator also attempts to uncover accumulation and distribution, but in a slightly different way. When the price closes up for the day, only a "piece" of the volume is added to the cumulative total, instead of the entire volume amount being added. The amount added depends on the percentage price change for the day. If the stock is up 5 percent, then 5 percent of the volume is added to the cumulative total. On the downside the calculation is the same, except the percentage of volume is subtracted from the cumulative total.

This construction technique allows for both the magnitude of price change and the volume to be directly incorporated into the indicator. Exhibit 6.12 shows how price-volume trend identifies accumulation and distribution for the same stock shown in Exhibit 6.11.

The accumulation/distribution index (ADI) is the third of this class of indicators. It is constructed by multiplying each day's volume by a certain number before it is accumulated with previous volume. The number used is the change in price di-

EXHIBIT 6.12 Divergence Analysis on the Price-Volume Trend

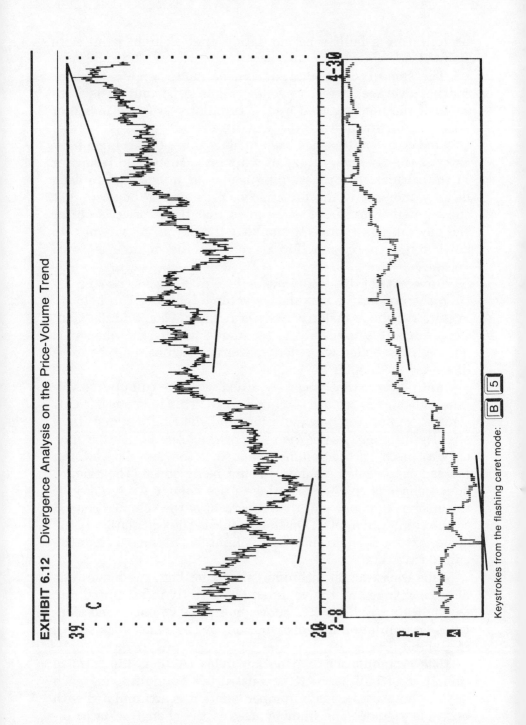

Keystrokes from the flashing caret mode:

vided by the trading range for the day. As an example, if the trading range is 1.00 (high minus low for the day) and the stock moved up by a quarter of a point, the accumulation/distribution indicator is adjusted by adding 0.25 of that day's volume to the previous total.

Exhibit 6.13 shows this indicator compared to the price history of GM. Because the cumulative volume adjustment is made based on percent of the price range, it tends to trace a pattern very close to that of the movement of prices; this correspondence makes any divergence easy to spot. On the chart, for example, the bottom is clearly identified as indicating an area of accumulation.

This indicator is also useful for spotting accumulation during periods of sideways or "quiet" movement. At these times, unusual activities stand out quite clearly when comparisons are made. Exhibit 6.14 provides an example of such a divergence in action.

Which of the three indicators is the correct one for displaying accumulation and distribution? None of them actually shows what we would really like to see: cumulative volume changes on a transaction-by-transaction basis. Each of the three has its proponents and opponents. Since it is so easy to construct these indicators, you should use all three to provide composite evidence of accumulation or distribution.

DAILY VOLUME INDICATOR

Are there extremes in buying or selling pressure?

The daily volume indicator (DVI) pinpoints major daily imbalances in the supply or demand for a stock. The stock's numeric value is a function of where the daily price closes with reference to its range. If it closes at the midpoint of the range for the day, the indicator shows no change. Closes above or below the midpoint cause the indicator to increase or decrease, respectively. The actual size of the change in the indicator depends on the volume for the day, the closing price, the magnitude of the trading range, and the distance between the midpoint of the range and the closing price.

EXHIBIT 6.13 Accumulation/Distribution Indicator

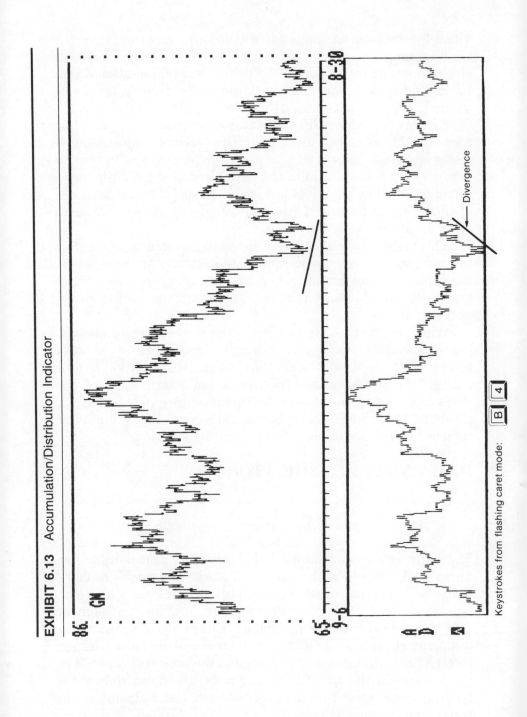

Keystrokes from flashing caret mode: B 4

EXHIBIT 6.14 A Large ADI Increase during Sideways Price Movement

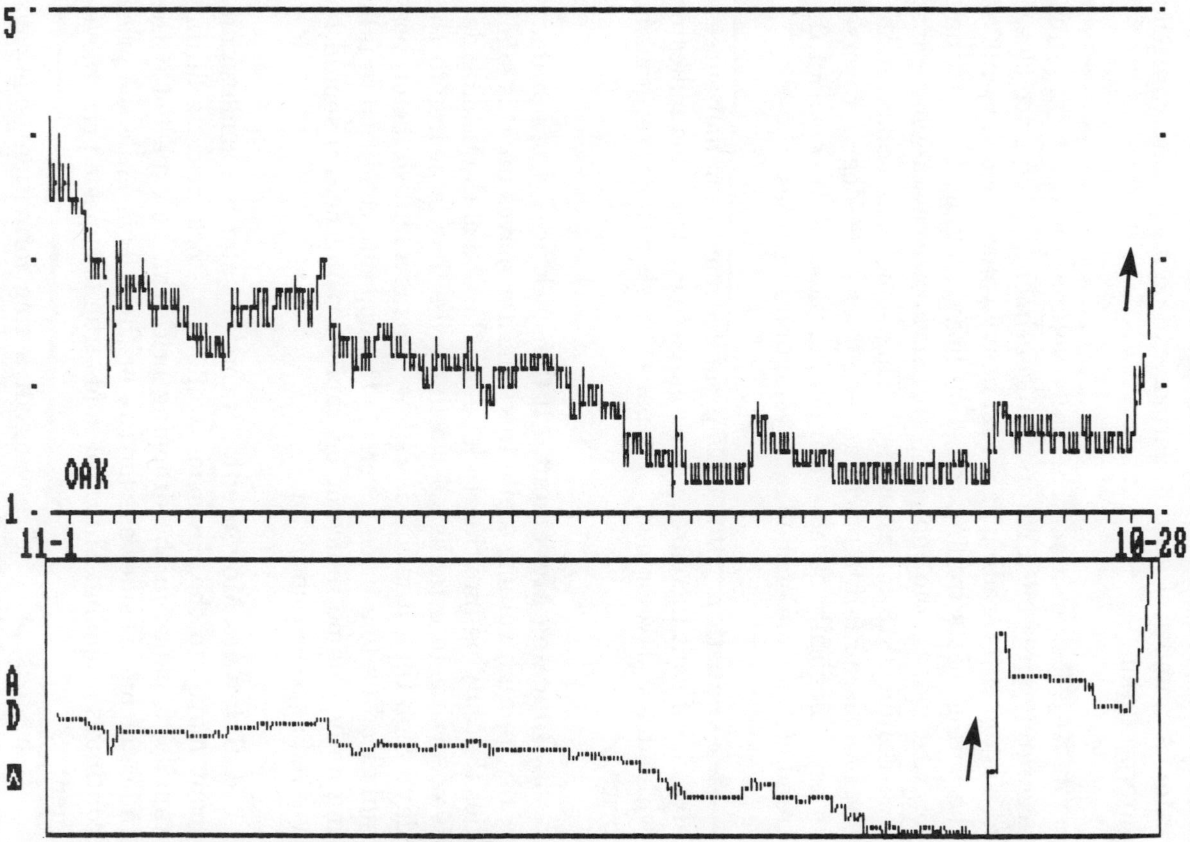

Keystrokes from flashing caret mode: [B] [4]

Exhibit 6.15 provides an example of the action of this indicator. A number of generalizations can be made concerning its interpretation.

1. Key Reversals.   The daily volume indicator can often accurately pinpoint a reversal in sentiment. If the price closes at the top of its trading range on heavy volume one day, and at the bottom of its trading range on heavy volume the next day (or vice versa), the indicator will form a free-standing spike (see Exhibit 6.15 for examples). This sometimes occurs at the end of a rise or fall in prices and signifies a 180-degree reversal in psychologically based sentiment. A pause or reversal in the trend at the time of the key reversal often ensues.

2. Exhaustion.   It is uncommon for more than four successive significant increases or decreases to occur in this indicator without the development of a pause or short-term reversal in price.

3. Opposing Movement.   If the stock price drops dramatically on high volume while the indicator moves up, this signifies that buying into the stock before the end of the trading day is occurring to establish a closing price that is nearer to the day's high than it is the day's low. This is a bullish factor, possibly leading to a price reversal. The opposite condition (a falling daily volume indicator on rapidly rising prices) should be viewed as a bearish factor.

4. Sideways Movement.   If the indicator has made significant moves to the downside while the stock price is falling rapidly, a pause in the dropping price can be expected if the indicator moves sideways for two or three days while the price continues dropping. This also holds true for upside price movement.

If a stock price is moving in a line formation (sideways movement) while the daily volume indicator is moving in a well-defined up- or downtrend, your expectations should favor the eventual movement of prices in the direction of the indicator. It is important to emphasize that the opposite is not true. Horizontal movement in the indicator while prices are trending

EXHIBIT 6.15 Action of the Daily Volume Indicator

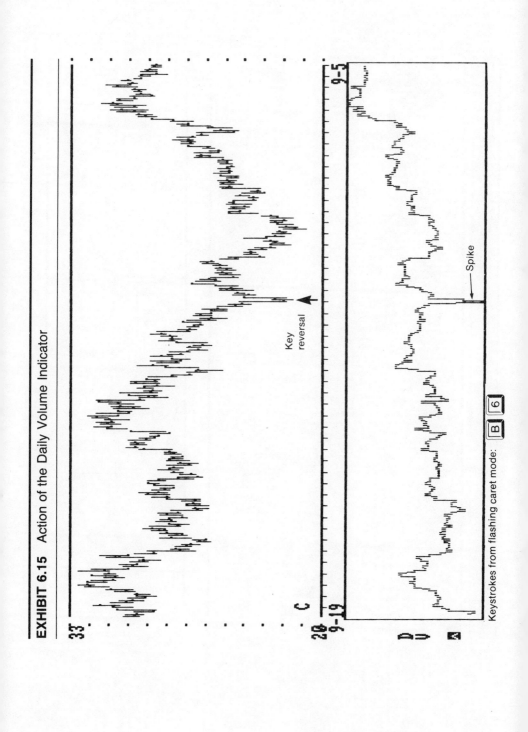

Keystrokes from flashing caret mode: B 6

EXHIBIT 6.15 *(concluded)*

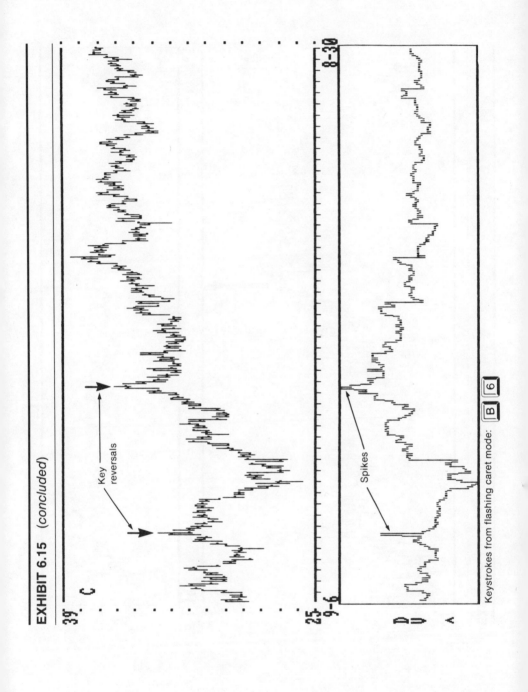

Keystrokes from flashing caret mode: B 6

up or down does not imply a return in price to horizontal movement.

THE BIG BLOCK INDEX

*Are actions of the institutions diverging from price action of
the overall market?*

Institutions account for more than 75 percent of all trading volume on the New York Stock Exchange. With this dominance, it is important for you to keep track of what they are doing.

Martin Zweig's Big-Block Index tracks large-volume trades.[2] It can be constructed easily and can be analyzed using the Dow Jones Market Analyzer PLUS or any other technical analysis software that permits manual data entry.

Data for the index is found in *Barron's* weekly statistical section. To construct the index, the total of all upticks plus downticks are divided into the upticks. The result is the percentage of big-block volume (50,000 or more traded shares) that resulted in higher transaction prices. Exhibit 6.16 shows how this is calculated from the *Barron's* data.

For analysis, Zweig uses a 10-week exponential moving average on the data. He then looks for three percentage point changes to provide contrary market reversal signals.

Exhibit 6.17 illustrates another way to analyze the index data. Major peak-to-peak and bottom-to-bottom divergencies between institutional activity and market price data are found and displayed. These divergencies show when "big money" is getting in while prices are dropping (a bullish sign) and when it is getting out while prices are rising (a bearish sign). When combined with other evidence, this information can be useful in helping you understand the status of the overall market.

OTHER VOLUME INDICATORS

Many other indicators can be constructed from components of total trading volume. If you have the time and interest to ex-

---

[2]See Martin Zweig, "Trusty Market Indicator, Bringing the Record of the Big-Block Index Up-to-Date," *Barron's*, January 24, 1983, pp. 11–12.

EXHIBIT 6.16   Sample Construction of the Big-Block Index
Using Barron's Data

NYSE LARGE BLOCK TRANSACTIONS

			UP TICKS	DOWN TICKS	NO CHANGE	TOTALS
	May	12	24	22	40	86
100,000	May	13	18	29	31	78
Shares	May	14	20	33	40	93
and Over	May	15	13	27	35	75
	May	16	16	33	38	87

			UP TICKS	DOWN TICKS	NO CHANGE	TOTALS
	May	12	43	32	62	137
50,000-99,999	May	13	31	37	60	128
Shares	May	14	68	56	87	211
	May	15	31	56	69	156
	May	16	30	37	71	138

Totals = 294   362   1189

Average
per day = 58.8   72.4   237.8

Big Block Index value:

$$\frac{58.8}{58.8 + 72.4} = .448$$

Average
daily volume
of NYSE
large block
transactions

plore this area, *Barron's* Market Laboratory provides an excellent source of data to start with.

Although the possibilities are endless, volume indicators may include odd-lot volume (purchases, sales, and short sales), volume ratios of the various exchanges, put-and-call option volume, short-interest volume, low-price-stocks volume, average price of stocks making new lows volume, and insider volume. The paperback, *The ABC's of Market Forecasting,* by Martin Zweig, provides a brief and understandable overview of many of these indicators.

EXHIBIT 6.17 Major Divergences between the Big Block Index and the Dow Jones Industrial Average

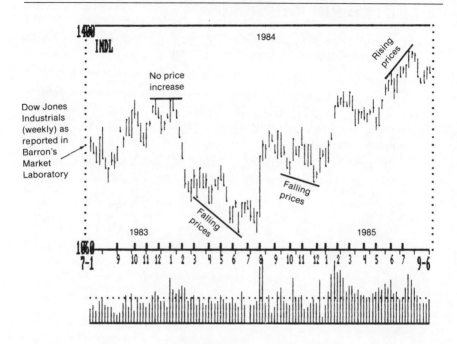

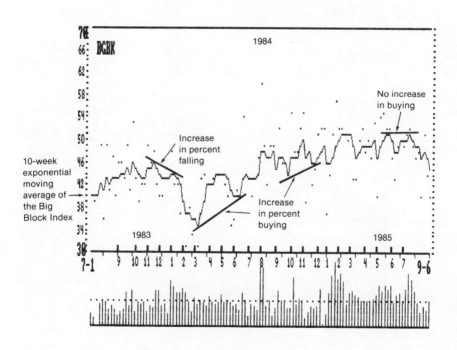

SELECTED REFERENCES

GRANVILLE, JOSEPH E. *Granville's New Key to Stock Market Profits.* Englewood Cliffs, N.J.: Prentice-Hall, 1963.

HILTZIK, MICHAEL. "Tuning in to Volume." *Personal Investor,* July 1985, pp. 40–42.

ZWEIG, MARTIN E. *The ABC's of Market Forecasting: How to Use Barron's Market Laboratory Pages.* Princeton, N.J.: Dow Jones & Company, Inc., 1984.

_____."Trusty Market Indicator, Bringing the Record of the Big-Block Index Up-to-Date." *Barron's,* January 24, 1983, pp. 11–12.

_____

CHAPTER SEVEN

Support, Resistance, and Price Patterns

The price of a stock at any point in time can be thought of as representing a struggle between supply and demand. If the current demand outstrips the supply, prices rise to induce an increase in supply (selling) to meet the demand. When current supply exceeds demand, prices drop to induce an increase in demand (buying) to meet supply. Over time, the pattern of price changes records the history of this struggle. This price history can be analyzed in an effort to identify price support and resistance, and to assess the potential for future price performance.

SUPPORT AND RESISTANCE

As the current price rises into an area of supply concentration, you can expect a stalling of the price rise. This region is called *resistance*. As the current price falls into an area of demand concentration, you can expect a stalling of the price drop. This region is known as *support*. Supply outstrips demand at a resistance area; demand outstrips supply at a support area.

In an effort to reveal concentrations of supply and demand, you can examine the price history traced by the stock. Both price levels and price-time relationships are useful for providing evidence of these concentrations.

PRICE–LEVEL SUPPORT AND RESISTANCE

> *At what price level might I expect to find support for falling prices or resistance to rising prices?*

Exhibit 7.1 shows a price pattern with support and resistance levels at X-Y-Z and 1-2-3, respectively. As the price rises to the 1-2-3 level, you should expect resistance to a further rise, and as it falls toward the X-Y-Z level, you should expect support for the falling price. What reasons have been cited for these expectations? Two major explanations have been proposed that seem to make sense: psychological reactions to past price action and the self-fulfilling prophecy concept.

Exhibit 7.1 indicates that many purchases were made between Point X and Point 1, driving the price up in the process. The price eventually reaches a high point (1 in the example) and then begins to drop back down. When this happens, your perceptions regarding the current price level are heavily influenced by past price action. This is because perceptions of "high" and "low" stock prices in the minds of investors are not made

---

EXHIBIT 7.1   Support and Resistance

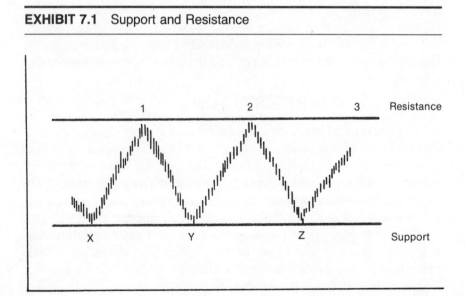

from an unbiased blank slate but are directly tied to highs and lows previously seen.

In psychology this is known as the "anchoring and adjustment" phenomenon. People develop current performance standards (anchors) based on past happenings. All judgments (for example, beauty and ugliness, good and bad, high and low) are based on previous experiences. Whether we realize it or not, new experiences are related back to the old and are not really viewed with a totally open mind.

If the stock gets down to Point Y we naturally view it as being at the "bottom," since our past experience has demonstrated that point to be a bottom. An attractive buying level, therefore, appears to be near the X-Y-Z level. Of course, this belief can be dominated by other information that would negate this view of the bottom (lower earnings estimates, for example) and create a belief readjustment, (causing us to look for a new bottom somewhere below Point Y). The same type of argument can be made for the price level at Point 2 as prices begin to rise from Y.

The more the price reverses from a previously established low or high level, the firmer is our psychologically based definition of "top" and "bottom," so the levels are more likely to constrain the price, given no new information.

A second reason cited for the sustained existence of support and resistance levels is based on the belief that many investors have heard of the concept, and these investors know that many others are also aware of the concept. As the price approaches Point 2 they know that other investors will recognize that point as a resistance point and will hesitate to buy as a result. No investors want to make the classic blunder of buying into overhead resistance, so they wait until others have made the big move to purchase a sufficient amount of stock to get the price through the assumed concentration of supply area. The level of resistance therefore becomes a self-fulfilling prophecy. The same type of reasoning can be used for the support level.

Many market technicians like to think of support and resistance in terms of zones rather than absolute price levels. Exhibit 7.2 shows how this concept is put into practice using the Dow Jones Industrial Average as an example. Instead of a single line to define support or resistance, a double line is used

---

EXHIBIT 7.2   Resistance Zone

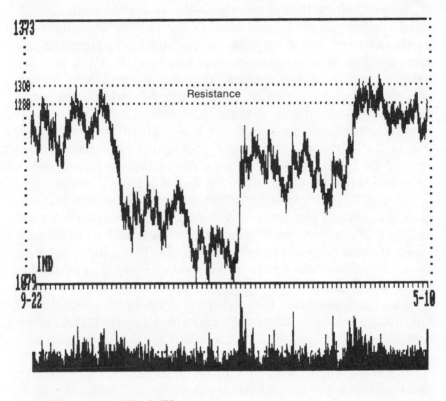

adv: 9784   days: 415 of 497

to form a zone. In general, the width of the zone is about the size as the high-to-low range of prices in the support or resistance area.

With the zone concept, supply and resistance are not viewed as a mirror that reflects the price back, but are viewed more as a demilitarized zone, where the price gets "shot at" until it stops advancing or leaves the zone. This is in keeping with a reasonable interpretation of the concept: that it provides *general* rather than absolute levels where price may be stalled or reversed.

Exhibit 7.2 also illustrates another concept related to support and resistance. There are times when support or resistance zones occur at or near psychologically "special" numbers, like the 10s, for stocks (e.g., 20, 30, 40, and so forth) and the 100s for widely followed averages like the Dow Jones Industrials.

The resistance zone in the exhibit lies near the 1,300 level. At this level, both the psychological and self-fulfilling prophecy explanations operate in strength. As the average nears the 1,300 level many investors hold back to see if the widely touted "milestone" price will be punched through. Moving from the 1,290s to above 1,300 is viewed as having more significance than moving only a few points. Crossing such a milestone is more like entering a new era; it becomes psychologically appealing to play it safe and refrain from buying until after the barrier is removed. This creates a tendency for buying to dry up as the average gets near that special level on the Dow.

When price works its way through a support or resistance zone, the penetrated zone takes on the opposite character. Support becomes resistance, and resistance becomes support. Exhibit 7.3 presents the same chart shown in Exhibit 7.2, except more elapsed time is shown. The resistance zone has been penetrated with a move into new territory. As prices drop back, you can see that the resistance zone has now become a new support zone for the falling prices. For falling prices that break through a support level, the opposite situation exists; the support level becomes a resistance level. Explanations can be cast in the same psychological framework as previously discussed.

PRICE–TIME SUPPORT AND RESISTANCE RELATIONSHIPS

Where might I expect to find support to price drops from important tops?
Where might I expect to find resistance to price rises from important bottoms?

One-third and two-thirds speed resistance lines are used to provide an expectation of how far prices are likely to go when reversals from important tops or bottoms take place. As Exhibits 7.4 through 7.7 show, this method is based on price-time rela-

EXHIBIT 7.3 Resistance Becoming Support

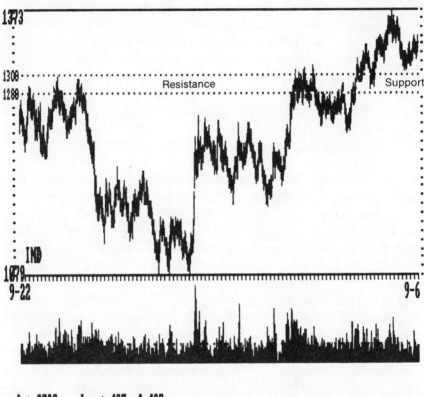

adv: 9790   days: 497 of 497

tionships and not simply on price levels or zones. Market psychology again provides the likely reason for its operation.

As price drops from a high, potential purchasers may wait until they feel the price has dropped far enough to make buying look like a "good deal." On the other hand, when price is rising from a low, investors may continue buying until the price appears expensive, at which time the buying (demand) tends to dry up. This, of course, assumes that no significant information surfaces during the rise or fall that will dominate the preexisting perceptions of value. Speed resistance lines provide rough guidelines for what appears expensive and what appears cheap.

EXHIBIT 7.4 Rising One-Third Speed Resistance Line

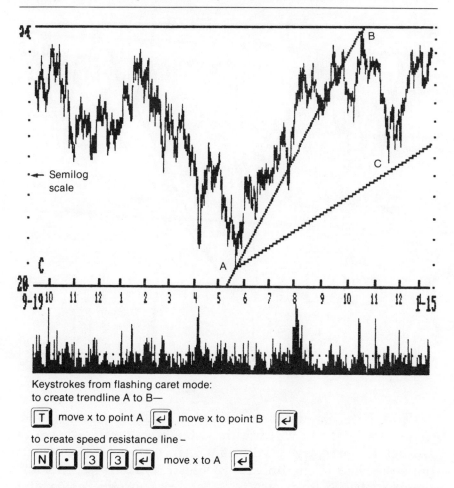

Keystrokes from flashing caret mode:
to create trendline A to B—

T move x to point A ⏎ move x to point B ⏎

to create speed resistance line –

N · 3 3 ⏎ move x to A ⏎

Looking at the chart in Exhibit 7.4, you can see that the price dropped from Point B to Point C, which is close to the point predicted by the one-third speed resistance line. To create this line, you should first identify the slope of the previous rise (A to B in Exhibit 7.4) with a trendline from the low point (A) to the high point (B) of the price rise. Then specify an anchor point at Point A and draw the one-third (0.33) speed resistance line. Note that the line can be drawn in advance of the drop to Point C. All you need to construct the line is a defined bottom point (A) and a defined top point (B).

EXHIBIT 7.5   Rising Two-Thirds Speed Resistance Line

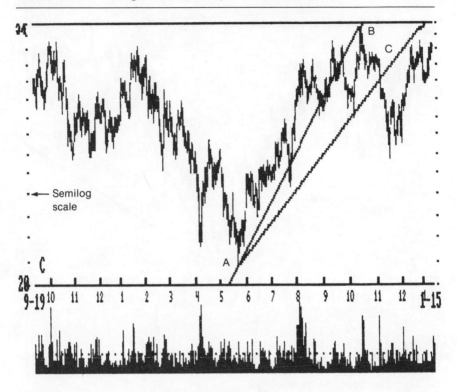

Two-thirds speed resistance lines are also frequently used. To create them you will use the same procedure as shown in Exhibit 7.4, except you will use 0.67 in place of 0.33 to determine the slope of the line. As Exhibit 7.5 illustrates, this line provides shorter-term objectives for price drops. The exhibit shows the price breaking through the line after a short period of consolidation above the line. As is often the case, a sharp break through the two-thirds line results in a rapid movement to the vicinity of the one-third line.

Price objectives for upward moves are made in similar fashion. First establish a trend line, then create the speed resistance line and anchor it to the high point. Exhibits 7.6 and 7.7 show how this is done.

Since the example used (Chrysler Corporation) was not selected to make the technique look good, you can see from these

EXHIBIT 7.6   Falling One-Third Speed Resistance Line

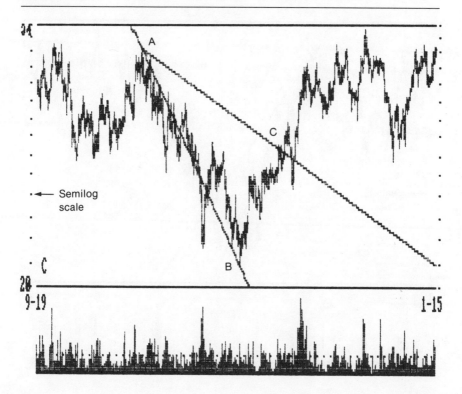

exhibits the type of results that often will occur in practice. Prices do not stall on the line in precise fashion. This is not disturbing for those who recognize that these lines represent expected regions of resistance to price movement, not absolute lines of resistance or support.

Another form of the speed resistance line is the bottom-to-bottom or top-to-top trendline. Trendlines were discussed in Chapter Three as a simple way to delineate the direction of prices. Trendlines can also be thought of as speed resistance lines with empirically derived slopes in place of the 0.33 and 0.66 slopes mentioned previously. Exhibit 7.8 shows how a trendline is used like a speed resistance line.

Everything else being equal, the trendline has a positive psychological impact on the investor. As long as the price is at or above the trendline, the investor views the trend as being in-

---

EXHIBIT 7.7 Falling Two-Third Speed Resistance Line

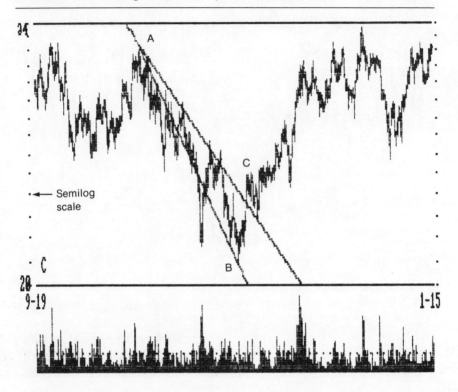

tact. If the investor believes in holding a stock as long as the trend is up, the stock will remain attractive above the trendline. Moreover, as the price drops to the level of the trendline it looks very attractive for purchase, since it is still in an uptrend, yet it is down from a recent high. Demand, therefore, can be expected to pick up as the stock price nears the trendline. If the price breaks below the line many investors will view the trend as broken and will sell the stock. The same line of reasoning can be applied to declining trendlines for explaining resistance (see Exhibit 7.9).

As long as the stock is below the line, the astute investor knows that it is widely viewed as being in a downtrend. Moreover, many investors would rather wait until a stock has provided evidence of turning around before sustained buying will occur. These investors will likely hold off on purchasing such

EXHIBIT 7.8   Trendline as a Line of Support

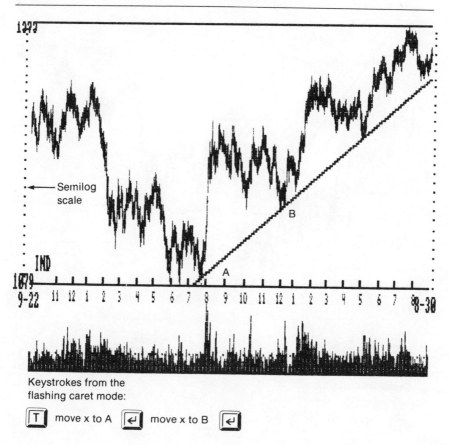

Keystrokes from the
flashing caret mode:

[T] move x to A   [↵] move x to B   [↵]

stock until others have turned the stock around and the down-
ward-sloping trendline has been broken. The line will therefore
appear to provide resistance to a further price rise, until the
trendline is broken and the demand is increased for the more
attractive "trend-reversed" stock.

How much faith should you put in the support and resistance methods discussed in this chapter? You should think of
them as providing a loose standard against which future prospects for price advances or declines can be assessed. Nothing
goes up or down forever, and knowledge of support and resis-

EXHIBIT 7.9   Trendline as a Line of Resistance

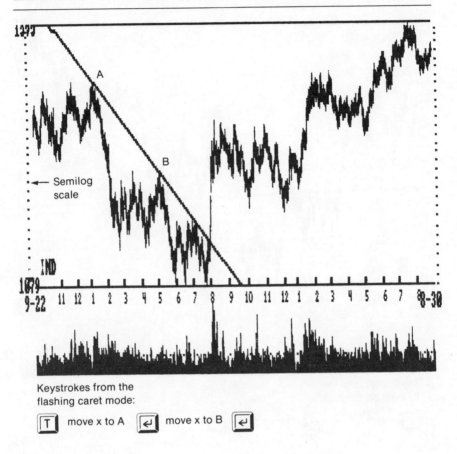

Keystrokes from the
flashing caret mode:

[T]   move x to A   [↵]   move x to B   [↵]

tance can provide you with a useful perspective on the overall
situation.

PRICE PATTERNS

Using chart price patterns is one of the most misunderstood
areas of technical analysis. There exists a spectrum of attitudes
concerning the meaning and importance of these patterns.
Some analysts believe that historical price patterns are empty
of information and should be ignored, while others think the
patterns can be used to directly forecast future price performance.

What is the proper interpretation of chart patterns? I have found four types of chart patterns to be especially useful in technical analysis. Following is a description and general interpretation of these patterns. Chapters Eleven and Twelve provide details on how price patterns can be used in supporting investment strategies. References at the end of this chapter provide sources for other interpretations and patterns.

Pattern 1: A Drop in Price of 80 Percent or More

This historical pattern reflects a severe sell-off in the stock price (see Exhibit 7.10). The value of this pattern is not in forecasting a rise in price but in selecting a subset of stocks from a larger set, using this pattern as the screening criterion. You can then use the identified group of stocks in making your analysis.

The reason you should have an interest in severely sold-off stocks is to find a group of distressed companies whose perceived value has been distorted. These stocks are sometimes battered down to a level where they are undervalued in price. By doing a price-pattern screening of stocks of this type you can rapidly identify candidates for additional analysis. Chapter Twelve, Investing in Unattractive Stocks, explains how you can make an analysis of these "ugly" stocks to build a portfolio with appreciation potential.

Pattern 2: A Bottom Formation

Exhibit 7.11 provides an example of this type of chart formation. Notice how the chart shows a retesting of the low point made at A. Like the previously discussed chart pattern, this one is also *not* used to forecast future prices. The value of this pattern is that it offers an excellent timing opportunity for you to perform a multifaceted technical analysis, which can provide a clear buy, sell, hold, or avoid decision.

This chart pattern provides the most opportune moment to make a divergence analysis, as Points A and B on the chart can be compared to similar points on the technical indicators of interest. As we will see in Chapter Eleven, divergences will be easy to spot.

EXHIBIT 7.10 Chart Pattern Showing a Major Sell-Off

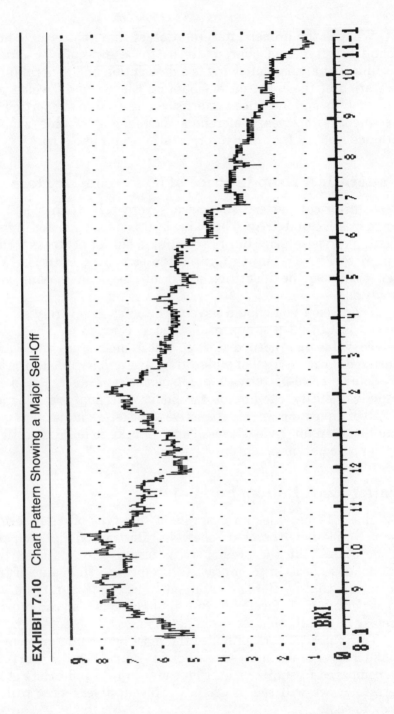

EXHIBIT 7.11   Chart Pattern Showing the Creation of a "Bottom"

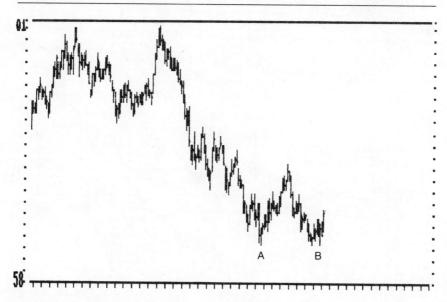

Triple-bottom chart formations and inverted head-and-shoulder formations can be interpreted for use in the same way. Moreover, chart patterns reflecting topping behavior (double or triple tops and head-and-shoulders formations) also provide a special timing opportunity.

Pattern 3: A Horizontal Line Formation

Stocks that trace a horizontal line over an extended period of time are interesting candidates for an ongoing analysis. Sideways movement indicates that neither selling nor buying pressure is dominating the market for the stock. Supply and demand are in an approximate balance (see Exhibit 7.12).

Like an innocent child whose mind is so easy to "read," stocks tracing this simple pattern often make good candidates for a straightforward technical analysis. Volume indicators are especially lucid during these periods.

EXHIBIT 7.12   Chart Pattern Showing a Horizontal Line Formation

---

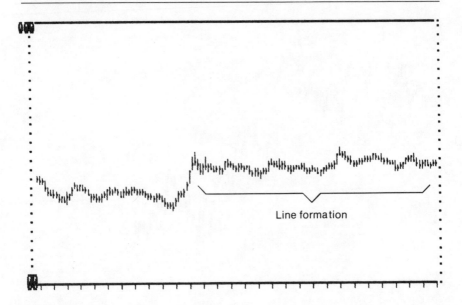

Line formation

Pattern 4: A Rising Price Trend

A pattern of rising prices is another important formation (Exhibit 7.8 shows an example). Trends often persist, providing an opportunity for investors to join the flow of movement for further gains. A major task of technical analysis is to choose the most advantageous entry and exit points for profitably riding the trend. These will be discussed in Chapter Eleven.

The chart patterns displayed up to this point have made use of standard bar charts. While this is the most popular charting format, another method, called point and figure charting, is also used by many technicians. With this approach, time is not displayed on the chart; only when the price reverses by a predetermined amount is the graph changed. Since the time feature is missing from the point and figure chart, it is inappropriate for use with most of the analytical techniques discussed in this part of the book. Exhibit 7.13 provides a sample point and figure chart with explanatory notation.

This charting approach provides no additional information

EXHIBIT 7.13   Point and Figure Chart

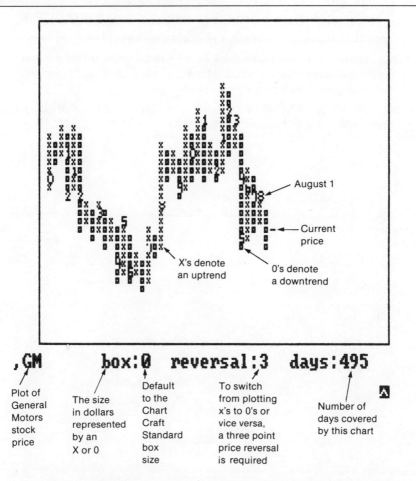

over the standard bar chart. However, because it removes much of the random component of price changes, it is often easier to interpret than the daily bar chart. For more information on this charting format, see the Cohen reference at the end of this chapter.

SELECTED REFERENCES

COHEN, A. W. *Point and Figure Stock Market Trading*. 8th ed. Larchmont, N.Y.: ChartCraft, Inc., 1982.

EDWARDS, ROBERT D., and JOHN MAGEE. *Technical Analysis of Stock Trends.* Springfield, Mass.: Stock Trend Service, 1954.

JILER, W. L. *How Charts Can Help You in the Stock Market.* New York: Commodity Research Publications Corp., 1962.

LERRO, ANTHONY J., and CHARLES B. SWAYNE. *Selection of Securities: Technical Analysis of Stock Market Prices.* 2nd ed. Morristown, N.J.: General Learning Press, 1974.

SHEINMAN, W. X. *Why Most Investors Are Mostly Wrong Most of the Time.* New York: Lancer Books, 1970.

PART THREE

Strategies

This section attempts to put the techniques discussed in Part Two into a usable framework. Its purpose is not to provide answers that promise to make you wealthy but to offer ideas from which you can develop your own system to meet your objectives. Both technical and fundamental evidence are used in the chapters that follow.

Chapter Eight offers advice for establishing an overall stock market investment plan. Chapters Nine through Twelve provide specific investment strategies and explore numerous ways in which they can be used to fit individual needs.

CHAPTER EIGHT

Strategy Development

Specific instances of short-term success occur in every endeavor: The rookie baseball pitcher who pitches a shutout in his first big-league appearance, the tourist who goes to Las Vegas and wins $1 million, the novice investor who buys a stock that doubles in a week are all examples of this phenomenon. The short run can deliver dramatic results. Unfortunately, the salient nature of quick success may distort perceptions of future possibilities while discouraging behavior useful to long-term achievements.

The typical investor has a time horizon for investment purposes that extends over many years. For this investor, an orientation toward achieving a good long-term record of annual percentage gains is much more important than a short-term focus on specific instances of dramatic success. This unfortunately runs counter to the human psyche, which reacts much more intensely to dramatic, single events than it reacts to long-run, orderly, and controlled results.

To be successful over the long run the investor must have an investment philosophy that has been translated into a specific plan of action. The investor creates this plan by establishing strategies that will support specific individual objectives. Once the strategies are established, specific techniques, like those discussed in previous chapters, can be applied to achieve the desired results.

Above all, it is important that investors keep the order correct: first the plan, then the strategies, and last the implementation of the specific techniques that lead to buy or sell decisions. In case after case the author has seen investors bypass the first two steps and jump right in with the haphazard implementation of stock market techniques, without first establishing an overall structure or framework for their decisions. The usual result is a mix of short-term successes and failures which, when summed, result in an average to poor overall investment performance.

Some thoughts and guidelines concerning important factors in establishing an investment plan follow. It is hoped that they will aid in the development of a "top-down" structure to your investment decision making, leading to the successful attainment of your objectives.

DIVERSIFICATION

Perhaps the most important investment planning principle is that diversification reduces risk. While everyone has heard of diversification, few individual investors seem to appreciate what a far-reaching, powerful, and important concept it is. There are three types of diversification: stock portfolio, strategy, and total asset.

Stock Portfolio Diversification

Stock portfolio diversification can be summed up with the "rule of eight." If you invest in common stocks, plan to establish a portfolio with a minimum of eight stocks. This is important because a portfolio of eight or more stocks can significantly reduce the chance of your losing a large amount of money from an unpredictable event that may affect a single stock. Natural disaster, fraud, bankruptcy, a prolonged strike, or other unforeseen events can destroy the gains of years of investing. If you are an investor over a long period of time, a disaster of this sort will almost certainly happen to one or more of your stocks. Moreover, any stock can be affected and there is no way to predict the occurrence. The question, in a practical sense, is not whether it will happen to you, but how long it will take you to financially recover from it when it does happen. The only reasonable way to protect yourself is by limiting the total percent-

EXHIBIT 8.1   Risk Reduction by Size of Portfolio

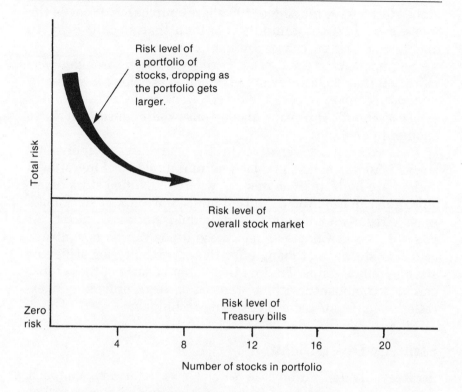

age of investment dollars that you put into any one stock. Exhibit 8.1 provides an indication of how rapidly total risk drops as the number of stocks in a portfolio increases.

If you do not implement stock diversification, you will be subjecting yourself to needless risk. Investors cite two common reasons why they fail to adequately diversify: lack of time to track more than a few stocks and not enough available capital to establish a diverse portfolio.

Investors can effectively eliminate the first problem with the use of a personal computer, financial software, and an information database. Numbers of stocks that would be impossible to keep up with manually can be computer analyzed on a technical and fundamental basis in the investor's home with a relatively small investment in time.

The second argument for not diversifying has some merit.

Assuming that the typical stock is selling for $25 a share, an investor would need a $20,000 investment to diversify into eight stocks with round-lot (100 share) purchases. What is the investor to do if substantially less than that amount is available and odd-lot purchases are not desired?

So important is the concept of risk reduction through diversification that the answer to the dilemma is, *"Don't invest in individual common stocks if you cannot or are not willing to buy at least eight."* Put your money elsewhere until you have enough to diversify.

An excellent alternative to the purchase of individual stocks is to buy and sell no-load mutual funds until investment dollars are built up to an amount where individual stock diversification can be effected. Mutual funds, having vast stock holdings, virtually eliminate the individual stock-risk factor. As you will see in Chapter Nine, these funds can be bought and sold like stocks, and many offer the opportunity for achieving sizable annual gains. Trading in and out of some of these funds can be accomplished with no transaction costs, providing an excellent vehicle for the use of timing techniques.

Strategy Diversification

Strategy diversification is a second risk reduction approach. There are many ways of making money in the stock market, with this book covering four major strategies that the author has found useful. There are, of course, many others. When devising an overall stock market investment plan, you should consider a mix of strategies.

By using more than one strategy simultaneously, you can reduce the risk of loss from problems associated with any one strategy. At one time or another the stock market humbles all of its participants, no matter how valid their approach to the market or how well they have done their research. Strategies that work well over one period of time may fall flat during other periods. There are times the market reacts well to balance sheet data, so strategies oriented to this information work like magic. At other times the market ignores the balance sheet and seems to concentrate on the income statement. At still other times, neither approach seems to be of importance, since overall economic issues dominate stock price movement. Trend-following strategies also come and go in their ability to produce profitable trades based on market action. When the market is volatile these strategies work well, but in quiet markets they may generate profit-robbing whipsaws.

Shifts in market responsiveness to various strategies can last from weeks to years and are very difficult to anticipate. If all your stock market investment funds are involved with a single strategy, there will be periods when the strategy will not work well. This is a sobering part of the reality that makes the market what it is. The wise investor will understand that there is no best way for making money in the market, but there are many good ways. Diversifying among more than one strategy reduces the effects of the market's inconsistencies and improves the odds that something is "working" all of the time.

Moreover, if you use a single strategy that requires very active personal involvement and you become ill or are away on an extended business trip or vacation, large losses could accrue. Partitioning funds between heavy-involvement and light-involvement strategies reduces the effect of this risk.

Finally, the strategies that involve subjective judgment or the mastery of complex techniques usually have a learning period associated with them. For these situations, strategy diversification can reduce the cost of your "education."

Total Asset Diversification

The third type of diversification involves the totality of an investor's assets. You should not view a stock portfolio in isolation but should see it as part of a larger portfolio, which may include real estate, bonds, savings deposits, vested pension plans, collectibles, and other assets of monetary significance. With this orientation, you should use an approach to manage your asset mix by developing a balance among the various areas to reflect economic conditions and personal objectives. By diversifying in this way, your overall exposure in any one area is limited, reducing the risk of loss.

There are two special circumstances where diversification takes on extra importance. The first relates to funds drawn out of an investment account: the second, to a large single influx of investment money.

As you get close to a time when you need to draw money out of your account, diversification becomes a critical factor in planning for the removal of funds. If you are not diversified and an unexpected event occurs that has a negative impact on your investment, gains reflecting years of effort can be wiped out without giving you sufficient time to recover.

Diversification is also extremely important when a large lump sum of money (for example, a bonus, inheritance, or insurance settlement) becomes available at one time for investment. The classic mistake that investors make when such a windfall occurs is to rush out and put the funds into a single investment, thereby unnecessarily increasing their exposure to risk.

BENCHMARKS

It is important that you have a standard or benchmark so you can assess your stock market performance and adjust your methods if necessary. As stated previously, the average annual rate of return is a much more important measure for determining how you are doing in the stock market than are individual instances of success or failure.

In assessing average annual performance, you should keep in mind some important performance benchmarks. The first is the rate of inflation. Unless the investment rate of return is above the inflation rate, no real gain has taken place. If you subtract the inflation rate from the investment rate of return, what remains is the real rate of return. Strategies that yield returns at or close to the inflation rate are preservation of capital strategies. While it is important to preserve existing funds, your investment plan is not providing increasing buying power unless its return consistently outpaces this standard.

A second benchmark is the risk-free rate of return. It is always possible to invest in government T-bills with virtually no risk and almost no time or effort on your part. Subtracting this rate from your performance will give you the extra percent profit that you made from all the time, effort, and risk exposure that you undertook.

The Standard & Poor's (S&P) 500 gain or loss on an annual percentage basis is another useful measure. Subtracting this number from your annual rate of return provides the excess in profits that you made over a strategy of throwing darts on January 1 at the financial pages of *The Wall Street Journal* to select a portfolio of 25 to 30 stocks, and then selling them on December 31.

Another benchmark is to compare your performance with other investors. Despite the claims of, "making a million in the market in one year," "doubling your money each year," and other claims that you see so often in magazine advertisements and on book titles, most professional money managers average between 15 and 25 percent a year. This is a rough and wide range but it provides some idea of what you can expect over a multiple business-cycle investment horizon. Strategies that yield consistent average profits over 30 percent are rare if they exist at all, and almost any strategy that utilizes a large portfolio of stocks and does not over-trade should yield an annual average (over many years) of close to 10 percent.

Two excellent sources of information on how specific professional investment advisers are doing on an ongoing basis are the *Hulbert Financial Digest* (643 South Carolina Ave., S.E., Washington, D.C.) and the *Timer Digest* (P.O. Box 03247, Fort Lauderdale, Fla. 33303). The *Hulbert Digest* provides information on portfolio rates of return, while the *Timer Digest* compares timing signal rates of return for the best 10 stock market timers to changes in the S&P 500.

In a practical sense, your stock market investment battle is to develop a plan that can push your gains, on average, above inflation, above the risk-free rate (assuming that your can tolerate some risk), and also above the random stock selection rate of return. The historical performance of experienced investors indicates that you can realistically expect an upper limit in the 20 to 30 percent range, on an annual basis across many market cycles. You might wonder if it is worth the time, effort, and expense to achieve an average performance in excess of the risk-free and random selection strategies. As Exhibit 8.2 illustrates, the answer is yes indeed!

The exhibit shows that a few extra percentage points per year over a long period of time can make a dramatic difference

---

EXHIBIT 8.2   Values of a Single $10,000 Investment at Given Annual
Compound Rates

Investment Horizon Years	8 Percent	12 Percent	16 Percent	20 Percent	24 Percent
5	$ 14,693	$ 17,623	$ 21,003	$ 24,883	$ 29,316
10	21,589	31,058	44,114	61,917	85,944
15	31,722	54,736	92,655	154,070	251,960
20	46,610	96,463	194,461	383,380	738,640
25	68,485	170,000	408,740	953,960	2,165,400
30	100,630	299,600	858,500	2,373,800	6,348,200

Effects of taxes are not included. Values given are for interest rate comparative purposes based on consistent year-to-year compound rates as shown.

---

in the ending sum. With a $10,000 initial investment, a 35-year-old investor with a 30-year investment horizon (assuming a need for the funds at 65 years of age) would have, at compound rates, $100,630 at 8 percent, $299,600 at 12 percent, $858,500 at 16 percent, $2,373,800 at 20 percent, and $6,348,200 at 24 percent.

Time plus compounding results in numbers that have to be seen and contemplated to be appreciated. A plan that yields an average annual return of just a few percentage points above the risk-free rate, for example, can make a major difference in your retirement lifestyle.

STOCK MARKET STRATEGIES

This book discusses four basic stock market investment strategies: mutual fund trading (Chapter Nine), high probability investing (Chapter Ten), trend and cycle trading (Chapter Eleven), and investing in unattractive stocks (Chapter Twelve). The strategies are presented in order of risk, from lowest to highest.

A typical novice investor is encouraged to begin his stock market investing experience with mutual funds. This same advice holds for those investors with low-risk tolerance or limited capital. For individuals with more market sophistication and sufficient capital and risk tolerance, other more advanced strategies can be undertaken.

High probability investing is a long-term strategy that makes use of academic research to indicate how a portfolio can be created that has exceptional appreciation potential. This is a strategy of moderate risk that requires a minimum amount of maintenance time.

Trading on trends and cycles is a strategy having a large measure of risk while providing the greatest return in excitement, potential for technical creativity, and, perhaps, profits. Seasoned investors having time, money, and the proper mental orientation will find this investment roller coaster ride to be a fascinating experience.

Investing in unattractive companies is a psychology-based strategy for finding stocks whose values have been distorted because of their state of perceived distress. It is a high-risk strategy that takes a considerable amount of time and effort to research and maintain.

As mentioned previously, there are advantages to your implementing more than one strategy at a time, and you should consider doing so. Moreover, you should develop your own customized market strategy or strategies, possibly based on ideas presented in this book, in order to achieve a proper match with your needs and objectives.

MAINTENANCE AND CONTROL

Whatever strategy or strategies you decide to implement, you must employ maintenance and control procedures over your portfolio. Keeping adequate records and knowing exactly where you stand with regard to all of your securities is one essential requirement. Another essential requirement is to have a loss control system in place at all times.

Record-Keeping

With a small amount of effort you can keep abreast of your securities with a computerized portfolio manager. The Dow Jones Market Analyzer PLUS has a portfolio manager program that is easy to use. Whenever a transaction takes place (buy, sell, sell short, or cover), data are entered into the portfolio manager

---

EXHIBIT 8.3 Manual Transaction Information for the Portfolio
Manager

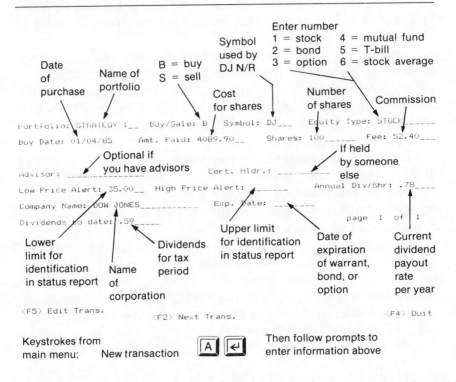

Enter number
1 = stock   4 = mutual fund
2 = bond   5 = T-bill
3 = option   6 = stock average

Symbol
used by
DJ N/R

Date
of
purchase

Name of
portfolio

B = buy
S = sell

Cost
for shares

Number
of shares

Commission

Portfolio: STRATEGY 1__   Buy/Sale: B   Symbol: DJ___   Equity Type: STOCK_____

Buy Date: 01/04/85   Amt. Paid: 4089.90__   Shares: 100_____   Fee: 52.40___

Optional if
you have advisors

If held
by someone
else

Advisor: _____   Cert. Hldr.: _____

Low Price Alert: 35.00__   High Price Alert: _____   Annual Div/Shr: .78____

Company Name: DOW JONES_____   Exp. Date: _____

Dividends to date: .59_____

page 1 of 1

Lower
limit for
identification
in status report

Name
of
corporation

Dividends
for tax
period

Upper limit
for identification
in status report

Date of
expiration
of warrant,
bond, or
option

Current
dividend
payout
rate
per year

<F5> Edit Trans.

<F2> Next Trans.

<F4> Quit

Keystrokes from
main menu: New transaction   [A] [↵]

Then follow prompts to
enter information above

---

program as shown in Exhibit 8.3. Valuations of all portfolio
stocks are kept current through updating from your quote disk.

You can generate a number of reports from the portfolio
data; each report is geared to meet a specific objective. If you
use more than one investment strategy it is important that you
maintain separate portfolio records for each. This will enable
you to make comparative judgments over time. It will also help
you to maintain purchase discipline. Actions taken outside of
your developed strategies (for example, purchases based on tips
or sales pressure) will have no "home" in your portfolio record
system.

To obtain current portfolio valuation, a simple updating
from the quote disk is required. This is done from **F** (From
Quote List) on the main menu.

Loss Management

Managing losses is probably the most difficult part of the investment process. Psychologically it means admitting to yourself (and perhaps to a spouse or stockbroker) that you were wrong. This may be more painful than the potential dollar loss from the decline in value. Putting off the sell decision eliminates this problem, at least for a while. If the stock slips far enough, you may find it appealing to think that the stock has moved too far down to sell, so you might as well hold it.

The best way to psychologically handle the loss problem is to develop a probabilistic attitude toward the investment process. When you make an initial investment, you should realize that there is a very good chance that it will not work out as planned. You can be absolutely certain that you will take losses sometime, no matter how effective your strategy is. You can compare your investment to a retail business in which some items will not sell well. Selling these items at a loss to get rid of them is part of the cost of doing business, and it should be for you too.

For those investors who are sensitive to evaluation by others, discount brokers provide the advantage of passing no judgments on investment decisions that do not pan out. You can reduce negative reactions from spouses by providing overall rates of return on a periodic basis instead of providing details about each transaction.

How far down should a stock go before you decide to throw in the towel? Exhibit 8.4 shows the folly of having too much patience with a poorly performing stock.

The larger the percentage loss, the more difficult it becomes to recover the loss and get back to the original position. A loss of 50 percent, for example, means that the stock must double just for you to break even. To maintain a reasonable amount of control, a decline tolerance range of 20 to 25 percent, requiring a 25 to 33 percent gain to break even, is a rational upper limit on a loss before giving up on a stock.

To support loss management, the Portfolio Status report in the Dow Jones Market Analyzer PLUS flags any stocks that have fallen below a level previously specified. On each portfolio update, this status report and column should be monitored.

EXHIBIT 8.4 The Recovery of Losses for a
$1,000 Investment

If You Lose		Amount Left	Percent Gain to Get Back to $1,000
5%	($ 50)	$950	$ 50/$950 = 5.3%
10	(100)	900	100/ 900 = 11.1
15	(150)	850	150/ 850 = 17.6
20	(200)	800	200/ 800 = 25.0
25	(250)	750	250/ 750 = 33.3
30	(300)	700	300/ 700 = 42.8
35	(350)	650	350/ 650 = 53.8
40	(400)	600	400/ 600 = 66.7
45	(450)	550	450/ 550 = 81.8
50	(500)	500	500/ 500 = 100.0
55	(550)	450	550/ 450 = 122.0
60	(600)	400	600/ 400 = 150.0
65	(650)	350	650/ 350 = 185.7
70	(700)	300	700/ 300 = 233.3
75	(750)	250	750/ 250 = 300.0
80	(800)	200	800/ 200 = 400.0
85	(850)	150	850/ 150 = 566.7
90	(900)	100	900/ 100 = 900.0

Any stocks exceeding the level that you have specified will require you to make an immediate decision. Some investors adopt the policy that, at minimum, 50 percent (or some other significant proportion) of the stock will be sold when the level is reached, no matter what the evidence or situation at that time suggests. Others use a two-phase system, with a certain percentage price drop (e.g., 20 percent) creating a warning signal and a further drop (e.g., 25 percent) resulting in a sell decision.

Levels can be based on a fixed percentage, on the existence of a support zone, or on a value given by a trend reversal indicator. Whatever you use, you must maintain selling discipline, so that the minor losses do not become irrecoverable.

CHAPTER NINE

Mutual Fund Switching

Mutual funds are one of the most popular investments of the 1980s. Their prevalence of use can be ascribed to the following advantages: (1) professional full-time management at low cost, (2) reduced company-specific risk through diversification, (3) simplified record-keeping, (4) high liquidity, (5) ability to add to an initial investment in small increments, (6) wide variety of fund types to choose from, and (7) possible free- or low-cost telephone switching between individual funds within a fund family.

It is the last advantage, the ability to easily transfer between funds, that has spawned a new investment strategy: mutual fund switching. Funds can be traded like individual stocks, providing a high level of personal control and the same type of action that stock trading provides.

Mutual funds are classified as load, low-load, or no-load, depending on the amount of the sales charge. These charges can occur at time of purchase, time of sale, or both. Load funds have charges ranging as high as 8.5 percent, while low-load fund charges range from 2 to 4 percent. No-load funds are free of front- and back-end sales charges, although some may have a hidden sales charge. This charge, known as a 12b-1 fee, will be explained in the next section.

Do load and low-load funds perform better than no-load funds? A considerably body of research has shown that the sales charge has no bearing whatsoever on the performance of a fund. This makes sense, as the load does not go to the fund managers but to the fund distributor and sales force. It is a marketing fee, not a management performance fee. Unfortunately, most load funds are *sold to* and not *purchased by* individuals. Financial planners, insurance agents, and broker sales representatives find it personally advantageous to push these funds since they receive a commission from the sales fee.

As a general rule, no-load funds should represent the universe from which specific funds should be selected. The only rational reason for buying a load or low-load fund is when a no-load equivalent cannot be found. As we will see, this is sometimes the case when specialty funds are desired for purchase.

There are two major approaches to trading mutual funds: switching between a stock fund and a money market fund and switching within a group of specialty funds.

The first approach involves investing in a growth fund when the market is advancing, then switching to a money market fund when the market declines. An analogy to this approach is having a convertible automobile—keeping the top down during good weather but putting it up at other times.

The second approach is specialty fund switching. This method is based on the observation that there is usually some industry group or economic sector that is doing well no matter how the general market is performing. The most favorable of these groups are identified and the representative equity fund is purchased. As group leadership changes, switches are made between funds to take advantage of the best performers.

For each of the switching approaches, mutual funds must be selected and a timing system developed. These requirements will be discussed in turn.

MUTUAL FUND SELECTION

The fund or funds to be selected must fit both your personal objectives and the needs of the switching approach that you have chosen to implement. You will need information about the objectives, structure, administration, and historical performance of the funds under consideration so you can make an informed choice. Fortunately, there are many good and readily available sources of information.

Exhibit 9.1 provides an example of information useful to

EXHIBIT 9.1 Key Information for Choosing a Mutual Fund

COMMON STOCK FUNDS 117

DREYFUS GROWTH OPPORTUNITY
(800) 645-6561/(212) 895-1206

The Dreyfus Corp.
600 Madison Ave.
New York, NY 10022

(Years ending 2/28)	1979	1980	1981	1982	1983	1984
Net Investment Income ($)	.11	.18	.15	.33	.22	.17
Dividends from Net Investment Income ($)	.05	.08	.18	.14	.29	.25
Net Gains (Losses) on Investments ($)	1.85	4.01	2.23	(2.98)	2.47	1.07
Distributions from Net Realized Capital Gains ($)	.23	.63	.59	.60	.81	.34
Net Asset Value End of Year ($)	7.30	10.78	12.39	9.00	10.59	11.24
Ratio of Expenses to Net Assets (%)	1.40	1.30	1.10	1.10	1.06	.99
Portfolio Turnover Rate (%)	86	40	29	35	68	60
Number of Shares Year End (000 omitted)	2,162	3,725	9,211	12,271	23,753	32,892
Total Assets: End of Year (Millions $)	15.8	40.2	114.1	110.4	251.5	369.7
Annual Rate of Return on Investment (%)	47.2	51.6	(14.9)	4.3	31.1	(12.1)

① ② ③ ④ ⑧

▶ Unlike the data items above, Rate of Return is on a calendar-year basis.

Five-Year Total Return	55.0%	Degree of Diversification	B	Beta	1.02	Bull	C	Bear	E

⑤ **Investment objectives/policy:** Primarily aims to promote growth of capital through investment in established companies up to 25% of which may be foreign. Income is secondary but in periods of market weakness the fund will emphasize investment in money market and other high-yielding securities.

⑥ **Portfolio:** (7/15/84) Common stocks 99%, short-term investments 1%. Largest stock holdings: paper 9%, railroads 6%, electrical and electronics 5%.

⑦ **Stocks held:** (7/15/84) 158
Year first offered: 1972

Distributions:
 Income April
 Capital gains April
12b-1: No ⑨ ⑩
Minimum investment: $2,500
Subsequent investment: $100
Minimum IRA: $750
Subsequent IRA: $100
Investor services: IRA, Keo, corp, 403(b), auto, withdr, ded, sep
Telephone exchange: With other ⑪ Dreyfus funds
Registered in: All states

the selection process. The following key data comments are referenced to the exhibit with numbered arrows.

1. Ratio of Expenses to Net Assets. The higher the fund's expenses, the lower the amount available to the fund's shareholders. While an exact cutoff point is not possible to define, an expense to net asset ratio over 1.50 percent should be eyed with some suspicion.

2. Portfolio Turnover Rate. The higher the turnover rate, the greater the chance that there will be a significant percentage of distributions taxed as short-term capital gains. For investors in high tax brackets this can materially affect the after-tax return. High turnover rates also contribute to high transaction costs, which will be reflected in high expense-to-asset ratios. Because of these factors, turnover rates of 1.0 or less are preferred.

3. Total Assets. With other factors equal, small funds tend to outperform larger funds. While this factor should not be the primary basis of a selection decision, if the choice comes down to a few funds and there are large differences in total assets, the issue of size should certainly be given consideration. As a rule of thumb, a small fund is one with total assets of 50 million shares or less.

4. Annual Rate of Return. This is the "bottom line" in terms of performance. Just because a fund has performed well (or poorly) in the past does not guarantee that it will do the same in the future. Nevertheless, past performance should be given a large measure of weight in fund selection. Making comparisons between funds for consistency and for performance levels is often more helpful than simply looking at one fund's performance record.

5. Investment Objectives/Policy. The mutual fund should have a relatively clear objective statement that is consistent with your purposes. Of special interest are statements concerning company size, growth phase, dividend payments, foreign stock ownership, exchange where traded, and industry group membership. Further, information about investments outside the arena of common stocks is important. Some funds utilize options, preferred securities, convertibles, bonds, money market instruments, and other investment vehicles.

Mutual funds can be classified in terms of their objectives.

Growth funds attempt to grow as safely as possible over long periods of time. Generation of income is not their primary objective, so dividend payouts are moderate to minimal. *Maximum capital gains funds*, sometimes called aggressive growth funds or performance funds, try to grow as rapidly as possible. They are high-risk investments paying little or no dividends. These funds may use leverage, may sell short, or may make use of arbitrage strategies. *Growth and income* funds attempt to grow as rapidly as possible under the constraints of low-risk and moderate dividend payouts. *Income funds* focus on the generation of income. These relatively low-risk funds purchase income-producing securities and often write covered call options. *Specialty funds* invest in a specific area, industry group, or economic sector. Examples include funds that specialize in international investments, the service sector, utilities, or gold.

6. Portfolio. The makeup of the portfolio should not be at variance with the statement of objectives. The prospectus provides specifics of actual securities making up the portfolio.

7. Stocks Held. Other factors equal, the greater the number of stocks held by the fund, the more the fund can be expected to behave like the market as a whole. However, for funds that specialize, this generalization will obviously not hold true.

8. Beta. The beta value is a measure of the historical variability of the fund as compared to the market as a whole. Beta values greater than 1.0 have been more volatile than the market: values less than 1.0 have been less volatile than the market.

9. Bull and Bear Ratings. Funds may perform quite differently during market advancing or declining phases. The measure shown here is an attempt at providing evidence of how well the fund fared during these periods in the past, based on an A (best) to E (worst) rating system. A similar feel for relative performance can be found by simply comparing the fund's annual performance with the respective annual percentage advance or decline of the market.

10. 12-b-1. In 1980 the Securities and Exchange Commission issued a ruling which in effect allowed fund management to "hide" sales fees by deducting marketing and distribution expenses from fund assets. With this method shareholders pay an annual sales fee, whether they know it or not, in place of an open fee at the time of purchase or sale. You might be wise to consider an alternate fund if a fund that otherwise looks interesting to you is utilizing this plan.

11. Telephone Exchange. If a fund has telephone exchange privileges, switching assets is as easy as calling your broker to buy and sell stocks. While this feature is not an essential one to support a switching strategy, it certainly makes life easier.

Besides the 11 key factors shown in Exhibit 9.1, there are other questions to ask. Are there restrictions on the number and frequency of switches? Some funds set a limit on the number of switches in one year. Others have a minimum amount of time for which you can hold the fund, once purchased (e.g., 30 days).

What is the cost to switch? Many funds have no switch fee, some charge a nominal amount (e.g., $5), and still others charge a more substantial sum. Another practice is to charge a fee based on the number of switches made each year. As an example, the Fidelity Select group of funds allows the first four switches at no cost, with subsequent switches costing $50 each.

The composition of the fund family is also important. If you are switching only between a growth fund and a money market fund, then these two members of the family are of sole importance. For other strategies, more family members will have to be examined. If a single family has all the funds that you are interested in switching between, and also has telephone privileges, a switching strategy becomes much easier to implement. All transfers can be made by phone, and no checks have to be mailed.

Money market funds require a special analysis, since there are differences in terms of yield and risk exposure. Those with the lowest risk primarily hold U.S. government and federal agency securities. Other money fund investments can include repurchase agreements, certificates of deposit, banker's bills of exchange, commercial paper, and (the riskiest) Eurodollar instruments. Potential investors in these funds have to weigh higher yields offered against possible risks.

Besides the AAII material referenced in Exhibit 9.1 there are many other sources of information on mutual funds. Daily quotes of net asset value can be obtained from Dow Jones News/Retrieval Current Quotes (//CQ), and quotes are also given in most newspapers with a financial section. *Barron's* magazine carries Lipper's performance ratings of major funds on a quarterly basis. *Money* magazine has a monthly "fund watch" section, and *Forbes* surveys the performance of funds every August. Many books and newsletters are also available. (See the reference section at the end of this chapter for examples.)

These sources can be used to initially screen funds. You can later obtain prospectuses on the few that you have a serious interest in by calling their toll-free telephone number.

SWITCHING BETWEEN A STOCK FUND AND A MONEY MARKET FUND

This basic switching strategy involves the movement of funds back and forth between a stock fund and a money market fund. The reason for making the switch is to avoid losing money during down markets while participating in up market moves.

After selecting a fund family containing the stock fund and money market fund that meet your objectives, you must next develop a system to time your switches. Two major approaches to timing will be discussed, one based on fund price performance and the other based on market analysis.

Switching on Fund Price Performance

One way to determine switch signals is to apply a trend-defining technique directly to the price of the shares of the fund itself. Exhibit 9.2 shows weekly closing price data for the Dreyfus Growth Opportunity fund, with a 4- and 10-week exponential moving average oscillator used to define trend changes. (See Chapter Three for an explanation of the moving average technique.) The crossover points can be used as switch signals, or they can be combined with other information to indicate when to switch out of the stock fund and into the money market fund.

EXHIBIT 9.2 Defined Trend Reversals for the Dreyfus Growth Opportunity Fund

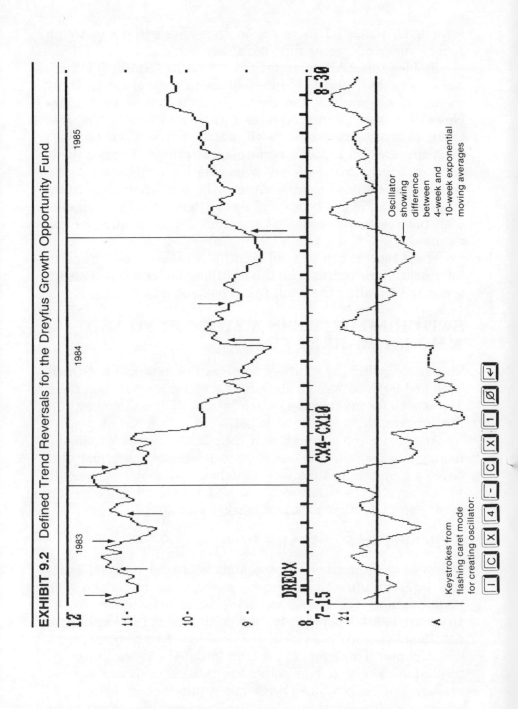

If the crossing points are used as pure switch signals, at each up arrow point the money market fund is liquidated and the money made available from the sale is transferred to the stock fund. At each down arrow point the stock fund is liquidated and the money is used to invest in the money market fund. Capital is preserved in this fund until the next switch signal is given.

Any of the trend-identification techniques explained in Chapter Three can be used to develop switch signals. You will certainly want to experiment to find a system that is consistent with your timing horizon (short, intermediate, or long) and has a history of success with your fund.

For most traders, weekly price data will be sufficient to effect a successful switching program. Daily data are more time-consuming and costly to gather, and generally provide an unneeded level of sensitivity for the price analysis of these diversified investments. By downloading Friday's daily quote on the mutual fund of interest each week and transferring the quote to your Dow Jones Market Analyzer PLUS data disk, you can build up a weekly price history of the fund. Exhibit 9.3 shows how this procedure works.

The symbol for mutual funds is found under //SYMBOL in Dow Jones News/Retrieval. Press 4 for mutual fund information and type in the name of the fund. Before a price history can be developed, the symbol provided by the Current Quotes database must be placed on your quote and data disks.

Building price histories on mutual funds is simple and requires just seconds of time each week. Developing a historical reference database is another matter, however, since Dow Jones News/Retrieval does not carry historical mutual fund data. One way to obtain the database is to start accumulating quotes week by week until sufficient data is stored on your disk to make a timing analysis. As an example, if you are using a 10-week simple moving average as part of your analysis, a minimum of 10 weeks of data will be required before the first value can be calculated. Another way to obtain the data is to first obtain a historical data set from another source and from then on update it from the Dow Jones Current Quotes database.

Barron's magazine is an excellent source of weekly data of all sorts, mutual funds included. Many stock market techni-

---

EXHIBIT 9.3 Building a Weekly Mutual Fund Price History

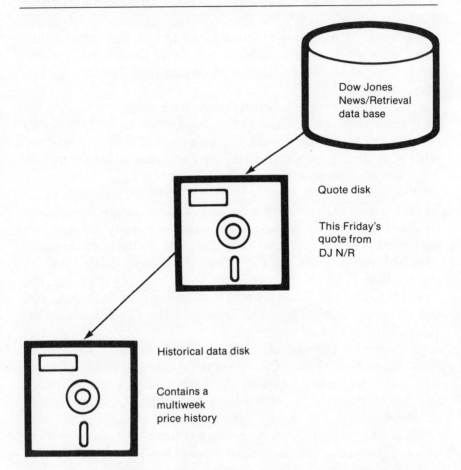

Dow Jones
News/Retrieval
data base

Quote disk

This Friday's
quote from
DJ N/R

Historical data disk

Contains a
multiweek
price history

cians keep a stack from the last six months to a year of this financial weekly publication on hand for just this purpose. Entering data values manually using the Dow Jones Market Analyzer PLUS is quite a simple task. From the main menu press **I** for New History from Keyboard and follow the prompts. The entry method is also a nice way to acquaint reliable teenagers with the world of finance and computers.

A complicating factor is using mutual fund price data arises from dividend and capital gain distributions periodically made by the funds. The quoted price is adjusted downward to reflect the distribution, affecting the continuity of prices before and after the distribution. For anlaytical purposes, the prices must be brought back together mathematically. This can be accomplished by changing all historical prices in the database before the distribution to bring them in line with subsequent quotes. As an example, suppose a fund closed at 21.00 on July 6 and had a 1.00 distribution on July 7. On July 7 the price would drop to 20.00 due to the 1.00 distribution, and future changes in price would start from this new value. To make the adjustment in historical prices, the stock split feature of the Dow Jones Market Analyzer PLUS is used in conjunction with the table in Appendix 9A.

To calculate the adjustment percentage, the reported distribution is deducted from the closing price on the *day before* the distribution (payment) day, and that amount is divided by the closing price. Mathematically;

$$\text{Adjustment factor} = \frac{\text{Closing price} - \text{Distribution}}{\text{Closing price}}$$

For our example, $(21.0 - 1.00)/21.00 = 20.00/21.0\,0 = 0.952$. This value is rounded off to two digits, then Appendix 9A is used to find the proper X and Y values for the Dow Jones Market Analyzer PLUS stock split feature. For our example, $X = 99$ and $Y = 94$. From the main menu, press selection **P** ↵ (adjust for splits), and follow the prompts.

Information on distributions for past data is available in *Barron's* magazine, to the right of the weekly quotes. Exhibit 9.4 provides an example for the Dreyfus Growth Opportunity fund.

At first glance, you may see price adjustments as a troublesome complication. In practice you will find it is a simple task that will have to be done infrequently (typically, one time each year).

Another option, which avoids manual entry and distribution adjustments, is to obtain data from a database that provides historical mutual fund pricing. Warner Computer Services has this information in weekly form for most mutual funds. To make use of this data, you must become a Warner subscriber and have software that can read their data. For the Dow Jones Market Analyzer PLUS, you will have to purchase the Warner Connector disk that will format the data properly.

Using the historical price of a mutual fund to time switches is straightforward and is easy to understand and implement. If

EXHIBIT 9.4 *Barron's* Fund Distribution Data

MUTUAL FUNDS 52-Week High	Low	Fund Name		Week's High	Low	Close NAV	Week's Chg.	LATEST DIVIDEND Dividend Inc.+Cap. Gains	Record Date	Payment Date	12 MONTHS Inco. Divs.	Cap. Gain
		Dreyfus Grp:										
15.36	13.39	A Bonds	n	15.06	14.90	14.90—	18	111	3-31-86	4-1-86	1.408	
15.22	13.29	CalTx	n	14.95	14.80	14.80—	19					
13.54	10.49	Dreyfus		13.24	13.06	13.06—	.19	.07	4-21-86	4-25-86	.59	1.75
15.89	14.90	GNM	n	15.59	15.42	15.42—	19	.131	3-31-86	4-1-86	1.316	
18.47	15.77	InsTx	n	17.97	17.74	17.74—	28					
13.82	12.66	Interm	n	13.62	13.53	13.53—	.11	.0797		2-28-86	1.0272	
21.37	15.71	Leverage		20.87	20.34	20.34—	.54	.78+1.94	11-13-85	11-15-85	78	1.94
13.01	9.57	GwthO	n	12.12	11.81	11.81—	.30	.205+1.095	4-7-86	4-11-86	.205	1.095
16.67	15.48	MA Tax	n	16.26	16.07	16.07—	.26					
23.37	14.68	NwLdrs		22.89	22.71	22.71—	22					
15.76	13.72	NY Tax	n	15.31	15.16	15.16—	.21					
9.88	7.52	SpclInc	n	u 9.88	9.70	9.83+	19	04	3-31-86	6-2-86	555	.241
12.76	11.35	TaxExmpt	n	12.48	12.37	12.37—	.14	0797		2-28-86	1.0193	
8.18	6.72	ThirdCntry	n	8.01	7.87	7.87—	.18	.205+.51	7-5-85	7-9-85	.205	51
8.34	7.19	EagleGth	Shs	8.24	8.18	8.18--	.01	.13+.23	12-11-85	12-27-85	13	23

Total distribution: .205 + 1.095 = 1.3

Date of distribution 4-11-86

SOURCE: *Barron's* May 19, 1986, p. 155. Reprinted by permission of *Barron's*, © Dow Jones & Company, Inc. 1986. All rights reserved.

the price undergoes well-defined swings, this method works well. However, it suffers from false switch signals during periods of prolonged sideways movements. Using price only to generate signals also ignores other, potentially useful, evidence. Despite these limitations, price-based switch signals are probably the most commonly used method for timing the stock fund to money market fund switch. A later discussion will indicate how the signals generated by this trend-following method can be combined with other information to improve the odds of success.

Switching on Market Evidence

This approach bases timing decisions on an analysis of the overall stock market. If the mutual fund price changes are correlated with the market as a whole, switch signals from this source can be used to effectively time the stock fund purchases and sales. Exhibit 9.5 shows the relationship between the S&P 500, Dow Jones Industrials, and three types of funds as measured by the Lipper indexes.

The indexes show a high degree of correlation with the market averages. The degree to which a specific fund rises and

EXHIBIT 9.5   Mutual Funds and General Market Movements

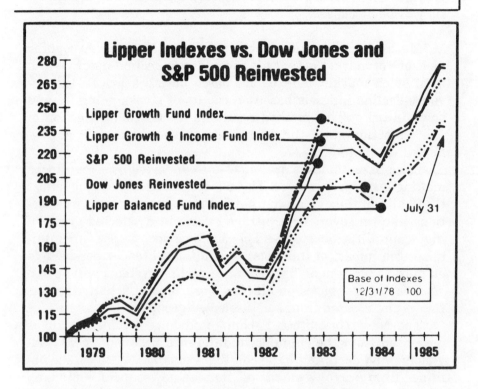

BARRON'S / *LIPPER GAUGE*

Lipper Indexes vs. Dow Jones and S&P 500 Reinvested

Lipper Growth Fund Index
Lipper Growth & Income Fund Index
S&P 500 Reinvested
Dow Jones Reinvested
Lipper Balanced Fund Index

July 31

Base of Indexes
12/31/78   100

SOURCE: Lipper Analytical Services. Reprinted with permission.

falls with the market is an issue that must be addressed on an individual fund basis. We saw in Exhibit 9.1 that the bull and bear ratings and the beta number are useful for determining this relationship. Another good indicator can be found in each August issue of *Forbes* magazine. This publication provides an annual rating for mutual funds separately for bull and bear markets. It seems safe to make the following generalization: If a timing system is developed based on the market, stock funds can be found that will work well with the switch signals generated.

To use this approach, favorable and unfavorable periods for

investment in the stock market must be identified and switch signals developed based on these findings. Two methods will be explained to aid in the accomplishment of these tasks. An advance-decline market timing model will be constructed and a procedure for making a comprehensive technical market analysis will be discussed.

Method 1: Advance-Decline Timing Model.   A popular measure of market activity is the advance-decline index. While most stock market indexes are based on stock prices, the advance-decline index is based on counts of stocks going up and down in price. This method results in a smoother reflection of market action since the magnitude of price change is not reflected in the index.

Price-based indexes are sometimes distorted by a few stocks making large price moves. These price changes may not reflect the health of the overall market but may simply result from actions like takeovers or arbitrage efforts in a selected group of high-capitalization stocks. The advance-decline system minimizes the impact of this noise, providing a broader perspective on market movement. Two advance-decline systems will be discussed, the first based on all New York Stock Exchange issues, the second created from a self-selected group of stocks.

The New York Stock Exchange advance-decline system is developed from the cumulative difference between weekly advancing and declining issues on this exchange. Data can be obtained from *Barron's* magazine, Sunday newspapers, and many other sources. To create the data set, the weekly declines on the New York Stock Exchange are subtracted from the weekly advances: the resultant number is added (or subtracted, if it is a negative number) from a cumulative running total. Each week's new number is appended to the existing data set. To aid in keeping the cumulative total positive, an initially large number (e.g., 15,000) is used to start the process.

As an example, if there were 1,400 advances and 500 declines in the first week of using the system, 900 would be added to 15,000 to provide a new cumulative total of 15,900. When the next week's advance-decline data became available, this number would be added to the 15,900 total to provide a new cumulative total.

The process is repeated each week, creating a new cumulative total which is appended to the previous data set. As the weeks go by, a larger and larger historical data set is created.

As with the price-based system explained previously, before this index can be used for timing it is necessary to have enough historical data so that an analysis can be made. Six month's to a year's worth of past data is sufficient to start. The historical data can easily be gathered from past *Barron's*, in the manner previously discussed.

Once the cumulative totals have been made and the data placed on a data disk, ongoing weekly additions will take no more than five minutes per week.

The cumulative advance-decline data is analyzed with a defined trend change system. Exhibit 9.6 shows a moving average crossing system for trend identification.

When the market cooperates and major movements occur (see the mid-1982 to mid-1983 and the 1985 periods shown), substantial gains accrue. However, when the market is going sideways, whipsaws occur. The second half of 1983 and mid-1984, for example, were characterized by a sideways movement that resulted in a number of whipsaws. Despite false signals, this method is very forgiving since mutual fund transaction costs are zero (or minimal), and the money alternatively rests in a money market fund earning interest. Moreover, if you choose your mutual fund carefully, the fund is likely to decline less than the market declines, providing another cushion to a potentially poor switch signal. The high frequency of whipsaw signals can, however, result in disadvantageous short-term tax consequences.

There is independent evidence to show that this type of timing system is successful in beating a buy-and-hold approach. Eugene D. Veilleux in his book, *How to Switch Your Money Market Fund for Maximum Profit*, (E.D. Veilleux, 1983) used switch signals generated by a weekly advance-decline index crossing a 10-week simple moving average of the index to time a number of mutual funds. He found an approximate doubling of returns from the switching strategy over a buy-and-hold approach. Another study, performed by Norm Nicholson, covered 10 years and used a 39-week moving average of the S&P 500 Index, triggered by the price of the index itself to generate

EXHIBIT 9.6 New York Stock Exchange Advance-Decline Timing System

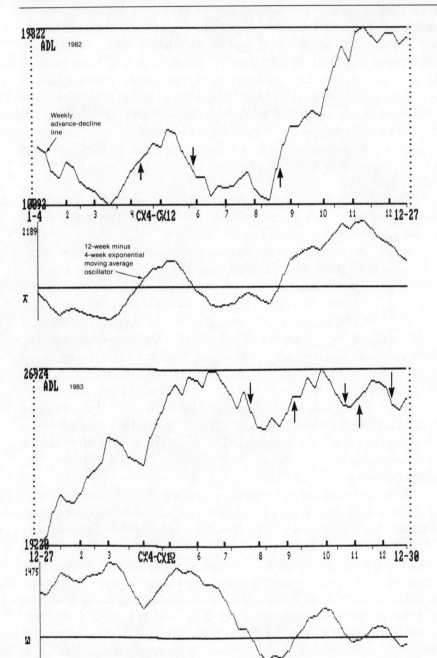

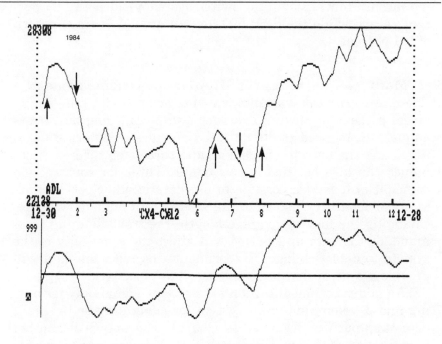

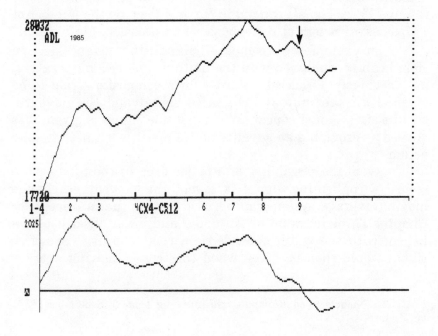

switch signals.[1] Despite the susceptibility of this trend-defining method to whipsaws, the switch system yielded an 11.7 percent return while the S&P 500 had an annual average return of 9.2 percent.

Modifications to the NYSE Advance-Decline System.

There are endless variants on the advance-decline timing model presented. Moving averages of different lengths, for example, can be used to define trend changes of differing durations, and the percentage change and three-step reversal techniques can also be used. (See Chapter Three for construction principles.) It is also possible to use data of other period units (daily or monthly) instead of the weekly unit data shown here. Changing the moving average length, the trend-defining technique, or the data-unit period will affect the sensitivity of the system to detect changes. Experimentation with the data will provide a system that best matches your objectives.

An additional modification is to use the signal only for buying and develop a different system for generating sell signals. (This approach is discussed in Chapter Eleven.) Still another modification is to combine switch signals to produce composite signals. These signals can aid in cutting down on the number of whipsaws, although at the expense of an occasional late signal.

As an example of a composite signal, the advance-decline signal can be combined with the mutual fund closing-price signal previously discussed. In order for a composite signal to be given, both the mutual fund price signal and the advance-decline signal must concur. When just one signal is given, it is viewed as providing an advance notice but it is not used to take action.

To avoid the possibility of a major drop in the fund's price before a confirming signal is given, the percentage change moving average system can be used on the fund's price. (See Chapter Three for details.) An upper and lower offset is established, with the width dependent on risk tolerance. A switch signal would then be given when the trigger moving average

---

[1]Norm Nicholson, ed., *Computerized Investing* 4, no. 5 (September 1985), pp. 2–4.

crosses the longer moving average and *either* the offset is crossed *or* the advance-decline signal is given.

In place of the New York Stock Exchange advances and declines, other data can be used. Your own group of "leading" stocks (a minimum of 25 for statistical purposes) can be chosen to create a truly unique timing system based on advances-declines of those issues exclusively. The Dow Jones Market Analyzer PLUS can easily make this index for any group that you select. Exhibit 9.7 shows an example.

To construct a customized advance-decline index, historical stock prices on your chosen stocks must first be downloaded from Dow Jones News/Retrieval. After obtaining this data, Edit Indicator from the main menu is accessed (**R** ←⎦) and the prompts are followed.

The advantages of making your own advance-decline indicator are many. First, it is easy to initially set up and maintain. All data are downloaded from the historical quotes database, so no manual data entry is required. Moreover, since your indicator is unique, the chances of placing your buy or sell order at the same time as others using a switch system are reduced. Furthermore, additional data are supplied with the index that can be important for analyzing the overall market. All of the volume indicators previously discussed can be used on your index, and the Daily Reports feature can be accessed to provide still more information. Finally, the index can be tailored to the type of stocks that comprise your mutual fund's portfolio. For example, if your fund invests primarily in over-the-counter stocks, your index can mirror that philosophy by being made up of these stocks.

The timing systems discussed so far can be classified as mechanical methods. They yield signals independent of the user's judgment. For the tyro they are an excellent way to "get your feet wet" while increasing personal knowledge of technical systems. The strength of systems of this nature is that they bring an unemotional discipline to buying and selling that may otherwise be lacking. The major weakness of mechanical systems is inexorably tied to its strength. Informed human judgment has the potential of providing better signals by assimilating vast amounts of information, weighting it, comparing it to past experience, assessing both the trends and changing interac-

EXHIBIT 9.7 Custom Large Company Stock Index

Components of the Index

Aluminum Corporation of America
American Express Company
AT&T
Boeing
BankAmerica
Coca-Cola
Delta Air Lines
Dow Chemical Company
Eastman Kodak Company
Exxon Corporation
Kmart Corporation
Kimberly Clark
Marsh & McLennan

General Electric Company
General Motors Corporation
The Goodyear Tire & Rubber Company
Intel Corporation
IBM
MCI Communications Corp.
Merck Sharp & Dohme
Merrill Lynch
3M
Motorola
Philip Morris Incorporated
Pacific Telesis

Advance-Decline Index

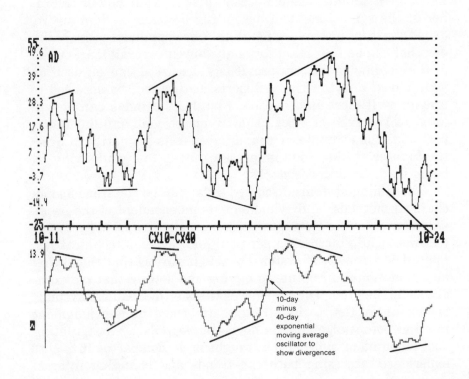

tions among the pieces of evidence, and coming to a decision that no mechanical system could ever match. We'll look next at an approach that allows this interaction and synthesis to take place.

Market Technical Analysis Timing Model

As we saw in Part Two of the book, technical analysis involves making numerous "tests" on historical data in an effort to gain an understanding of the current price situation. From this knowledge set probabilistic-based assessments of the future can be made. Exhibit 9.8 provides a guide for this form of analysis by indicating questions to be asked along with techniques available for use and where they can be found in this book. The set of questions presented are minimums. Your own indicators and techniques should be added to the list.

Data for use in the analysis can include the Dow Jones Averages, the NYSE advance-decline index, and your own market indexes. Other data to support the requirements of specific indicators (see Appendix 9B) may also be used.

To facilitate the analysis on a repeated basis using the Dow Jones Market Analyzer PLUS, Chart Auto Run should be used. From the main menu press **Z** (Learn Run) followed by an enter. The Learn Run procedure allows you to select precisely the procedural steps that you want to save for future analyses. Subsequent access to the Auto Run feature is made from the main menu **A** (Auto Run) followed by an enter.

How often should a market anlaysis be made to support a mutual fund switching strategy? In most cases, once each week is sufficient for a full-blown intermediate-term market analysis. If an aggressive growth fund is used with a record of high volatility, a closer watch is necessary. This can be made easy through a daily downloading of market price and volume data followed by a View Summary and View Trend screen. If unusual activity has occurred that day it will be quickly spotted and a further investigation using Chart Auto Run can be undertaken. If unusual behavior is not evident, the market analysis can be skipped that day.

Information gleaned from the market analysis is used to support switching decisions. This is done by assessing each

EXHIBIT 9.8 Basic Technical Market Analysis

Questions	Techniques	Chapter for Explanations and Examples	Comments
1. What is the current trend of the market? Has a trend change signal been given?	Moving averages. Trendlines. View trend indicators.	3 3 3	Develop your own system from the available techniques to determine the long-, intermediate-, and short-term trends. Many technicians like to use advance-decline data along with market average data for this purpose.
2. Is there evidence of trend overextension?	Price minus moving-average oscillator. Moving average minus average oscillator.	3 3	Check for the intermediate to long term. If double peaks or bottoms exist, be sure to use divergence analysis. Do *not* use regression for market analysis.
3. Are any time or business cycles currently favorable or unfavorable to the market?	Backward look. Simple moving average. Moving-average crossings.	4 4 4	Two major cyclic influences for the market: presidential election (time cycle), interest rates (business cycle).
4. What are relative strength measures saying?	Internal relative strength	5	Check for nonconfirmation on consecutive rising peaks or falling bottoms.
5. What is volume "saying" about current price action?	Utilities to the Dow. Volume generalizations. The DJMA Plus volume indicators. Big blocks.	5 6 6 6	If Dow is in a consolidation phase (sideways movement) find the utility's relative strength. You should commit to memory the volume generalizations. Be careful when using the DJMA Plus indicators. Use them in the proper circumstances.
6. Where may there be support or resistance?	Resistance zones. Speed resistance lines.	7 7	These provide rough guides, not precise points.
7. What other evidence do I have about the status of the market?	—	—	The previous analysis represents just a beginning. There are many other sources of evidence. Appendix 9B provides a sample.

market test and developing a value judgment based on the combined results of all tests. In essence, when the bulk of evidence turns unfavorable, a sell signal is given, and when the opposite occurs, a buy signal is given. Many investors use an incremental switching policy when market analysis buy and sell signals are given. A percentage of money is switched instead of the total amount, with the portion moved depending on the strength of the evidence.

The aggregation of the evidence for decision purposes can be performed subjectively, or more formal approaches can be used. Appendix 9C provides a worksheet that can be used to guide this evaluation. The trading strategies discussed in Chapter Eleven can also be used.

With experience that is derived from repeated market analyses, you will begin to get a feel for the market's health. Before long the weekly "snapshots" of the market will turn into a dynamic "motion picture" and you will see unfolding before you vibrant market moves that falter and poor markets that become strong. You will see markets that appear to be going nowhere on the surface, but underneath you will find the building of evidence for a move in one direction or another. In short, with experience will come an in-depth understanding of current conditions and a sense of probabilities for the future. This level of market awareness could only be attained in the past by dedicated full-time market professionals. With a computer, comprehensive market analysis software, and online data retrieval it is now attainable by any motivated investor.

To speed up the learning phase of market analysis, simulations can be made on past data. A friend can download stock data, make a copy, change the name to X, and remove a few months of data before supplying it to you. After making your analysis the original disk is furnished so you can see how your analysis relates to the later price and volume action that you did not see. This can be repeated over and over to cover many different situations. Two investors can swap disks created in this manner for a mutual learning experience. For more realism, an index can be constructed from a chosen set of stocks. Use of a common index like the Dow Jones Industrial Average may not work well, since its recent pattern is highly recognizable by most investors. There's nothing like knowing what happened to bias one's views of technical indicators.

Some market technicians make and keep a copy of their market analysis (similar to Appendix 9C) whenever a buy or sell decision is made. This allows them to later review their good and bad market decisions for improving future performance.

You may wonder if there is a way to remove human effort and judgment from the market analysis. It would be easier to simply download information and have a system developed that would make the comprehensive market analysis for you while providing discrete signals at the right moment.

Many of these automatic multifactor timing systems have been developed, with various degrees of success. One of the most well known is the Wall $treet Week "Elves" indicator developed by Robert Nurock and provided each day in *Investor's Daily*. With this system, 10 indicators are assessed and each is given a weighting of plus one, zero, or minus one, depending on whether it is yielding a favorable, neutral, or unfavorable indication. If the sum of all the indicators reaches plus five, a buy signal is flashed; if it drops to minus five, a sell signal is given. The indicator has made many important calls but its record has not been perfect.

You can make your own automatic timing index using computer spreadsheet software. The spreadsheet link feature of the Dow Jones Market Analyzer PLUS (and other software products) in association with a computer spreadsheet program like Lotus 1-2-3 makes the job easier. The required procedure is to develop a spreadsheet template that both accommodates the data you have chosen and defines the relationships within and among the data. For the Dow Jones Market Analyzer PLUS, a data file understandable to the spreadsheet is established by O ← (Spreadsheet Data) from the main menu.

A description of how the Wall $treet Indicator is made using the spreadsheet approach is given in the article "The Elves of Wall $treet Week," by Andrew T. Williams.[2] This article of-

---

[2]Andrew T. Williams, "The Elves of Wall Street Week," *PC World* 1, no. 3 (1984), pp. 186–91.

fers an excellent starting point for constructing your own automatic system.

Despite the conceptual attractiveness of this method, creating a reliable multifactor system is a difficult task indeed. The development of mathematical weights for each of the factors in your index is a major problem. Should they be given equal weight (as in the Wall $treet Week Elves indicator), or should the more important factors be given greater weight? Moreover, should the weights remain constant? In bull markets one factor may be very important as an indicator of market tops but not a very good indicator of market bottoms. Furthermore, there may be interactions among the factors that may also change across market time. These and other questions of a more theoretical nature make the task of creating these models a formidable one.

Switching among Specialty Funds

In the last few years specialty mutual funds have emerged as an important investment alternative. These funds concentrate their investments in a single area, allowing the investor to participate in individual industry group or economic trend changes. This concentration of assets brings with it both advantages and disadvantages. On the positive side, at almost any time one or more specialty funds are likely to be doing well. Identifying the good performers offers the potential for making money in any market, be it bull, bear, or sideways. There is, however, a potential problem. The price movement of the stocks in a specialty fund are highly correlated with one another. Economic or other effects that make one stock go up or down in a specialty portfolio will often affect all stocks in the portfolio in a similar manner, leading to high volatility and increased risk.

There are three fund families that have groups of specialty funds and that allow switching between them. Fidelity Select Portfolios was the first fund family to offer a diverse group of specialty funds. This family was followed by the Vanguard Group and the Financial Programs Group. Exhibit 9.9 provides data on these fund families.

EXHIBIT 9.9 Specialized Mutual Fund Families

Fidelity Select
  Energy Portfolio
  Leisure and Entertainment Portfolio
  Technology Portfolio
  Financial Services Portfolio
  Precious Metals and Minerals Portfolio
  Health Care Portfolio
  Utilities Portfolio
  Defense and Aerospace

Brokerage and Investment Management
Chemicals
Computers
Electronics
Food and Agriculture
Software and Computer Service
Telecommunications

Fidelity Investment
82 Devonshire Street
Boston, Mass. 02109
800-225-6190

2 percent sales charge.
1 percent redemption fee.
Minimum investment: $1,000.
Telephone switching allowed.
$50 fee for each switch over four per year.

Financial Group
  Energy Portfolio
  Gold Portfolio
  Health Sciences Portfolio
  Leisure Portfolio
  Pacific Basin Portfolio
  Technology Portfolio

Financial Programs
P.O. Box 2040
Denver, Colo. 80201
800-525-8085

No sales charge.
Minimum investment: $1,000.
No sales charge on switches.
Telephone switching allowed.
Excessive switching discouraged.

Vanguard
  Energy Portfolio
  Gold and Precious Metals Portfolio
  Health Care Portfolio
  Service Economy Portfolio
  Technology Portfolio

Vanguard Group of Investments Company
Vanguard Financial Center
Valley Forge, Pa. 19482
800-523-7025

1 percent redemption fee.
Minimum investment: $1,500.
No sales charge on switches.
Telephone switches allowed.

The basic approach in using these funds is to place your money in a fund that is doing well and to leave it there until it shows signs of reversal or is overtaken by a significantly stronger fund. This approach is like riding the fastest horse you can find, and when it tires, switching to another fast-moving horse.

Specialty fund switching offers the potential for greater profits than does the growth fund to money market fund

EXHIBIT 9.10 Procedure for Specialized Fund Switching

Procedure	Comments
Initial determination What funds should be monitored?	The funds shown in Exhibit 9.9 are a good starting point. You must choose enough to represent wide economic diversification, but not so many as to promote whipsaws (5 to 10 is a reasonable number).
Initial evaluation Which funds are in defined uptrends? (If none, buy the money market fund, otherwise, see below.)	Possible techniques: Percent up, percent down trend. Moving average crossings. Percentage change. Three-step reversal. Trendline.
Of these, which is the strongest: (Buy the strongest.)	Possible techniques: Percent price above moving average. Slope of moving average. Wilder strength indicators. Relative strength comparisons.
Periodic evaluation Is your currently held fund still in an uptrend? (If not, it's time to switch. If none are in an uptrend, switch to money market fund. Otherwise, see below.) Which uptrending fund is currently the strongest? (If not your current fund, switch to the strongest if it is significantly stronger than your fund. Also switch to it if your fund is no longer in an uptrend.)	Weekly or monthly. Significance is in terms of a fixed percentage difference between the currently held fund and the stronger.

switching approach. Moreover, it represents the most exciting way to make use of mutual funds. Exhibit 9.10 provides the general procedure for participating in this strategy.

The first step is to determine which mutual funds should have membership in the set from which you will make your switches. It is important to have sufficient representation across economic sectors to help ensure that something is likely to be doing well at all times. Specialty fund switching will work only if there is a fund to switch to that is making gains to the upside. If all the funds in your chosen universe are going sideways you may be whipsawed between them with possible losses accruing. If there are too many funds under consideration, the chances for unnecessary switching between funds increases. As a general rule, you should think in terms of 5 to 10 funds from which to make your analysis.

The three fund families shown in Exhibit 9.9 make a good starting point for obtaining information on specific funds. Other single management funds should also be considered. Information about these candidates can be obtained from many sources. The reference at the end of this chapter should prove helpful.

Once the funds are chosen, an evaluation is made resulting in a fund purchase. From that time on, periodic reviews are made with switches taking place when required.

A basic switching model using the procedures in Exhibit 9.10 will be explained next, followed by a discussion of possible modifications and enhancements. You will see that this strategy allows considerable room for personal creativity.

A Basic Switching Model

For this switching model, a one-year weekly closing price history for each fund is required. As mentioned previously, this can be obtained from past *Barron's* and manually entered into the system or downloaded from Warner Computer Services. After the data are on your data disk, it can be automatically kept up-to-date by downloading quotes each weekend from Dow Jones News/Retrieval.

The initial evaluation involves finding for purchase the strongest fund in an uptrend. To define an uptrend on this basic switching model we will use the three-step reversal technique (see Chapter Three) on a 40-week weighted moving average. The funds are graphed and those with uptrends are noted. If none of the funds are in an uptrend, a money market fund is purchased.

If at least one fund is in an uptrend, the Dow Jones Market Analyzer PLUS View Summary report is next used to order funds on c/adc on the same 40-week basis. Exhibit 9.11 shows a sample of what this report looks like for six Fidelity Select

---

EXHIBIT 9.11   View Summary Report for Speciality Fund Basic Switch
Model

---

		1 day change		40 day average			14 day volatility	
stock	close	change	% ch	c/adc	v/adv	vlty	posn	rstr
HLT	24.04	-0.63	-2.6	1.11	1.10	2.16	5	56
FNC	24.89	0.04	0.2	1.10	1.09	1.04	46	71
UTL	19.75	-0.03	-0.2	1.06	1.06	1.35	34	59
ENE	10.80	-0.08	-0.7	1.04	0.94	1.48	92	58
TEC	19.56	-0.24	-1.2	0.95	0.95	2.32	49	46
MET	9.10	-0.13	-1.4	0.91	0.86	4.16	0	41

Ratio of the closing weekly
price to the average weekly
close for 40 weeks

(ordered from largest to
smallest value)

---

funds. Although the report indicates a 40-day average, a 40-
week average is actually computed, as the historical data is in a
weekly form.

The c/adc column represents the ratio of the current closing
price to its most recent 40-week moving average value. A number greater than 1.00 indicates a closing price that is above its
40-week moving average, while a value less than 1.00 indicates
a closing price less than the moving average. The strength
measure for the basic switching model is this c/adc value. The
larger it is, the stronger the trend is defined to be. The largest
of these values that represent a fund in an uptrend would
therefore be purchased.

After the initial purchase is made, a monthly evaluation
takes place. This evaluation is first accomplished with the c/adc
data in the View Summary report. If the currently held mutual
fund has dropped below its 40-week moving average (c/adc less
than 1.00), a switch is made out of the fund and into the fund
with the highest c/adc reading above 1.00 that is in an uptrend.
If none of the funds are above 1.00, a money market fund is
purchased. If the currently held mutual fund has not fallen below 1.00, it is held until another fund has become stronger by
.03 or more on the c/adc scale and is in an uptrend.

This evaluation process takes place each month, with
switches made, when necessary, into stronger funds. As an example of this procedure on past data, Exhibit 9.12 shows re-

EXHIBIT 9.12 Switching Activity for Basic Fund Switching Model

		Monthly Ranking for c'adc over 1.0						Fund Held	Approximate Change (Percent)
		1	2	3	4	5	6		
1984	January								
	February								
	March								
	April	Metals	Energy					Money Market	
	May	Energy	Metals	Financial	Utilities			Money Market	
	June	Metals	Energy					Money Market	
	July	None						Money Market	
	August	Utilities	Health	Financial				Money Market	
	September	Utilities	Health	Energy	Financial	Technology		Money Market	+5.5
	October	Utilities	Financial	Energy	Health			Utilities	
	November	Utilities	Financial	Health	Energy			Utilities	
	December	Financial	Utilities					Utilities	
1985	January	Financial	Utilities	Health				Utilities	+9.6
	February	Financial	Health	Utilities	Technology	Energy		Financial	
	March	Health	Financial	Utilities	Technology	Energy		Financial	+1.5
	April	Health	Utilities	Financial	Energy			Health	
	May	Health	Financial	Utilities	Energy			Health	
	June	Health	Financial	Utilities	Energy			Health	
	July	Health	Financial	Utilities				Health	
	August	Health	Financial	Utilities	Energy	Technology		Health	+14.5
	September	Health	Financial	Utilities					
	October								
	November								
	December								

sults of the basic switching model in six Fidelity Select funds. Exhibit 9.13 provides graphs of the funds over the period of evaluation, with buy and sell points marked.

Modifications and Enhancements to the Basic Model

The basic switching model is just one of many possible configurations within the framework of the procedure shown in Exhibit 9.10. The following alternatives for change are presented as possibilities for your consideration.

1. Evaluation Period. The periodic evaluation can be shortened to a weekly or daily basis, or lengthened to a quarterly basis. Shortening the period will make the system more sensitive to changes, resulting in more switches but reducing the chance of a large loss between periods of analysis. A daily evaluation period will generate the most switches. This period would only be feasible for use on those funds that have unlimited switching at no charge or for monetary investments so large that the fees to switch are comparatively negligible.

Lenghthening the period to a quarterly basis on these volatile funds can be very risky. One professional mutual fund timer uses quarterly periods on the Fidelity Select funds in order to ensure that the $50 charge for more than four switches per year would never have to be paid. This approach is not recommended, as the possibility of loss over a three-month period is probably greater than any potential switch fee savings.

2. Trend Definition. The trend-defining technique can also be changed, with any of the methods explained in Chapter Three available for use.

3. Strength of Trend. The strength of trend is another area where a different approach can be taken. The Welles Wilder measures of trend strength offer a great opportunity for applicability here. As an example, all funds could be filtered based on strength of trend, with the fund having the largest value that is also in an uptrend (percent up trend above its percent down trend) being defined as the best candidate for purchase. Other strength-of-trend measures include the slope of

EXHIBIT 9.13 Basic Switching Model Results for Six Fidelity Select Funds

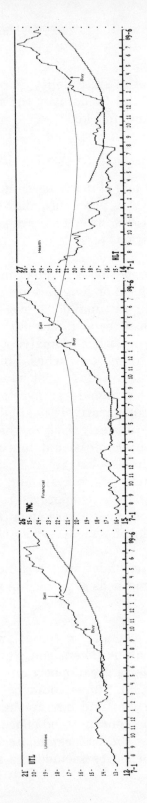
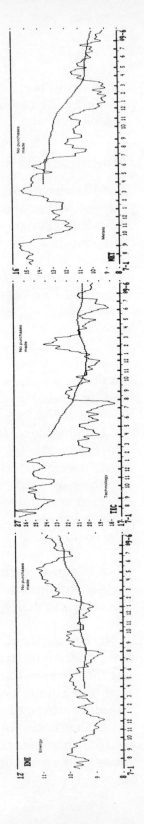

the defined trend (the greater the slope, the greater the trend strength) and the ratio of a short-term moving average of price and the current value of a trend-defining moving average.

If Welles Wilder measures are used, it is necessary to obtain data having high and low values as well as closing prices, since all three are used in calculating the Wilder indicators. This precludes the use of daily data and of Dow Jones News/Retrieval mutual fund quotes, since these have closing prices only. The Warner database and *Barron's* are convenient sources.

4. Indexes. In place of using fund prices, indexes can be constructed based on fund composition, and the required data can be downloaded from an information utility that maintains it.

The index method is a rapid way to obtain data and has the added advantage of yielding daily high, low, and close price information and volume figures. An index for specialty funds is created by finding 5 to 10 stocks that represent the group covered by the fund, then downloading the data and making an index for these stocks. The fund's prospectus is an excellent source of company names for this purpose. Because most specialty funds are so concentrated in one investment area, a small sample will usually give excellent results. Exhibit 9.14 shows a Fidelity Select Technology fund index created from a listing of eight of the largest holdings as given in its prospectus.

One disadvantage of using a custom index for this task is that it can be troublesome to maintain if you are following many specialty funds. Stock splits, mergers, and trading suspensions, for example, must be continually addressed. Moreover, some funds are not amenable to a straightforward representation by an index. Metals funds that have domestic and foreign holdings, for example, are difficult to construct an index for. If the index is to model the actual fund's price-change behavior, chosen stocks have to reflect the approximate proportions of each holding group. This is often difficult to maintain as fund management makes adjustments to the portfolio. Other funds, unaccommodating to representation with indexes because of their portfolio diversity, are service-sector funds and international funds.

EXHIBIT 9.14 Custom Index to Represent the Fidelity Select Technology Fund

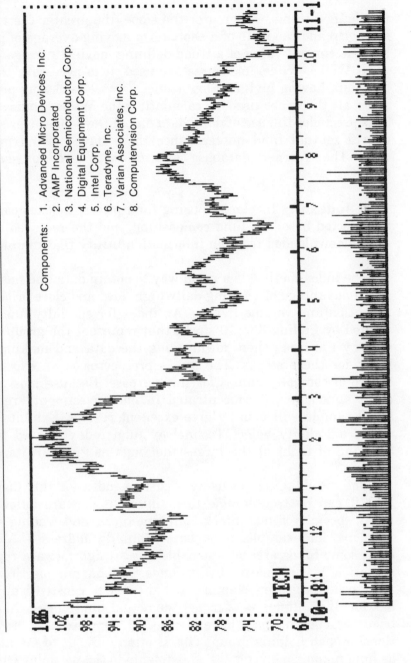

Components:
1. Advanced Micro Devices, Inc.
2. AMP Incorporated
3. National Semiconductor Corp.
4. Digital Equipment Corp.
5. Intel Corp.
6. Teradyne, Inc.
7. Varian Associates, Inc.
8. Computervision Corp.

Despite these problems, building your own custom index is a viable alternative for representing many sector funds. The indexes can be updated at each evaluation period, and the switching analysis procedure can be performed on them as if they were the funds themselves.

5. Use of Judgment. Human judgment is an alternative input to mechanical timing systems. For example, when the moment to switch arises, a further analysis can be made to support (or refute) the fund switch signal. This is an especially valuable input when a new fund appears stronger than the currently held fund (which may still be moving up) and a signal to switch is given. Is the new fund really stronger, or is it experiencing a blow-off period of overextension that will lead to a possible reversal in trend? Assessing the situation through the combined use of the trend overextension indicators discussed in Chapter Three, the Wilder RSI measure explained in Chapter Five, the relative strength technique shown in Chapter Five, and the volume indicators detailed in Chapter Six (if an index is used) can aid in preventing the purchase of a fund that is rising into a short-term price peak.

6. Investment Diversification. As an alternative to purchasing only one specialty fund at a time, positions in the top two or three funds can be maintained. Spreading your investment dollars between two or three funds reduces the overall loss that would accrue from a precipitous drop in one fund's price. Diversification is also important if you want to follow a large number of funds, since profit-robbing whipsaws between single funds will be reduced. Of course, attendant with these advantages is a lowering of return during periods when one fund is performing much better than any of the others.

APPENDIX 9A: MUTUAL FUND DISTRIBUTION ADJUSTMENT TABLE

Historical Data Adjustment Factor	X Value	Y Value
0.99	99	98
0.98	99	97
0.97	99	96
0.96	99	95
0.95	99	94
0.94	99	93
0.93	99	92
0.92	99	91
0.91	99	90
0.90	99	89
0.89	99	88
0.88	99	87
0.87	99	86
0.86	99	85
0.85	99	84
0.84	99	83
0.83	99	82
0.82	99	81
0.81	99	80
0.80	99	79
0.79	99	78
0.78	99	77

APPENDIX 9B: SELECTED MARKET EVIDENCE

Indicator	*Comments*
Market Price Action	
1. Percentage of stocks above their moving average.	If you have your own market index (see Chapter Nine), you can use the daily reports feature to get this information. Using a 55-day intermediate moving average, above 75 percent is overbought, below 25 percent is oversold.
2. Short-term trading index (TRIN) average declining volume divided by average advancing stock volume.	Widely available on FNN and other stock quotation services. Under 1.0 is bullish, over 1.0 is bearish.
3. New York Stock Exchange Tick. The sum of last price changes (positive or negative) of individual stocks.	Another widely available indicator. Positive tick is bullish, negative tick bearish for the short term.
4. High-Low index. There are many forms of this index with the most popular being an exponentially smoothed new highs, over new highs plus new lows.	Under 25 percent is bullish, over 80 percent is bearish.
5. Percent rise and fall of market index.	In a typical bull market, prices rise above 75 percent from base to peak. In a typical bear market, prices drop about 30 percent from peak to base.
Economic-based evidence	
1. Long-term interest rates minus short-term rates.	When this difference is negative, it is a bearish sign for the market.
2. Bond yield to dividend yield.	Over 3.0, bearish; under 2.0, bullish.
3. Federal Reserve actions.	Norman Fosback's Federal Reserve rules: Two easing actions will result in a higher market; three restrictive actions and the market will fall.
4. Cash position of mutual funds.	Bullish if over 10 percent. Bearish if under 8 percent.
5. Dow Jones price-to-dividend ratio.	Bearish if over 30. Bullish if under 20.

Market participant evidence

1. Insider purchases and sales.	Six to nine months after heavy selling the market usually peaks (buy/sell ratio of 0.15 or less). Conversely, with heavy buying (buy/sell ratio of 0.50 or more), the market can be expected to rise.
2. Odd-lot short-sales divided by total odd-lot sales.	When above 3.0 percent provides an indication of a market bottom.
3. NYSE member short-sales divided by total short sales.	Bullish if under 70 percent. Bearish if over 80 percent.
4. Advisory sentiment index— percentage of bullish investment advisers.	Investors intelligence tracks. Bullish and bearish newsletters. At extreme levels, can be used as a contrary indicator.
5. Big block index of upticks over upticks plus downticks.	When divergence is seen with overall market action, a warning signal is given. See Chapter Six.

APPENDIX 9C: MARKET ANALYSIS WORKSHEET

Evidence	Favorable	Neutral	Unfavorable	Analysis Comments
Trends and trend changes				
Long term	___	___	___	
Intermediate term	___	___	___	
Short term	___	___	___	
Trend overextention				
Long term	___	___	___	
Intermediate term	___	___	___	
Short term	___	___	___	
Cycles				
Presidential election	___	___	___	
Fundamental (e.g., interest rates)	___	___	___	
Other	___	___	___	
Relative strength				
Internal	___	___	___	
Utilities to industrials	___	___	___	
Volume relationships				
Total volume	___	___	___	
Negative volume	___	___	___	
Positive volume	___	___	___	
Indication of accumulation/distribution	___	___	___	
Daily volume indicator	___	___	___	
Big block volume	___	___	___	
Support	___	___	___	
Resistance	___	___	___	
Other evidence (including fundamental factors)	___	___	___	

SELECTED REFERENCES

DONOGHUE, WILLIAM E. *William E. Donoghue's Complete Money Market Guide*. New York: Harper & Row, 1981.

———. *William E. Donoghue's No-Load Mutual Fund Guide*. New York: Harper & Row, 1983.

GORDON, MARION, and JANICE HOROWITZ. "Inside Moves, Market Timing with Mutual Funds." *Personal Investor*, July 1985, pp. 32–39.

LASSER, J. K. *J. K. Lasser's Guide to Mutual Funds*. New York: Cloverdale Press, 1985.

PERRITT, GERALD W., and I. KAY SHANNON. *The Individual Investor's Guide to No-Load Mutual Funds*. Chicago: American Association of Individual Investors, 1985.

POPE, ALAN. "Loading Up: What Is the Total Cost to Mutual Fund Investors?" *AAII Journal*, January 1985, pp. 19–21.

RUNDE, ROBERT. "The Alluring Lineup of Sector Funds." *Money*, November 1984, pp. 175–78.

———. "Services that Time Your Trades." *Money*, May 1984, pp. 71–73.

SCHOLL, JAYE. "12b-1 Plans: A Revealing Look at Hidden Costs." *Barron's*, August 12, 1985, pp. 46–48.

WEISS, GARY. "Is Small Beautiful? For Some Funds, Profitable, Too." *Barron's*, August 12, 1985, pp. 44–45.

WILLIAMS, ANDREW T. "The Elves of Wall $treet Week." *PC World* vol. 1, no. 3 (1984), pp. 186–91.

CHAPTER TEN

High Probability Investing

This strategy involves the creation of a portfolio of undervalued stocks purchased during periods when the general market is selling at a discount. The stocks are held for the long term, until there is evidence that the stocks are fully valued and that important fundamental factors are slowing. This strategy is called "high probability" because each of the factors making up the strategy has a research underpinning, associating it probabilistically with favorable stock price movements.

Unfortunately, most investors and stockbrokers will not view this stock investment strategy as attractive, for it offers one of the surest ways of achieving above average returns in the stock market. For individual investors it is one of the most boring and unappealing of all the strategies covered in this book. Years can pass with the strategy taking no action, and when action is required it happens at a time of market decline, making it psychologically difficult to act. For brokerage firms this strategy generates extremely low commission income, so it provides little financial incentive for them to become involved with it.

The basic idea is to make use of research, primarily academic in nature, to identify factors that are correlated with stock price movements. The results of this research are then placed into an overall framework for action. Like the casinos of Las Vegas and Atlantic City, the overall situation is structured so that the odds of success favor the established system. This approach will offer no assurance of the profitability of individual stocks over the short term, but it will provide near certain success for a portfolio of stocks over the long term.

The specific variables addressed by this strategy are time, investor interest, stock price, and selected fundamental factors.

HIGH PROBABILITY VARIABLES

Time

Over the long term there is a built-in upward bias in stock prices. Instead of wandering aimlessly and randomly, prices tend to move higher over extended periods of time. Exhibit 10.1 shows closing monthly prices of the S&P 500 since 1948, plotted on a semilogarithmic scale. While the price motion is anything but smooth, the long-term uptrend is obvious. Over the time period covered by the chart, the S&P 500 has increased at an annual compound rate of more than 10 percent, while the inflation rate was increasing at less than half that amount.

If an investor buys a portfolio of stocks that emulates the market and just holds on for a long period of time, say 10 years or more, the odds of making money and also of beating inflation are a near certainty. As the holding period is shortened, the effects of the up and down moves that are riding on the overall uptrend take on more importance and increase the possibility that a loss could be sustained. Shorter holding periods also imply increased commissions which further reduce returns. Time, if you have it, is a tremendous ally in increasing the probability of obtaining substantial after-inflation returns in the stock market. All else being equal, the odds favor long-term investments over short-term investments.

The major up and down market swings that are evident in Exhibit 10.1 are tied to the business cycle and occur at intervals of approximately every four or five years. The cyclic upswing typically lasts from 24 to 40 months and the down phase from 12 to 18 months. (See Chapter Four for a discussion of this cycle.) An investor wishing to take advantage of the market's long-term up-bias would like to further improve his return possibilities by avoiding purchases near cyclic peaks. A long-term investor entering the market at a peak would face the possibility of enduring years of holding paper losses until the cycle

EXHIBIT 10.1   The Long-Term Upward Bias in the S&P 500

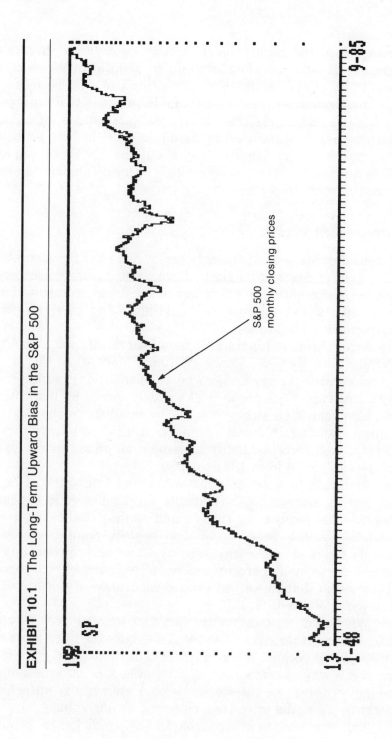

S&P 500
monthly closing prices

returned to the higher level. A high probability investment strategy should therefore attempt to significantly reduce the possibility of making investments at peak market periods.

To summarize, time as a variable provides two high probability messages: (1) time is a great accomplice since price changes have a significant upward bias over the long term, and (2) prices fluctuate significantly about the bias in an approximate four- to five-year cycle, making entry points for long-term investing very important.

Ignored Stocks

A considerable body of recently performed research has related the level of investor neglect of stocks to future price performance. The results show that neglected stocks, in terms of analyst reports and institutional holdings, tend to significantly outperform other stocks.

Avner Arbel in his book, *How to Beat the Market with High-Performance Generic Stocks* (William Morrow & Co., 1985), found returns for stocks ignored by institutions outperformed by about two to one those stocks widely owned by institutions. He also compared stocks ignored by analysts to those widely followed and again found a significant difference in return (16 percent to 9 percent). Returns were on an annual basis for the nine-year period from 1971 to 1980.

Another study by Steven Carvel and Paul Strebel as described in *Market Logic* (Institute for Econometric Research, No. 254, September 20, 1985) found similar results for the period 1976–1981. Based on analyst neglect, annual returns for widely followed stocks increased by 13 percent, moderately followed stocks by 20 percent, and neglected stocks by 29 percent. They found that this effect existed regardless of the size of the company followed.

What could account for the fact that ignored stocks perform better than other stocks? Avner Arbel believes these stocks are underpriced because of uncertainty. The discounted price is the market's way of compensating for the lack of information surrounding them. As the stocks become known, the uncertainty decreases and the price rises closer to its fair value.

This explanation is supported by the psychological principle that relates liking, disliking, and familiarity. There is a human bias that makes people more likely to view the known more positively than they view the unknown. This bias helps account for suspicions about people that live on the next block or in another country. As we get more familiar with the customs, habits, and nature of others, our natural defensive bias against them is reduced, and we can make judgments based on actual characteristics instead of on blanket feelings. In human relations, distance and lack of information flow often determine the unfamiliar disliking bias.

A natural initial reaction of a stockbroker when asked about an ignored stock is: "My advice is not to deal with those risky unknown stocks," or "Why look at a dog like that with all the well-known stocks available for purchase?" Lack of information automatically implies a degradation of value. An irony of the ignored stock effect is that it makes full-service brokers less attractive than discount brokers for the very reason that they think of themselves as being better: use of their research facilities for choosing stocks.

Level and Movement of Prices

There are two important effects concerning prices of individual stocks: the level of prices and volatility, and long-term trends and their persistence.

Low-priced stocks tend to be more volatile than high-priced stocks. For a given move in the stock market a portfolio holding low-priced stocks can be expected to experience greater percentage movements than will a portfolio holding much higher-priced stocks. The mathematical expression that relates the differential movements is called the *square root rule*. For a given change in the market, stocks change in price by adding a constant amount to the square root of their beginning prices. As an example, if the average stock advances from \$36 to \$49, the square root of the average price has moved from $\sqrt{36} = 6$ to $\sqrt{49} = 7$, for a square root increase of 1. Other stocks would be expected to do the same on a square root basis, resulting in greater percentage gains for lower-priced stocks.

A portfolio of \$9 stocks should advance to \$16 ($\sqrt{9} = 3$, $\sqrt{16} = 4$) for a percentage gain of *78 percent*. A portfolio of \$25 stocks should advance to \$36 ($\sqrt{25} = 5$, $\sqrt{36} = 6$) for a percentage gain of *44 percent*. A portfolio of \$100 stocks should gain to \$121 ($\sqrt{100} = 10$, $\sqrt{121} = 11$) for a gain of *21 percent*. The square root rule tells us that, over the long term, probabilities for greater percentage price changes are increased by creating a portfolio of low-priced stocks.

Price persistence is the second high probability price factor. In Chapter Three a number of trend-identifying techniques are discussed. The purpose of applying these techniques is to take advantage of trend persistency: "the trend is your friend" effect. Academic research has found that past trends are indeed important as factors in assessing the chances of future price changes.

Terry Zivney and Donald Thompson found that the most important factor in predicting future stock prices is the current trend in stock prices.[1] They constructed a series of 10 stock portfolios, with the differences between them being the direction and strength of the five-year trend in stock prices. For each stock, its current price was compared with its five-year average, and the stocks were assigned to portfolios ranging from low relative price (long-term downtrend) to high relative price (long-term uptrend). Results over a 10-year period (1971 to 1981) found stock portfolios that were highest in price relative to their average price outperformed the other portfolios. Differences were quite dramatic, with the highest two relative price portfolios (strongest uptrends) outperforming the market by 18 percent and 40 percent, respectively, over the 10-year period.

Their study found this effect to be so powerful that it subsumed other important factors, including company size, price-earnings ratio, dividend yield, price, and net working capital.

Fundamental Factors

For very short-term stock price changes, randomness is a major factor. In the intermediate term, psychology appears to have a

---

[1]Terry Zivney and Donald Thompson, "Buy High? Relative Price Screens Shows Above Average Returns," *AAII Journal* 7, no. 7 (August 1985), pp. 9–14.

great influence on the struggle of supply with demand. In the long run, however, fundamental considerations appear to be the most important factor in establishing common stock prices. Ultimately, the price of a stock reflects the factors of economic performance and value. Notwithstanding the power of technical analysis, stock portfolios to be held for the long term should consider important fundamental evidence to provide clues to future price behavior.

What fundamentals should be given special attention? Literally hundreds of fundamental factors have been used by long-term investors. Four that seem to hold special promise for increasing the probability of success include the price-earnings ratio, earnings growth rate, total capitalization, and price-sales ratio.

Price-Earnings Ratio

The price-to-earnings ratio is one of the most popular indicators of a stock's value. In general, stocks with a low P/E ratio are thought to be undervalued: stocks with a high price-to-earnings ratio are thought to be overvalued. Of course, this generalization must be tempered by the standards of the industry group to which an individual stock belongs.

A considerable amount of academic research has confirmed the benefits of building stock portfolios with stocks having low P/Es. A readable summary of these results can be found in an article by David Dreman.[2] In one study, buying a group of stocks having the lowest 20 percent of P/Es and holding them for nine years netted returns nine times greater than buying and holding the 20 percent group of stocks with the highest P/Es! The data across academic studies appears to be consistent: for long-term investment, low P/E stocks outperform both the market and high P/E stocks.

Earnings Growth Rates

In the long run, price levels reflect earnings growth rates. The relationship is anticipatory and is difficult to relate mathemat-

---

[2]David Dreman, "A Market-Beating System that's Batting .809," *Money*, December 1979, pp. 68–70.

ically, but it certainly exists. Exhibit 10.2 shows four 12-year stock charts with prices and earnings displayed.

The examples show long-term price movements responding to earnings changes, albeit not in a precise manner. To satisfy yourself of the validity of this relationship, you may want to obtain a long-term chart book that displays earnings along with price, and examine a number of chart patterns. You will see page after page of examples like the ones in Exhibit 10.2, with rates of change in reported earnings closely associated with changes in long-term prices. The charts also show numerous examples of trends in earnings that persist over many years.

Capitalization

Many formal research studies have confirmed the "small stock effect." Companies with small capitalizations (market values of less than $100 million) tend to outperform the rest of the market. The previously mentioned study by Carvel and Strebel, for example, found annual return differences of 26 percent for small stocks to 16 percent for large stocks over the five-year period of their study. Similar results have developed from other research efforts. With all else equal, investing for the long run in small-capitalization firms will provide greater average annual returns than will investing in the market as a whole or in larger capitalization stocks only.

Price Sales Ratio

Kenneth Fisher, in his book *Super Stocks* (Dow Jones-Irwin, 1984), finds price-sales ratio analysis to be a powerful gauge for assessing the prospects for long-term growth of stock prices. A number of controlled studies were performed, with results showing low price-sales ratio stocks outperforming high price-sales stocks over the long term. Moreover, the author's research found low price-sales ratio stocks to outperform low price-earnings stocks by about two to one.

Price-sales ratios that are considered low are a function of the type of company being assessed. For small, growth-oriented or technology companies 0.75 is considered a low ratio. For

EXHIBIT 10.2 Long-Term Price Movements and Changes in Earnings

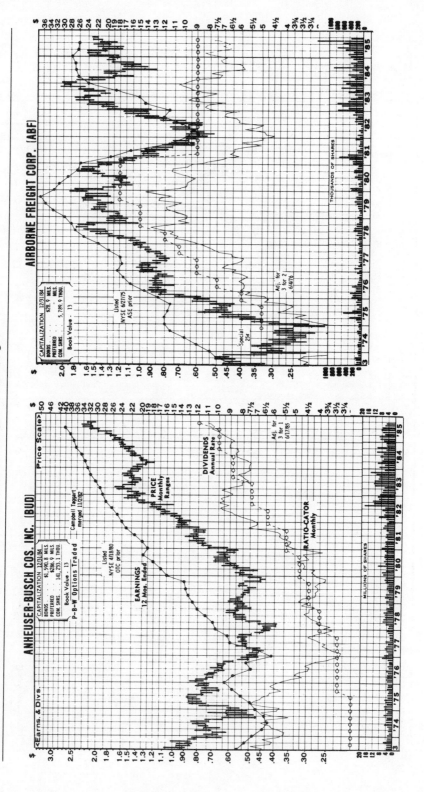

EXHIBIT 10.2 *(concluded)*

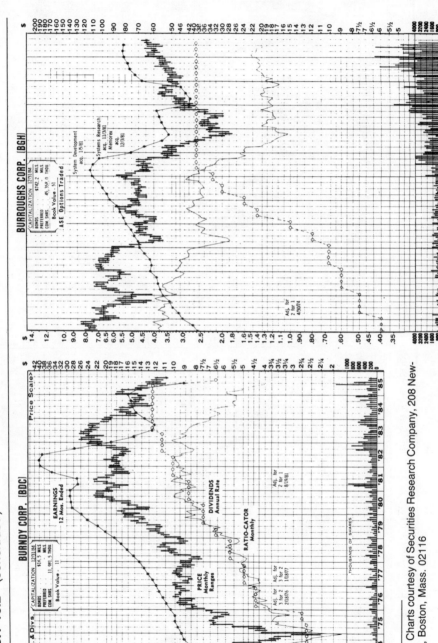

Charts courtesy of Securities Research Company, 208 Newbury, Boston, Mass. 02116

what would be considered companies without growth attributes or companies with multibillion dollar sales, a 0.20 ratio is low. For thin-margin companies (like supermarkets), 0.03 is considered to be a low ratio. Fisher's corresponding high ratios for these company types are 1.5, 0.4, and 0.06.

Along with earnings, size, and sales measures, many other fundamental indicators, which have a long history of successful application, are worthy of interest. Of major importance are return on equity, net current asset value per share, estimated takeover value, cash flow, and dividend growth rate.

BASIC MODEL FOR THE HIGH PROBABILITY INVESTMENT STRATEGY

Integrating the various research findings is a difficult task. Most research efforts make use of just a few variables, so the findings are difficult to relate to important factors addressed in other studies. Furthermore, time spans often differ from one study to another, making them hard to compare.

The approach taken in the basic model is to use the previously discussed factors in combination to aid in timing and selecting stocks. It is assumed that any interaction among the factors will not result in a significant decrease in their effectiveness.

Exhibit 10.3 provides an overview of the procedure for implementing the high probability investment strategy. As the exhibit shows, selecting the time to invest comes first, followed by stock screening, portfolio creation, monitoring, and eventual selling.

Timing

Buying with the intent of holding for the long term is viable only if your investment horizon is substantial. This strategy requires you to be in no hurry to sell your stocks; it also requires that you be in no hurry to buy them. For people in their 20s to early 50s with a retirement objective, there is enough time. For those within 10 years of needing the investment funds, another strategy (for example, mutual fund switching) may be more appropriate.

EXHIBIT 10.3   Basic Procedure for Implementing the High
Probability Strategy

Procedure   *Comments*

Timing
  Has the S&P 500 declined from a   No action is taken unless the market
  high for the last 15 months?   has experienced a prolonged
                                         decline.

Screening
  Have you found a group of stocks   Exhibit 10.5 provides these
  that satisfy screening requirements?   requirements.

Selecting
  Have you assembled a portfolio of   Stocks should be as widely diversified
  eight stocks *minimum* using the   as possible.
  DJN/R data?

Buying
  Has the S&P 500 closed up on a   Before taking action wait for an
  month-ending basis?   actual turnaround in price.

Monitoring
  Has a month passed for price   Don't monitor these stocks too
  monitoring? Have three months   frequently! Don't react to price
  passed for fundamental   drops unless a 25 percent reversal
  monitoring?   has taken place. You're in for the
                                         long term.

Selling
  Twenty-five percent below
  purchase price?
  One year from purchase date
  without a gain?
  Twenty or more institutions
  holding the stock?
  Earnings breakdown by 25 percent
  or more?

For a buy and hold strategy it is important that you not enter the market during a peak period. If this happens, an immediate loss will likely accrue and it may take you years just to break even. While past research has found an approximate four- to five-year cycle in the market, the accurate timing of this cycle is difficult to pinpoint. As we saw in Chapter Four, the election cycle was a good timing device in the past, but whether this will hold in the future is anyone's guess.

One infallible way to identify market peaks is to discover them after they have occurred. For many strategies this is not

---

EXHIBIT 10.4   Long-Term Defensive Buy Signals Using the Clear
                    Backward Look Technique

Chart A

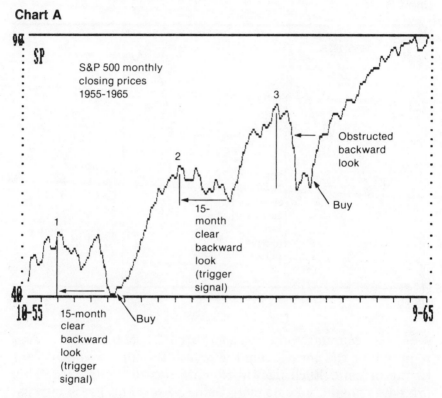

useful because the identification is too late. For the long-term
investor this approach is a workable one since the identification is primarily for defensive purposes. The peaks are important to discover for knowing when *not* to act, not when *to* act.

Exhibit 10.4 shows the clear backward look technique (see
Chapter Four) applied to the S&P 500 Index for avoiding long-
term entry during peak periods. Each chart covers a 10-year
period. As you can see, over the past 30 years there have been
only six times when a buy signal has been given using this
approach.

Using monthly data on an index like the S&P 500 is best
for this procedure since it identifies long-term broad-based
trends. To start the analysis historical data are not required
unless the stock market has formed a peak and is currently in

---

EXHIBIT 10.4 *(concluded)*

Chart B

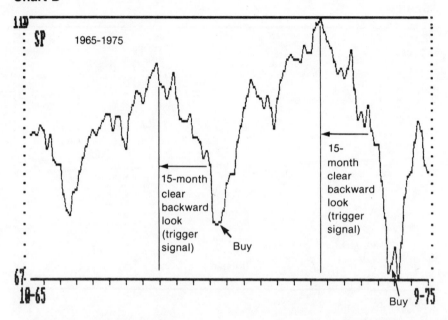

a decline. Manually entered monthly S&P 500 data are then required for the period from the month the high was made until the present. Each month the data has to be updated. This procedure should take no more than five minutes per month using the Dow Jones Market Analyzer PLUS.

Long-term buy points are established by counting the number of months since the market made its last high. After 15 months of retreating from its high point, a trigger signal is given when the index makes a new low from that high. The trigger signal indicates that a buy point is near and may occur as soon as within one month. If 15 months have elapsed and the index is not making a new low but is in a rising phase, the trigger signal is delayed until the average actually works its way to a new low. If the average instead goes higher and eventually surpasses the previous high, the count is ended and the procedure is held in abeyance until the next peak has formed.

After the 15-month trigger signal has been given, stock screening takes place in anticipation of the buy signal to come.

EXHIBIT 10.4 *(concluded)*

Chart C

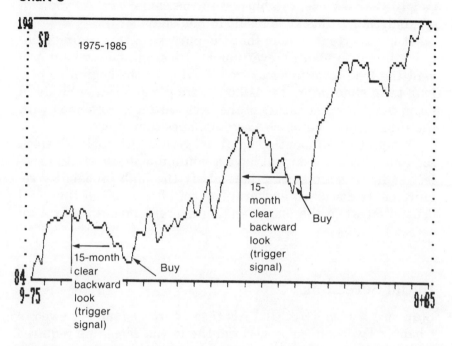

The buy signal occurs the first time the monthly closing average closes up after the trigger signal is given.

Chart A, showing the 1955–65 period, illustrates two buy
signals. Looking first at Peak 1, 15 months are seen passing
with the market declining to new lows from the peak. The base
of the arrow is at the price 15 months after the high was established. A backward look after the 15-month period allows a
clear look at the line drawn down from the peak, so a trigger
signal is given. The actual buy point occurs after the first
month-ending increase, as shown in the chart. The same situation exists with respect to Peak 2.

A buy signal is not generated by the decline from Peak 3,
however, as the duration of the decline is insufficient to make a
new low after 15 months. As the arrow shows, the price after
15 months does not provide a clear backward look to the vertical line drawn down from the peak, so no trigger signal is

given. The market reversed before the 15-month period had a chance to run.

Charts B and C in the exhibit show buy points for the other two 10-year periods, established in the same way. As you can see, only major reversals result in buy signals.

It is important to note that the purpose of this timing technique is not to identify every market bottom, but to help prevent the long-term investor from buying at the beginning of a long-term slide in prices. Although simple and rather crude in form, the defensive nature of the backward look combined with the first month-ending rise accomplishes this objective.

When the 15-month signal is given, the task of stock screening begins. You will have a minimum of one month to select eight or more stocks that satisfy the high probability requirements discussed earlier. (The actual amount of time will depend on when the month-ending average makes its first increase.)

Initial Screening

Standard & Poor's STOCKPAK II software system (reviewed in Chapter Two) can easily perform the initial screening required by the basic procedure. It rapidly narrows the S&P universe of over 4,500 available stocks down to those that meet established standards, within the capabilities of the system. Exhibit 10.5 provides screening parameters required for the initial screen using the basic high probability strategy.

Because the initial screen is made during a prolonged market decline, there will be an unusually large number of stocks with low P/E ratios, P/S ratios, and prices. The STOCKPAK II output can be expected to yield hundreds of stock candidates for further analysis.

If you have sufficient time, you can make the further screens on all the stocks that survive the initial STOCKPAK screen. A more time-effective approach is to rank the stocks in terms of price-sales ratio and proceed through the list from the lowest toward the highest until a sufficient number of stocks have met the requirements of the subsequent screens.

EXHIBIT 10.5 Screening Factors for Basic High Probability
Investing Model

High Probability Factors	Criteria	Rationale
Initial screening		
Capitalization (#123 TOTALCAP).	$20–$100 million.	Utilize the small-firm effect while avoiding illiquidity.
Price/Earnings ratio (#119 PE).	Less than 10.	Avoid buying dear.
Price (#38 PRICE).	5 to 20.	Square root rule while helping to avoid "junk."
Positive earnings, last two years (#23 EPS1, #24 EPS2).	Greater than 0.	Eliminate distressed companies.
Price/Sales ratio (#38 PRICE/#45 SALES).	Less than 0.75	Avoid overpriced based on sales.
Secondary screening		
Evidence of being ignored.	10 institutions or less holding.	Psychologically undervalued.
Final screening		
Relative price. Earnings growth.	Closer to five-year high than low.	Price persistence.
Betas up/Betas down. Industry group membership. Earnings estimates. Other.	Favorable conditions.	"Fine-tune" selections to your specifications.

Secondary Screening

The secondary screen makes use of Standard & Poor's monthly
Stock Guide. Available from Standard & Poor's and at most
libraries, this publication provides data on numbers of institutions holding shares in publicly traded stock.

Starting with the first ranked stock, the procedure is to
look at the *Stock Guide* column that shows the number of institutions holding the stock. If the number is over 10, you can
strike the stock from the list. If the number is 10 or less, the
stock is assumed to be in the ignored category, so a further
analysis is appropriate.

As an example, the stock Motor Club of America satisfies

EXHIBIT 10.6 The Number of Institutions Holding Motor Club of America Stock

150 **Mor-Nan** Standard & Poor's Corporation

¶S&P 500 •Options Index	Ticker Symbol	Name of Issue (Call Price of Pfd. Stocks)	Market	Com. Rank. & Pfd. Rating	Par Val.	Inst. Hold Cos	Inst. Hold Shs. (000)	Principal Business	Price Range 1971-83 High	1971-83 Low	1984 High	1984 Low	1985 High	1985 Low	Sep. Sales in 100s	September, 1985 Last Sale Or Bid High	Low	Last	%Div. Yield	P-E Ratio
1	MORR	Morrison Inc	OTC	↓A−	2	52	3874	Public & contract food svcs	21¼	2⅛	19⅛	13⅛	22⅛	16⅜	4210	20⅛	17⅝	18⅞B	2.5	15
2	MRN	Morrison-Knudson	NY,M,P	A+	3⅓	86	5078	Constr & engr'g svs: shipbldg	46½	3⅝	34¼	26⅞	47	33	3504	45¾	41⅜	43	3.4	10
3	MRS	Morse Shoe	NY,B,M	B	1	36	3251	Self-serv shoe depts: stores	39¾	1	33	18⅛	23½	18¼	1097	22½	20¼	20⅜	3.9	14
4	MTG	Mtge Growth Inv	AS	NR	1	28	2175	Real estate investment trust	20	2⅞	18⅛	12⅞	19⅝	16⅞	954	18½	17⅝	17⅝	8.9	6
5	MIP	Mtge Investments Plus	AS	NR	1¢	...	....	Real estate investment trust	....	....	....	....	10	9	3143	9¾	9	9¼	8.6	...
6	MRT	Mtge & Rlty Trust	NY,M,P	NR	1	24	522	Real estate investment trust	29¾	3¼	18	12	21	16⅝	1577	18½	16⅝	17	10.6	9
7	WS	Wrrt(Pur 1.5 com at $30.75)(**8)	AS	...	...	...	....		....	....	....	....	4⅛	1⅞	568	2⅞	1⅞	1⅞	...	...
8	MTI	Morton Thiokol	NY,B,M	A	1	190	27180	Aerospace specialty chem,salt	26⅞	3⅛	31⅜	20	38	26	16600	34⅞	30	32	2.0	8
9	MR	MorTronics Inc	AS	C	No	4	134	Coin-oper video games:restr	13½	⅜	4¼	¾	2⅛	1	1091	1¾	1½	1⅝	...	d
10	MSCM	MOSCOM Corp	OTC	NR	10¢	...	....	Electr eqp for telecom ind	....	....	....	....	6½	4½	2732	6½	4½	4⅞B	...	d
11	MOSE	Moseley Hallgarten	OTC	B−	1	13	1371	Security trad'g,3d mkt,bonds	50	1⅝	7	4	7⅝	2¾	8328	3½	2¾	2⅞B	...	d
12	MOSI	Mosinee Paper	OTC	B+	2½	16	771	Paper & paper products	15⅛	1⅛	15¾	11⅜	16¼	11¾	1149	16¼	14½	14½B	2.5	9
13	MOTR	Motor Club of Amer	OTC	B−	50¢	5	130	Motor club: insur: financing	29½	1⅝	20	12⅜	15¾	12½	804	14¾	14⅛	14¼B	2.1	7
¶14•[1]	MOT	Motorola Inc	NY,B,M,P,Ph	A	3	484	6[illegible]701	Semiconductors:communic eq	50	8⅝	46⅞	29¼	39⅜	29½	72409	36⅜	32⅜	34½	1.9	36
15	MSM	Mott's Super Markets	AS	B+	1	10	410	Chain of Shop-Rite supermkts	14¾	1⅛	12¾	10⅝	13¼	9⅛	15	9½	9⅛	9⅛B	2.2	d
16	MTN	Mountain Med.Eq	AS	NR	10¢	7	714	Oxygen concentrators	25	3¼	14	2⅞	6⅜	3⅞	370	5	4⅜	4¾	...	13
17	MVS.A	Movie Star Cl A	AS	B	50¢	6	[illegible]02	Makes lingerie & loungewear	15⅞	3¼	21	15	20⅜	13½	10	14	13¾	13¾B	...	15
18	MOV	Movielab, Inc	AS,P	C	50¢	2	[illegible]48	Film & TV processing lab	9¼	½	8⅝	4¼	9⅝	5⅛	132	7⅞	6⅝	6⅝	...	d
19	MOXE	Moxie Indus	OTC,B	C	1	5	3[illegible]4	Specialty food/drink prod	6¼	⅛	1½	¾	1⅛	½	22	⅝	½	⅝B	...	d
20	MPSG	MPSI Systems	OTC	NR	5¢	15	216[illegible]	Softwr for strategic plann'g	19⅛	7¾	17	5¾	7¼	3½	505	4⅝	4	4⅝B	...	40
21	MRFY	MRFY Corp	OTC	C	1	...	....	Hldg:regional motor carrier	14	2¼	7¼	2½	3½	1¼	25	2½	2¼	2½B	...	d
22	SSS	MSA Rlty	AS	NR	....	2	55	Real estate investment trust	....	....	10⅛	7⅜	9⅞	7⅞	319	8⅜	7⅞	8⅛	9.8	d
23	WS	Wrrt(Pur 1 com at $9)(**5)	AS	...	....	7	1899		....	....	2⅛	1	1¾	⅞	331	1¼	1	1	...	...
24	MSI	MSI Data	AS	B	1	15	371	Portable data collection sys	37	2¾	21⅜	9⅛	12⅝	6¾	701	9¼	8⅛	9	...	d
25	MSR	MSR Exploration	AS,To,Vc	B	No	4	615	Oil/gas explor,dev,prod'n	18	3⅝	5⅝	3	4⅛	2⅜	1009	3	2⅜	2⅜	...	26
26	MTSC	MTS Systems	OTC	B+	25¢	19	870	Mfr testing systems: services	24⅞	1⅛	20¾	12⅜	21¼	15	1215	19	16	16¾B	1.4	11
27	MTVN	MTV Networks*4	OTC	NR	1¢	30	3874	Satellite TV programming	....	....	18½	13¼	32¼	18	7540	32¼	30⅞	32B	...	34
28	MUEL	Mueller (Paul) Co	OTC	B	1	6	242	Stainless steel process eq	35½	6¼	32¼	17¼	23⅜	19½	42	21	19¾	20B	8.5	23
29	MLTF	Multibank Fin'l	OTC	A−	6¼	31	1463	Multibank hldg:Massachusetts	17⅝	1¾	23⅜	17⅛	31¾	21	2161	30¾	27	27B	2.4	9
30	MMED	Multimedia Inc*5	OTC	A	1	89	7517	Newspapers & broadcasting	43¾	2½	42½	29¾	64½	36¼	23195	62¼	55½	58½B	1.1	23
31	MFD	Munford, Inc	NY,M	B	1	29	1336	Convenience food stores	24	2⅞	24¼	15¾	26⅞	19¾	1853	22	21	21⅜	2.5	12
32	MUN	Munsingwear Inc	NY,M	C	1	8	435	Intimate apparel: men's wear	19⅜	4¾	11 11/16	7	14¾	8⅝	291	13⅞	11¾	13½	...	41
33	MIH	Murphy Industries	AS	C	1	9	545	Electric wiring assemblies	12¾	1⅝	5¼	3	4⅝	1⅞	568	2⅝	2	2⅛B	...	d
34•[2]	MUR	Murphy Oil	NY,B,M,P,Ph	A−	1	143	16175	International integrated oil	64	4⅛	38½	24½	31½	23½	5402	30⅛	28¾	29⅛	3.4	12
35	MYO	Murray Ohio Mfg	NY,M	B	2½	31	1285	Mfr bicycles & pwr mowers	31¼	6⅞	24⅝	18⅝	22⅝	16½	1401	18⅝	17⅞	18⅛	3.3	14
36	MAC WS	Muse Air Wrrt(So'west Air)	AS	...	...	...	....	Sub of Southwest Air	7⅝	½	3⅞	⅛	1	⅛	340	⅛	⅛	⅛	...	...
37	MUO	Mutual Omaha Int Sh	NY,M	NR	1¢	6	19	Closed end invest:income	19⅝	10	13	11	14¾	12½	669	14¼	13¼	13⅜	10.6	...
38	MYR	Myers (L.E.)Gr	NY,M	C	1	1	15	Constrn sv for elec utilities	39¼	3⅝	15⅞	3⅝	4⅞	1⅛	604	2⅝	2	2	...	d
39	MYE	Myers Indus	AS	B+	No	14	728	Tire serv eq & supplies	12	¾	9⅝	7⅛	12	8⅞	133	10⅝	10	10	2.8	9
40•[3]	MYLN	Mylan Labs	OTC	B	50¢	39	2556	Pharmaceutical products	5½	1/16	18 11/16	4⅛	26¼	12	67385	19⅝	14½	14⅞B	0.7	27
41	NAF	NAFCO Fin'l Group	NY,M	B	1¢	26	884	Hldg:Svg & ln Southwest Fla	30½	8⅞	25⅝	16	21½	15¾	445	17⅞	16	16	6.2	15
42	NAWE	Nahama Weagant Entpr	OTC	C	No	2	36	Oil & gas exp,dev,prod'n	7⅝	2¾	4⅜	2⅝	3⅝	2¼	119	3⅛	2¼	2¼B	...	37
43	NLC	Nalco Chemical	NY,B,M	A	37½¢	208	29046	Specialty chemicals	37	6½	33¼	21	28⅜	22½	12677	25	22⅜	22⅞	5.2	11
44	NKIN	Nankin Express	OTC	NR	No	...	....	Chinese fast food restaurants	3¾	2	3⅞	1¼	1⅞	¼	787	½	¼	¼B	...	d
45	NANO	Nanometrics Inc	OTC	NR	No	14	621	Mfr electr inspection sys	....	....	9⅛	7¾	14	4¼	937	5¼	4¼	4¼B	...	10
46	NAN	Nantucket Indus	AS	B	10¢	12	569	Mfr hosiery & underwear	[illegible]1⅜	1/16	10¼	5½	9½	5¾	408	9¼	8⅝	8⅝	...	15

Uniform Footnote Explanations—See Page 1. Other: [1]AS:Cycle 1 Pilot Program. [2]P:Cycle 2. [3]ASE:Cycle 1. *1△$0.04,'82. *2®$4.12,'84. *3Incl $0.0668 cap gains'84. *4Incl $0.009 cap gains'84. *5Fr 1-16-91. *6Com price 140% of exercise price-20trad days. *7△$1.98,'82. *8 2.3 shrs of Institut'l Networks. *9△$0.17,'83. *0Subsid pref in $M. *1$0.3286 nontaxable'84. *2 9 Mo Dec'84. *3Fr 4-1-87. *4Viacom Intl plans acq,$33.50. *5Approve recap:$41.24/$26.54debs:court blocks. *6Fiscal May,'83 & prior. *7 12 Mo May,'84,$d0.02. *8$6cash,0.125com&0.125wrrt to pur 1 com at $35. *9Stk dstr of Myers(L.E.)Int'l Gr,0.18 shrs. *0△$0.08,'84.

5 institutions

Reproduced with permission of Standard & Poor's Corporation, 25 Broadway, New York, N.Y. 10004.

the initial screening requirements in Exhibit 10.5 and will be used to demonstrate this and other screenings. A look at Standard & Poor's *Stock Guide* (Exhibit 10.6) shows that only five institutions hold the stock. This stock therefore "survives" the secondary screening effort and is a candidate for final screening.

Final Screening

For stocks that pass the institutional holdings test, it is necessary to make a final screening to pick specific candidates for purchase. The Media General Database (//MEDGEN) is used to provide up-to-date fundamental information for making these choices. Exhibit 10.7 illustrates the important information that this database provides, again using Motor Club of America as an example.

The first data that you will want to look at is the current

EXHIBIT 10.7 Final Screening Information Using the Media General
(//MEDGEN) Database

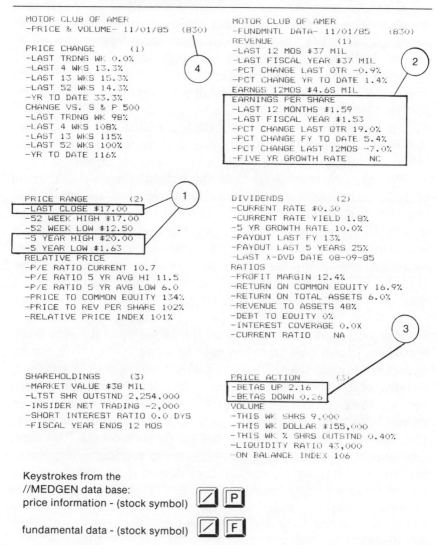

```
MOTOR CLUB OF AMER
-PRICE & VOLUME- 11/01/85   (830)

PRICE CHANGE      (1)
-LAST TRDNG WK 0.0%
-LAST 4 WKS 13.3%
-LAST 13 WKS 15.3%
-LAST 52 WKS 14.3%
-YR TO DATE 33.3%
CHANGE VS. S & P 500
-LAST TRDNG WK 98%
-LAST 4 WKS 108%
-LAST 13 WKS 115%
-LAST 52 WKS 100%
-YR TO DATE 116%


PRICE RANGE      (2)
-LAST CLOSE $17.00
-52 WEEK HIGH $17.00
-52 WEEK LOW $12.50
-5 YEAR HIGH $20.00
-5 YEAR LOW $1.63
RELATIVE PRICE
-P/E RATIO CURRENT 10.7
-P/E RATIO 5 YR AVG HI 11.5
-P/E RATIO 5 YR AVG LOW 6.0
-PRICE TO COMMON EQUITY 134%
-PRICE TO REV PER SHARE 102%
-RELATIVE PRICE INDEX 101%




SHAREHOLDINGS      (3)
-MARKET VALUE $38 MIL
-LTST SHR OUTSTND 2,254,000
-INSIDER NET TRADING -2,000
-SHORT INTEREST RATIO 0.0 DYS
-FISCAL YEAR ENDS 12 MOS
```

```
MOTOR CLUB OF AMER
-FUNDMNTL DATA- 11/01/85   (830)
REVENUE         (1)
-LAST 12 MOS $37 MIL
-LAST FISCAL YEAR $37 MIL
-PCT CHANGE LAST QTR -0.9%
-PCT CHANGE YR TO DATE 1.4%
EARNGS 12MOS $4.6S MIL
EARNINGS PER SHARE
-LAST 12 MONTHS $1.59
-LAST FISCAL YEAR $1.53
-PCT CHANGE LAST QTR 19.0%
-PCT CHANGE FY TO DATE 5.4%
-PCT CHANGE LAST 12MOS -7.0%
-FIVE YR GROWTH RATE    NC


DIVIDENDS         (2)
-CURRENT RATE $0.30
-CURRENT RATE YIELD 1.8%
-5 YR GROWTH RATE 10.0%
-PAYOUT LAST FY 13%
-PAYOUT LAST 5 YEARS 25%
-LAST X-DVD DATE 08-09-85
RATIOS
-PROFIT MARGIN 12.4%
-RETURN ON COMMON EQUITY 16.9%
-RETURN ON TOTAL ASSETS 6.0%
-REVENUE TO ASSETS 48%
-DEBT TO EQUITY 0%
-INTEREST COVERAGE 0.0X
-CURRENT RATIO    NA



PRICE ACTION        (3)
-BETAS UP 2.16
-BETAS DOWN 0.26
VOLUME
-THIS WK SHRS 9,000
-THIS WK DOLLAR $155,000
-THIS WK % SHRS OUTSTND 0.40%
-LIQUIDITY RATIO 43,000
-ON BALANCE INDEX 106
```

Keystrokes from the
//MEDGEN data base:
price information - (stock symbol) ⧄ P

fundamental data - (stock symbol) ⧄ F

price relative to the five-year high and low prices (marked 1 on
the chart). As research has shown, the closer the current price
is to the five-year high, the better the chances of the stock
outperforming the market in the future. At minimum, look for
the price to be above the midpoint of the high to low range. The

exhibit shows Motor Club of America to be very favorably positioned in its five-year range.

Earnings growth (number 2 in the exhibit) is the second factor to check. You would like to see a substantial rate of earnings growth (10 percent or higher) occurring in the stock. Severe declines in the current earnings picture will result in the stock being removed from further consideration. For the example stock, it appears that earnings are up over the last quarter (19 percent) but down for the past 12 months (− 7 percent). This is not grounds to eliminate the stock at this point but does put it at a possible comparative disadvantage to stocks with better earnings histories, everything else being equal.

You may have noticed that the exhibit shows a P/E ratio of 10.7, although it was previously stated that the stock had "passed" the initial screening which calls for a P/E ratio of 10 or less. In screening stock data you will find this type of apparent contradiction occurring again and again. For the current situation, the Media General online data are much more current than the Standard & Poor's data, which are furnished on a disk. For long-term investing, unless there are major differences, these minor discrepancies can be ignored.

You will next want to look at the betas-up and betas-down statistics. These measures indicate how much the stock can be expected to move relative to the market as a whole. A betas-up reading of 3.0, for example, means that, for the last eight market upmoves of 5 percent or more, the stock registered average gains three times that of the market. The betas-down measure provides the same information but for down markets. The ideal case would, of course, be a large betas-up reading and a small betas-down reading. Motor Club of America has an excellent record in this regard (number 3 in the exhibit). The stock has increased over twice as much as the general market during upmoves and has only declined about one fourth as much during downmoves.

The industry group number (marked as number 4) is also important. When screening takes place it is not unusual to find some industry groups overrepresented in the screened set of stocks. To reduce the level of risk in your portfolio of chosen stocks it is important to diversify among industry groups (Appendix 10A provides the code number translations). Motor Club

---

EXHIBIT 10.8   Final Screening Information for
Motor Club of America from
Earnings Estimator (//EARN)
Database

```
    CORPORATE EARNINGS ESTIMATOR
  ZACKS INVESTMENT RESEARCH INC.
        CHICAGO, ILL.
THIS WEEKLY DATABASE PROVIDES
CONSENSUS FORECASTS OF EARNINGS
PER SHARE FOR 3,000 COMPANIES
BASED ON ESTIMATES PROVIDED BY
1,000 RESEARCH ANALYSTS AT MORE
THAN 60 MAJOR BROKERAGE FIRMS
FOR CONSISTENCY, ESTIMATES ARE
CONVERTED TO PRIMARY EARNINGS
BEFORE EXTRAORDINARY ITEMS.
```

```
PLEASE ENTER DESIRED STOCK
SYMBOL AND PRESS RETURN
```

```
STOCK SYMBOL ENTERED NOT FOUND
```

of America belongs to industry group 830, which Appendix 10A
identifies to as "other insurance."

As part of the final screening effort, an earning estimate
check (//EARN) should be made. This check can provide two
important pieces of evidence. It can indicate if earnings growth
or decline is expected, and it can confirm the ignored status of
the stock. For Motor Club of America, as Exhibit 10.8 shows,
the stock is so ignored that no earnings estimates are available
for it. This is a positive sign for the stock.

Monitoring and Selling

The final screening will allow you to make an informed choice
of stocks for inclusion in your portfolio. When the market turns
up and purchase is made, an ongoing monitoring of the stocks
is required so proper selling decisions can be made.

Since this strategy is based on a long-term valuation adjustment, it is important that an overly sensitive approach to monitoring not be used. In general, pricing information should be updated no more frequently than once a month; and fundamental data, no more than once each quarter. If you look again at the monthly price charts shown in Exhibit 10.2, you will see the major swings in price that this strategy is trying to catch. The objective of monitoring is to provide breathing room in your portfolio for the few stocks that will make long runs to the upside, while selling the losers before they decline to untenable levels.

In high probability portfolios it can be expected that a small percentage of stocks will not amount to much and will be sold for a loss; the majority will average out at about market levels, and the rest will make large gains. Some stocks will likely advance 500 percent or more over the years in which they are held. It is the big movers that you will want to nurture so your overall annual percentage gain from the portfolio will be as large as possible.

How do you determine when to sell? First, any stock that falls 25 percent below the purchase price should be sold. Second, any stock that has not advanced above the purchase price after 12 months of the purchase date should also be sold. These two rules will help eliminate the "bad merchandise" from your inventory before it does excessive damage. The portfolio Status Report feature of the Dow Jones Market Analyzer PLUS can be very supportive of these rules, as it can display both an expiration date and a low-limit price.

The rest of the stocks should be held until they become well known. The measure used is the same as that used before: the number of institutions holding the stock. When it exceeds 20, the stock can be assumed to be so well known that the "unfamiliarity bias" is no longer operating. The stock then becomes a candidate for selling by technical analysis. This is discussed in Chapter Eleven.

The only other reason for selling a stock before its unknown status is shed is if fundamental factors turn bad. If earnings in any quarter drop by 25 percent or more from the same quarter the year before (extraordinary items removed), the stock immediately becomes a candidate for selling by technical analysis.

POSSIBLE MODIFICATIONS

The basic high probability investing model will yield returns well in excess of the general market. Nevertheless, there are many ways to modify this strategy to provide a better match with individual objectives. The following represent some possibilities.

1. The Timing System. The timing system can be changed in a number of ways. The 15-month backward look will undoubtedly miss many good buying points, as it did in the past (see Exhibit 10.2). For the more aggressive investor a shorter trigger period may be appropriate. As a hedge against a further drop in the market after the trigger signal is given, an incremental system (dollar cost averaging) can be used for committing funds.

Another possibility for change is to use a forward-looking system to identify market bottoms. This can be attempted with a technical market analysis using the techniques discussed in Part Two of this book. Appendix 9C provides a worksheet for making this analysis. (The procedure is discussed in Chapter Nine.)

2. Initial Screening. Because the high probability strategy requires very infrequent screenings, using STOCKPAK II is not a very cost-effective approach, unless you plan to use the system to support other investment strategies as well. An additional consideration is that the STOCKPAK II system does not support all of the variables that are needed to implement the strategy, so additional manual screening is still required.

Readily available prescreened stock lists are an alternative. The American Association of Individual Investors (612 N. Michigan Avenue, Suite 317, Chicago, Ill. 60611) publishes each January in their *AAII Journal* a list of 440 "shadow stocks." These are stocks that are screened on three criteria: lack of interest, capitalization, and earnings. Specifically, the list provides stocks that are ignored by financial institutions and advisory services, have a capitalization between $20 million and $100 million, and have positive earnings over the past two fiscal years. The association also occasionally provides further screens of their 440 group that can be of use. Examples include rankings by P/E, relative prices (trends), dividend yield, and price-sales ratios.

The Institute of Econometric Research (3471 North Federal Highway, Fort Lauderdale, Fla. 33306) also publishes a list of ignored stocks. Their list is based on the number of earnings estimates provided by institutional analysts. They also screen to remove distressed companies by requiring the current earnings estimate to be above the previous year's earnings and a P/E ratio of less than 10 to 1.

Using these ready-made screens, you can use the S&P *Stock Guide*, Dow Jones News/Retrieval, and other sources to obtain the rest of the information needed to select a final set of stocks.

3. The Screening Criteria.   The screening criteria represent another possibility for change. Although based on empirical research and logic, the factors shown in Exhibit 10.5 certainly reflect the biases of the author. There is much fertile territory here for modifying the high probability strategy.

4. Final Screening.   Considerably more effort can be put into the final screening process. More fundamental factors can be assessed for each candidate before the purchase decision is made.

Textual information (//DJNEWS) on each candidate can also be obtained. Is there any news on the company that implies an unusual measure of risk (for example, a major lawsuit pending, accounting changes, impact of new government regulations, effect of changes in a major economic variable)? Is the company distressed, or is there some factor that clouds the stock's future? What are the prospects for the industry group? Not only are the news stories important, but the number of stories can be used to confirm the extent of neglect for the stock.

Other databases that can be useful for final screening include Standard & Poor's Online (//SP) for additional fundamental information. DISCLOSURE II (//DISCLO) for details of company operations, Text Search (//TEXT) for news stories, and Investext (//INVEST) for possible research reports.

APPENDIX 10A: MEDIA GENERAL INDUSTRY GROUP CODES

Natural Resources

Metals—Iron and steel
001 Iron and Steel Mills

Metals—Nonferrous and coal
010 Copper Mining and Refining
012 Aluminum Refining
013 Lead, Nickel, Tin, Zinc Mining and Refining
015 Other Mining and Refining

Metals—Rare
020 Rare Metals

Wood and Forest Products
030 Lumber and Wood Products
031 Paper Products

Building Materials
040 Cements
041 Glass and Clay Products
043 Paints
044 Other Building Materials

Oil, Natural Gas Services
050 Oil, Gas Field Services
051 Oil Drilling, Exploration

Oil, Natural Gas Production
060 Oil, Natural Gas Producers

Oil Refining and Marketing
070 Oil Refining and Marketing

Chemicals
080 Chemicals and Synthetics

081 Sulphur and Nitrates
082 Specialty Chemicals

Industrial Products

Electrical Equipment
100 Industrial Equipment
101 Transmission Equipment
102 Controls and Switches
103 Other Electrical Equipment

Electronics
110 Electronic Circuitry
111 Electronic Components
112 Electronic Devices
113 Electronic Systems
115 Computer Parts

Machinery—Heavy
120 Farm Equipment
121 Construction Equipment
122 Handling Equipment
123 Mining Equipment
124 Special Industry Machines
125 General Industry Machines
126 Railroad Equipment
127 Engines and Turbines
128 Pollution Controls

Machinery—Light Equipment
130 Machine Tools and Accessories
131 Small Tools
132 Screw Machine Products

133 Machine Accessories
134 Light Equipment

Metals Fabrication
140 Fabricated Metal Products

Building Heavy
150 General Contractors
151 Other Building—Heavy
153 Construction Materials and Components

Aerospace
160 Aerospace Manufacturing
161 Aerospace Components
162 Aircraft Manufacturing, Parts and Service

Computers and Business Equipment
170 Computers, Subsystems and Peripherals
171 Office Machines
172 Copying Machines
173 Other Business and Institutional Equipment
174 Office Supplies

Precision Instruments
180 Scientific Instruments
181 Mechanical Devices
182 Electronic Controls and Instruments

Containers
190 Metal Cans
191 Paperboard Containers
192 Other Containers

Consumer Durables
Automotive
200 Auto Manufacturers
201 Auto Parts and Accessories
Rubber and Plastics
210 Tires and Inner Tubes
211 Rubber and Plastic Products
Construction
220 Residential Construction
221 Plumbing and Heating
222 Air Conditioning
223 Mobile Homes
Housewares—Furnishings
230 Appliances
231 Radio and TV Manufacturers
232 Furniture, Home Furnishings
233 Housewares and Fixtures
235 Rugs and Carpet Manufacturers
236 Other Housewares—Furnishings
Recreation and Luxury Products
240 Sporting Goods
241 Sports Vehicles
243 Photo Equipment and Supplies
244 Other Luxury Products
247 Jewelry
248 Toys and Games

Nondurables
Food Production
300 Farm Products
301 Canned, Cured and Frozen Foods
Food—Packaged Goods
310 Soaps and Cleansers
311 Grain Mill Products
312 Bakery Products
Food—Meat and Dairy
321 Meat and Poultry
322 Dairy Products
Food—Confectioners
330 Sugar Manufacturers
331 Confection Manufacturers
332 Soft Drinks
Textiles
340 Textile Mills
342 Apparel
344 Lingerie and Hosiery
Footwear and Leather
350 Footwear and Leather
Cosmetics
360 Cosmetics and Grooming Aids
Distillers and Brewers
370 Distillers
371 Brewers and Wineries
Tobaccos
380 Cigarettes
381 Other Tobacco Products
Drugs
390 Ethical Drugs
391 Proprietary Drugs

Retail Trade
Food Stores
400 Food Chain Stores
Department and Apparel Stores
410 Department Stores
411 Apparel and Accessory Stores
412 Shoe Stores
Discount and Drug Stores
420 Discount and Variety Stores
421 Drug and Proprietary Stores
Retail—Miscellaneous
430 Auto and Auto Parts
431 Building Materials
433 Electrical, Electronic, Radio and TV Stores
434 Grocery Wholesalers
435 Metals Distribution
437 Miscellaneous Wholesalers
438 Miscellaneous Retailers

Services
Business Services
500 Advertising Agencies

501 Insurance Brokers
502 Printing
503 Security and Personnel Systems
504 Engineering and Consulting
505 Computer Software and Data Processing
508 Waste Management and Janitor Services
509 Miscellaneous Business Services

Publishers
510 Newspaper Publishing
511 Periodical Publishing
512 Book Publishing

Broadcasting
520 Broadcasting

Movies and Sports
530 Motion Picture Production and Distribution
532 Sporting Events

Hotels, Motels and Restaurants
540 Hotels and Motels
542 Restaurants

Health Services
550 Hospital and Laboratory Instruments
551 Hospital and Laboratory Supplies
552 Hospitals and Laboratories
553 Health and Care Services

Personal Services
560 Personal Services
562 Auto Services

Utilities
Utilities
600 Telephone Utilities
601 Telegraph and Satellite Utilities

Electric Utilities
610 New England Electric Utilities
611 Mid-Atlantic Electric Utilities
612 Southeast Electric Utilities
613 Midwest Electric Utilities
614 Middle-South Electric Utilities
615 Southwest Electric Utilities
616 Northwest Electric Utilities
617 Electric and Gas Utilities
618 Foreign Electric Utilities

Gas Utilities
620 Gas and Oil Pipelines
621 Northeast Gas Utilities
623 Southern Gas Utilities
624 Midwest Gas Utilities
625 Western Gas Utilities
628 Other Utilities

Transportation
Airlines
700 Airlines

Railroads
710 Railroad Systems

Freight, Handling, and Shipping
720 Trucking Companies
721 Water Transport
722 Air Freight and Forwarding
724 Equipment Leasing

Financing
Banking
800 New England Banks
801 New York Banks
802 Middle Atlantic Banks
803 South Atlantic Banks
804 East North Central Banks
805 East South Central Banks
806 West North Central Banks
807 East North Central Banks
808 Mountain States Banks
809 Pacific States Banks

Credit
810 Credit

Life, Accident, and Health Insurance
820 Life, Accident, and Health Insurance

Other Insurance
830 Other Insurance

Real Estate
840 Real Estate

Real Estate Investment
850 Mortgage Banks, Brokers, and Insurance
852 Mortgage Investment Trusts
853 Equity Investment Trusts

Savings and Loan
860 Savings and Loan Associations

Investments
870 Investments
873 Closed-End Funds

Multiindustry
Multiindustry
900 Multiindustry Companies

SELECTED REFERENCES

ARBEL, AVNER. *How to Beat the Market with High Performance Generic Stocks.* New York: William Morrow and Company, 1985.

CAPPIELLO, FRANK A. *Finding the Next SuperStock.* Cockeysville, Maryland: Liberty Publishing, 1982.

DREMAN, DAVID. "A Market Beating System that's Batting .809." *Money*, December 1979, pp. 68–70.

————. *The New Contrarian Investment Strategy.* New York: Random House, 1982.

FISHER, KENNETH. *Super Stocks.* Homewood, Ill.: Dow Jones-Irwin, 1984.

FOSBACK, NORMAN G. *Stock Market Logic.* Fort Lauderdale, Fla.: The Institute for Econometric Research, 1985.

ZIVNEY, TERRY, and DONALD THOMPSON. "Buy High? Relative Price Screens Show Above Average Returns." *AAII Journal* 7, no. 7 (August 1985), pp. 9–14.

CHAPTER ELEVEN

Trend and Cycle Trading

Trading on trends and cycles is a strategy that attempts to put the investor in harmony with price movements occurring in the market. While it is the highest-risk strategy covered in the book so far, it offers a large measure of personal excitement combined with the potential for quick and substantial profits on many trades.

To be a trend and cycle trader requires capital that can be placed at a higher-than-average level of risk and a continuing availability of time to devote to the strategy. Moreover, it is important to have patience and a genuine interest in the technical approach to investing.

Many conservative investors have a small trading account along with their major investments so they can participate in the action. For them, the psychological enjoyment of this strategy is as real a return as a cash dividend.

The essential elements of a trend and cycle trading strategy are quite simple. Purchases are made when technical evidence indicates an uptrend, and selling takes place when technical evidence points to a downtrend. As we will see, there are many variations on the form of implementation. Exhibit 11.1 provides an overview of the basic procedure.

A BASIC TRADING PROCEDURE

The approach to trend and cycle trading requires an analysis from the macro level to the micro level. The stock market (or a

---

EXHIBIT 11.1   Basic Procedure for Trading on Trends and Cycles

---

Procedure	*Comments*
Market analysis	
What is the current trend and prognosis for the market?	Your analysis should be periodic. Auto Run will facilitate the analysis.
Choice and grouping of trading stocks	
Grouped or ungrouped?	If stocks are ungrouped, the market as a whole will be the reference group.
	If stocks are grouped, establish at least five groups, including interest rate sensitive, cyclical, and inflation sensitive.
Implementation of trading strategy (three possibilities)	
1. Determine strong groups; trade stocks only within those groups.	You must make regular and consistent technical analyses of your stocks.
	Match the techniques emphasized to the situation.
2. Use the groups to generate purchase timing decisions.	Purchase the strongest stock in the group.
	Sell on individual stock evidence.
3. Switch between the strongest stock groups.	This approach is essentially the same as specialty fund switching.
	See Chapter Nine for details.

---

representative group index) is first assessed, followed by an analysis of the individual stocks themselves.

Market Analysis

If the climate is ripe for equity investments, money will be flowing into the market, resulting in an upward biasing effect on individual stock prices. The converse is true on the downside, with stock weakness accentuated by the general market decline.

The prime goal of market analysis is to avoid trading on the wrong side of the market. During market uptrends a purchase strategy is used; during downtrends either the trading account is closed out, a short-sale strategy is implemented, or investments are made in industry groups that are moving contrary to the market.

There are a number of ways to determine favorable and unfavorable market periods. One simple way is to use a long-term
trend-defining technique on a market average. An advance-
decline system (see Chapter Nine) is one approach and the
three-step reversal method with a long-term weighted moving
average is another (see Exhibit 11.2). A more sophisticated
method involves making a consistent and periodic full-blown
technical analysis on the market (see Exhibit 9.8). This provides the greatest potential for understanding the current situation and providing informed estimates of future possibilities.

Stock Selection

To be a successful trader, you should think in terms of concen-
trating your energies on a manageable number of securities. It
is best to select a set of stocks, get to know them well, and use
them as your universe for trading purposes. This approach will
allow you to get to know the technical "personality" of your
trading vehicles and will help prevent you from rushing to purchase a stock based on a hot tip.

I once had occasion to work with a successful trader who
concentrated all his energies on understanding the 30 Dow Industrials. For him, this was the entire universe of stocks available for trading. With over 20 years of trading these stocks exclusively, he was able to develop a sense of understanding that
the casual observer could not come close to matching. He would
often say that a certain stock "had a cold," another was "feeling
frisky," or still another was acting "unusual." While he missed
a lot of fast plays over the years in other issues, his level of understanding of those few stocks allowed him to plod along year
after year making money as a trader in the market. This is a
feat that is not overly common among individual investors using a trading strategy.

In place of choosing the 30 industrials, you will probably
want to choose stocks that you have a greater interest in. It is
important not to choose so many that you will not have time to
keep up with them. While you should not feel that you are
stuck with your group forever, try not to make too many swaps.
You want to have a core set of stocks that you can get to know

EXHIBIT 11.2 Three-Step Reversal Method for Favorable Period Identification

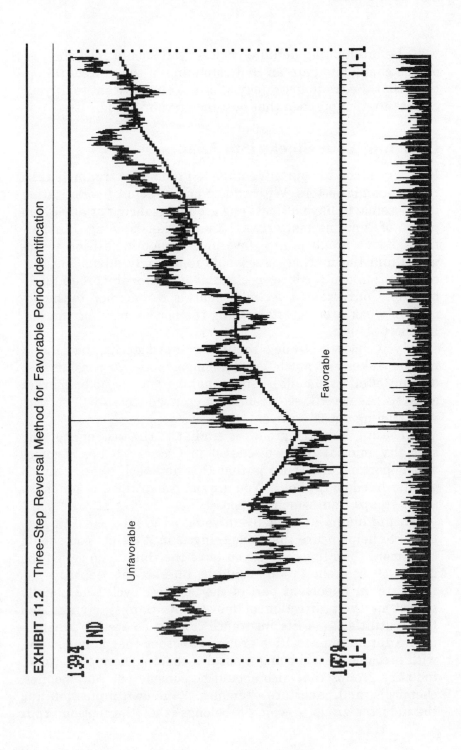

well. Before making definite choices, you should read the rest of this chapter to gain an understanding of the procedural options that the trading strategy allows. You will want to fit your choices to the approach that best meets your needs.

Grouping Your Stocks into Sectors

It is very much to your advantage to group your trading stocks into economic sectors. With wide enough sector diversification it is possible to have at least one group advancing at any given period of time, no matter what the market is doing. Furthermore, if one group is in a favorable economic position to advance and the market as a whole is strongly advancing, the combination can produce spectacular gains for the group membership. Conversely, a declining market can accelerate the decline of weak groups, establishing the opportunity for successful short selling.

If you choose to trade a set of ungrouped stocks, the general market takes on much greater importance. A considerable amount of effort should be spent making your periodic market analysis. As we will see, trading ungrouped stocks will restrict your trading opportunities.

Choosing industry groups is similar to the task of choosing specialty mutual funds discussed in Chapter Nine. A major and important difference is that this approach offers a much greater freedom of choice. You are not constrained to a narrow set of groups from which to choose.

At minimum, at least five diversified groups should be selected to help ensure that something is in a trend. You should keep more than five only if you have the time to do so. Of the groups chosen, one group should be interest-rate sensitive, as rates are an important part of the business cycle and usually persist in their direction of movement. Banks, savings and loans, utilities, and life insurance companies are all possibilities. An inflation-sensitive group is another that is important, with precious metals being a natural choice. There are "cyclic" industry groups that also should be considered. Automobiles, chemicals, and paper are examples. Your own profession and the industry group to which it belongs is another option. Your working knowledge of the industry may provide you with an intuitive feeling (or hard evidence) about special events or developing trends that might have an impact on certain companies.

After partitioning your trading stocks into groups, you should develop an index for each group. There are two possibilities for doing this: You can create your own indexes using individual stock data from Dow Jones News/Retrieval, or you can obtain ready-made index information from another source. Custom indexes created from historical quotes offer the most advantages for the individual trader, so they will be discussed first (a later discussion will indicate how the other option can be effected).

To make a custom-made index using the Dow Jones Market Analyzer PLUS you simply download the historical stock quote information on each stock to be included in the index, then choose **R** (Edit Indicator) ↵ from the main menu and follow the prompts.

For each industry group you will want to use enough stocks in the index to provide a representative pattern of movement for all stocks in the group. Some industries do not have many members (automobile manufacturing, for example), so the index will of necessity have only a few members. Other industries may have many participants (e.g., savings and loan associations), so more stocks can be represented.

There are many sources for finding specific companies to make up your indexes. Two readily available possibilities are the Value Line Investment Survey and Standard & Poor's Trendline. The Value Line Investment Survey is organized by industry group, and it's easy to choose stocks from any of the listed groups of interest. Trendline's Current Market Perspectives chart book has stocks arranged in 73 different industry groups, making a selection a simple task.

Once the indexes are created, the industry groups need to be monitored and analyzed to determine how favorable or unfavorable each is for trading purposes. The procedure used for analysis will depend on which implementation procedure you have chosen for use.

There are three alternatives for making trades within the

structure of the procedure presented in Exhibit 11.1. The first approach involves eliminating from consideration the stocks in weak groups, thereby allowing the freedom of individual stock selection to take place only within the stronger groups. The second alternative requires an analysis of each group, with stocks timed for purchase based on group timing. The third approach uses the method described in Chapter Nine (Exhibit 9.10) to switch from group to group.

Alternative I: Trading Strong Group Stocks Only

A simple and straightforward way to trade stocks within groups is to restrict purchases only to groups that are experiencing an uptrend. Exhibit 11.3 shows an example of five group indexes marked to show favorable periods during which purchases can take place, using a three-step reversal technique on a 50-day weighted moving average for trend determination. (See Chapter Three for an explanation of this technique.) The stocks within the groups are essentially switched "on" or "off" for consideration by the trend of the group to which they belong.

If your stocks are not categorized by group, the general market trend can be used as a switch for your trading. Exhibit 11.2 shows the switch being turned on, again by a weighted moving average, establishing a buy period for a diversified set of ungrouped stocks.

The use of a weighted moving average as shown in the exhibits is a minimal effort for implementing this strategy. If you have the time, you should make a comprehensive analysis of each index on a periodic basis using the procedure outlined in Exhibit 9.8.

Whatever procedure you use to determine favorable and unfavorable investment periods, you must define a zone of time that is longer in its scope than your trading horizon. As an example, a short-term trader using a moving average system would choose an intermediate-term moving average length for trend definition. Choosing a longer span provides enough time for short-term trades to develop within the intermediate-term trend. For the intermediate-term trader, a long-term definition

EXHIBIT 11.3 Custom-Made Indexes Marked with Favorable and Unfavorable Periods

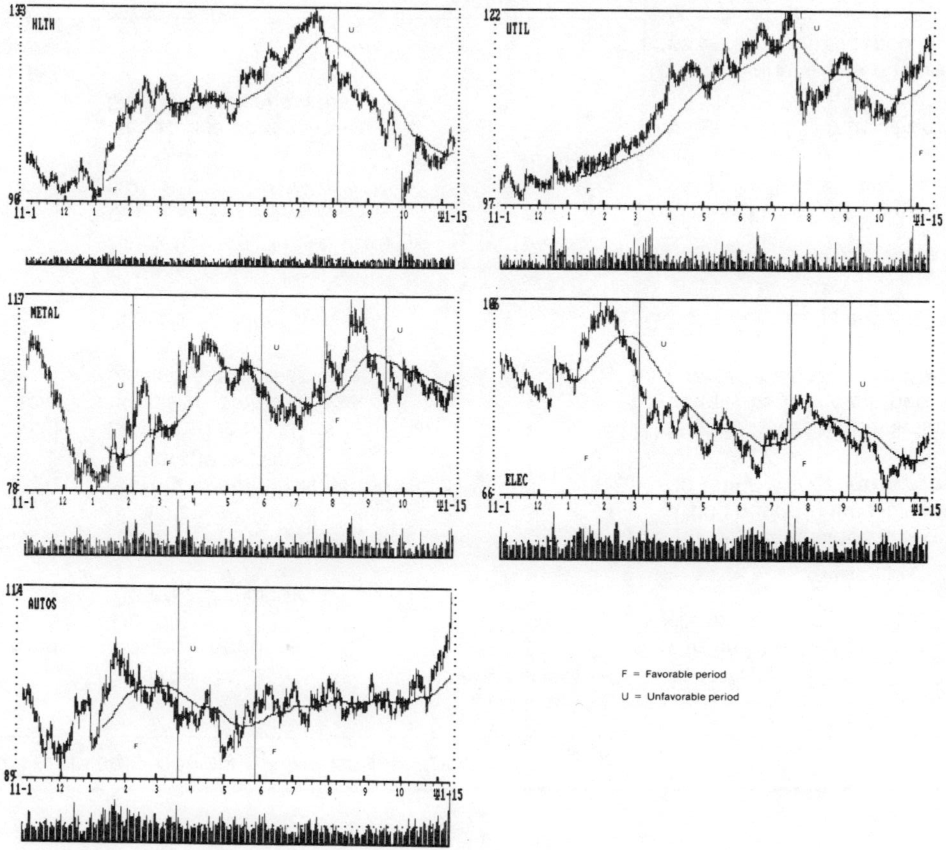

F = Favorable period
U = Unfavorable period

EXHIBIT 11.4 Basic Technical Analysis for Individual Stocks

Questions	Techniques	Chapter for Explanation	Comments
1. What is the current trend of the stock? Has a trend change signal been given?	Moving averages. Trendlines. View trend indicators.	3 3 3	Try to find the technique that best fits the historical character of the data.
2. Is there evidence of trend overextension?	Price minus moving-average oscillator. Moving average minus moving average oscillator.	3 3	A strongly advancing stock may stay overextended for a long period of time. Do not make a decision based on entry into overextended territory.
3. Are any time or business cycles currently favorable or unfavorable to the stock?	Backward look. Simple moving average. Moving-average crossings.	4 4 4	Use time cycles with special care. It is usually best to cast them in a trend or trend-overextension framework.
4. What are relative strength measures saying?	Internal relative strength Stock to Dow. Stock to group index.	5 5 5	Group reference is especially important at buy points.
5. What is volume saying about current price action?	Volume generalizations. NVI, PVI, ADI, PVT, CVI, DVI.	6 6 6	You must fit them to the proper circumstances or they will provide confusing evidence.
6. Where may there be support or resistance?	Resistance zones. Speed resistance lines.	7 7	Don't expect too much from these indicators.
7. What other evidence do I have about the stock?	—	—	Technical analysis is a never-ending search for new methods and evidence.

of favorable and unfavorable periods is necessary for the same reason.

The trading of individual stocks within groups experiencing favorable price movement requires technical tests to be made on the price and volume data. Exhibit 11.4 provides an overview of the procedure for making a technical analysis of individual stocks. If you are a short-term trader, this analysis should be made on each stock in your favorably defined groups on a daily basis. If you are an intermediate-term trader your technical analysis should take place no less often than once each week. In either case, Auto Run will simplify the process. It is essential that your analysis be accomplished consistently on a daily (or weekly) basis. This strategy is not forgiving of inattention.

The objective of the analysis is to find profitable entry and exit points for buying and selling stocks in the favorable group or groups. There are four types of price behavior that are especially important for accomplishing this task. Each of the four requires that extra attention be given to certain technical indicators when the analysis is made.

1. Defined Trend Changes. Trend-change signals provide a potential opportunity to make successful trade decisions. As an example, Exhibit 11.5 illustrates how a defined trend change can yield a profitable trade. The difference oscillator shown below the price chart indicates a buy at Point A ($66) and a sell at Point B ($75). When substantial price movements like this one take place, trend change signals work well. However, as we have seen so many times in the past, the problem with using defined trend changes to provide automatic timing signals is that whipsaws often occur, with losses resulting.

Pairs of trend-change signals never define the absolute distance from the bottom of a trend to the top but, instead, define a section out of the middle of the move. If the move is long enough, the section will be large enough to yield a profit. If not, a loss will accrue, as shown in trade C to D in the exhibit.

One method that often increases the odds of success is to use different techniques to define entry and exit points. For example, defined trend changes can be used to signal a purchase, and trend overextension reversals can be used to indicate a

EXHIBIT 11.5   Buying and Selling Based on Defined Trend-Change Signals

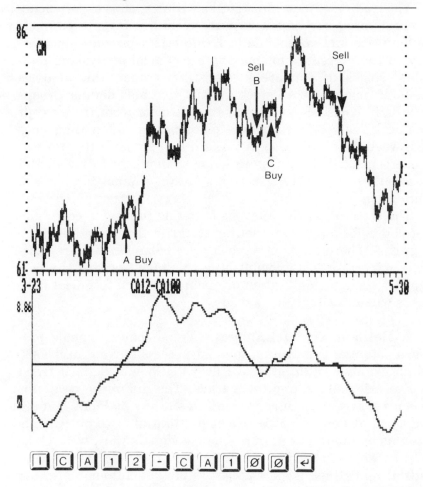

sale. Exhibit 11.6 illustrates how this is accomplished. For this example, the internal relative strength measure (see Chapter Five) is used to define sell signals. As before, when the trend-defining oscillator rises through the horizontal line, a buy signal is given. Sell signals, however, are given when the internal relative strength indicator shown above the price chart drops under the 70 level, after having gone above it.

For this system to work, movement is a necessity, so stocks chosen should have a history of volatility. Academicians often

EXHIBIT 11.6 Moving Average Oscillator to Generate Buy Points, Trend Overextension to Establish Sell Points

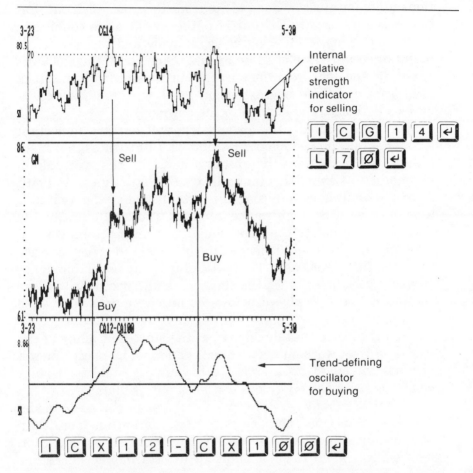

rate investments based on a risk volatility measure, with the greater the volatility, the greater the risk. For this system, the opposite is true. The riskiest stocks are those that do not experience substantial swings in price but that instead drift and produce whipsaws.

It is important to understand that this strategy does not predict the length of time of the trend, nor does it assume the rising and falling price behavior is part of a recurring periodic cycle. It simply makes use of the undulations, whether they are part of a regular cycle or not.

When creating buy and sell systems like this one, it is necessary to specify the rules for the trade, along with specifications for what must be done if the trade does not work out. For the procedure used in Exhibit 11.6, the specification could take on the following form: A purchase is made and the position is maintained until one of three events takes place: the stock declines by 5 percent from the purchase price (stop loss), the stock falls from a defined overextension level, or the stock experiences a defined trend change to the downside.

Having specified rules in advance will be very important for managing "busted plays." Exhibit 11.7 illustrates this eventuality and underlines the absolute necessity that you take a probabilistic view of this (and all) trading strategies. At Point A on the oscillator a buy signal is established as the oscillator breaks upward through the center line. The oscillator quickly reverses itself before the upper indicator can make its way up through the 70 level. This results in a sale at a lower price than the buy, creating a loss. At Point B the oscillator again signals a buy, after which the stock price uncooperatively takes a tumble. The stop placed below the purchase price limits the loss to 5 percent.

You can be absolutely sure from the start that many of the trades will not work out as planned. You must be ready and not hesitate to sell in accordance with your preestablished rules when the price behavior does not work out as planned.

There are many ways to make changes to the basic model just described. One approach is to use different (or more than one) technical indicators for deciding when the trend has commenced and when it has exhausted itself. Chapter Three discusses many of these technical measures, and through experimentation you may be able to find a more effective match for the stocks that you follow. You can also use the buying signal as a *possible* buy point, instead of a certain one. Based on other evidence (technical, fundamental, and intuitive), you can either accept the signal or reject it.

The selling rule can also be modified. You will often find that this strategy will produce a small profit but will miss the longer move which comes immediately after you have sold out. This can be avoided by selling only part of the total trade at

EXHIBIT 11.7   Failures in Trading on Defined Trend Changes

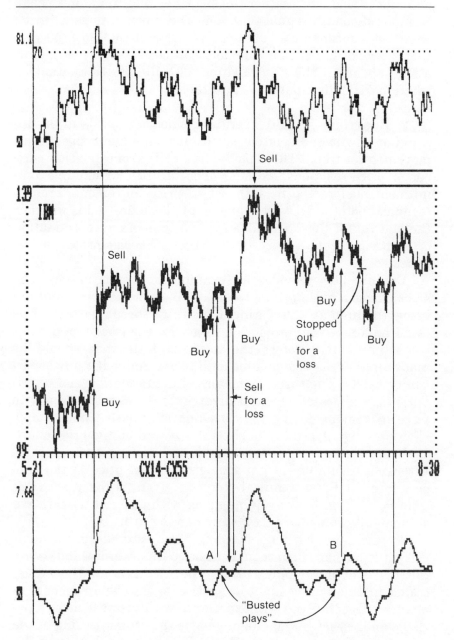

the signal given by the trend overextension indicator. The remainder is sold when either the stock declines from later peaks or a trend-change signal is given. The amount to sell can be based on a mechanical rule (e.g., 50 percent sold now, 50 percent later), or it can be a judgment call based on how each situation appears at the time. Exhibit 11.8 illustrates a situation where partial distribution is profitable.

2. Reactions within Trends. When a stock is in an uptrend or downtrend it often pauses at points along the overall movement of trend. These pauses are called consolidation periods or price reactions and offer opportunities for making commitments before the next thrust in price movement. From a technical point of view, the question to be addressed is whether the slowing of the price advance is a temporary consolidation or if it represents a price top from which lower prices can be expected.

Exhibit 11.9 provides an example of this situation. The stock shows a nice uptrend from A to B, with the prices stalling below the high at B. Creating a one-third speed resistance line (see Chapter Seven) provides a target for the price reaction.

Exhibit 11.10 shows the minimal tests that should be made on the price and volume data to determine if a buy opportunity exists. The three indicators of accumulation and distribution are assessed to see if divergence exists with respect to price movement during the consolidation phase. The example shows no divergence to the rise from A to B on the price chart. Both the internal relative strength and moving average overextension oscillator show a strengthening of price at the support level at B. A technical "buy" is given as the price rises from Point B on heavy volume along with a rise of the positive volume indicator above its 50-day moving average.

To gain a proper understanding of this procedure, the analysis must be made on a regular basis so the technical indicators can be seen "developing" before you. A static analysis illustrated in this book cannot do justice to the dynamic motion-picture effect that you will experience with your consistent, periodic analyses. On a day-to-day basis the strengthening of the price from Point A to Point B will be clearly evident, and the

---

EXHIBIT 11.8   Partial Distributions

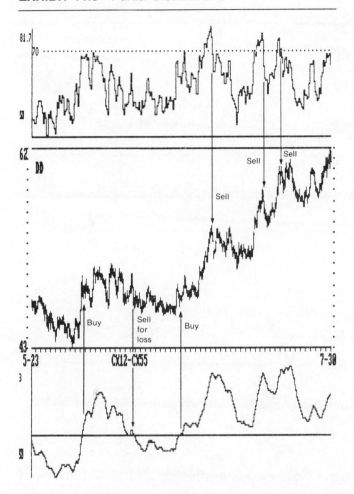

sharp rise in price from the support level at B on high volume will provide a dramatic signal to buy.

As with the previously discussed method, a procedure should be developed for selling. For short-term traders, a 5 percent tolerance on the downside coupled with a trend-overextension signal of reversal is appropriate. Intermediate-term traders may want to distribute on trend reversals or wait until clear evidence of a topping formation (to be discussed later) appears.

EXHIBIT 11.9   Example of a Rapid Rise Followed by a Price Reaction

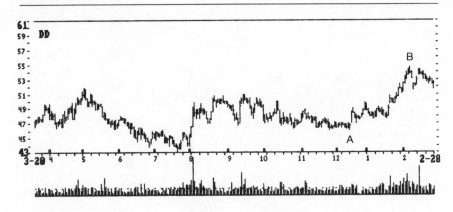

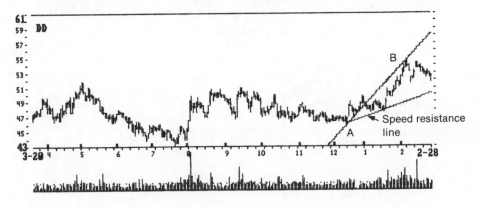

3. Controlled Bottom Formations.   At the beginning of a buy zone for a group, some stocks may be making what appears to be a bottom after a decline in price. When a stock reaches a point comparable to Point B in Exhibit 11.11, it is in an extremely favorable position for certain technical indicators to flash a buy or don't-buy signal.

It should be noted that uncontrolled bottoms—prices falling rapidly and often accompanied by price gapping, necessitate the use of other techniques. This situation will be discussed in the next chapter, Investing in Unattractive Stocks.

The pattern shown in Exhibit 11.11 is sometimes called a

EXHIBIT 11.10   Technical Analysis of Price Reaction

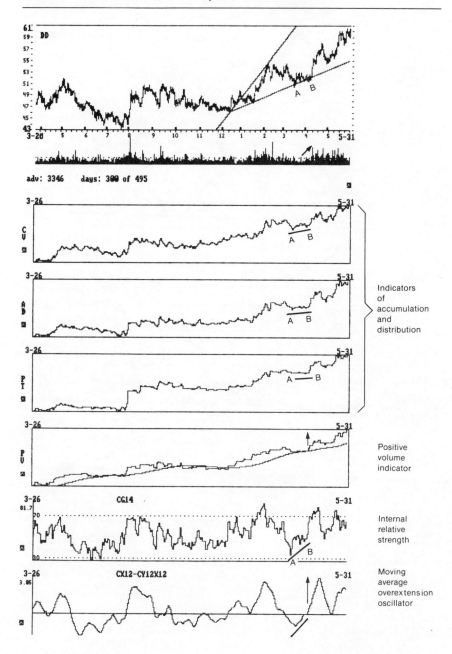

EXHIBIT 11.11   Technical Analysis of Controlled Bottom Formations

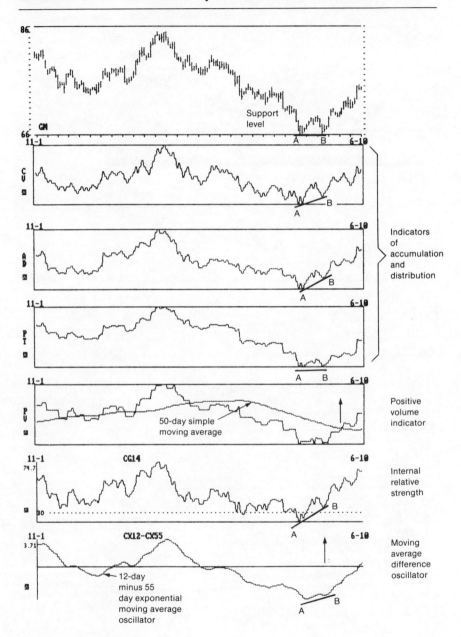

double bottom and has been hailed by some stock market technicians as representing an excellent buy point. In reality, the pattern has no value in itself for predicting the course of future prices. It is, however, extremely useful as a point for making a focused technical analysis. Divergencies, if they exist, will be glaringly apparent, telling us if the odds favor buying. It also ensures that if a buy is made, it will occur at a relatively low point near a support level. This has some merit in itself.

The exhibit illustrates the minimum tests that should be made at Point B. The first three indicators below the price chart are volume-based indicators of accumulation and distribution. If the indicators show a rising trend from Point A to Point B, this provides an indication that the stock is undergoing accumulation. (See Chapter Six for a further discussion.) The exhibit shows two of the three indicators suggesting significant accumulation, with the third giving a neutral reading.

The PVI shows a rise coming off B, lending conviction to the persistency of the rise. The internal relative strength and the moving average difference indicator are used to indicate changes in price dynamics. Both show divergencies from Point A to B, lending support to a purchase at Point B. Given that the stock group also looks favorable, a purchase commitment would be made.

As always, it is important to place a stop loss below the purchase price. A 5 percent level is again reasonable for making these trades. Sale of the stock for a quick trade would be based on trend overextension reversal, with intermediate-term trades using partial distribution and a top formation analysis.

4. Horizontal Line Formations. Another excellent opportunity to seriously analyze a stock is when it has been trading in a narrow range (10 percent or less) for a number of months. The narrow price range implies an approximate balance of supply with demand, with neither winning the battle to move prices one way or the other in a decisive fashion. Despite the outward appearance of equilibrium, under the surface of price behavior there may be evidence of one side or the other getting the upper hand.

Exhibit 11.12 shows a line formation lasting about four months, during which time the stock is trading in a range of about 10 percent. Looking below the price to the volume indicators shows interesting behavior during the horizontal movement period. All three of the accumulation and distribution indicators exhibit an uptrend, implying that the stock is gaining strength throughout the four-month period.

The positive volume indicator is seen breaking above its 50-day moving average, then staying well above it as the price drops back down to Point A. This is a very bullish indication of an uptrend in progress. As the price rises from Point A, the negative volume indicator does not initially rise, hence it does not provide evidence of an early end to the upmove. From a technical point of view, the stock looks like a purchase candidate at Point A.

It again must be mentioned that a protective stop is always necessary when using a trading strategy. If the stock moves in an unexpected way you must get your money out quickly and with the bulk of it intact so you will be free to try again when conditions look right. Trend overextension and top formation analysis will again form the basis for selling.

Alternative II: Trading Based on Group Timing

With this trading approach, the group indexes are treated as if they are stocks. When a buy decision is made on a group, instead of buying the group, the strongest stock in the group is purchased. As the group is being treated as if it were a stock, all the "tests" provided by the technical indicators described for use on stocks (Exhibit 11.4) are appropriate for use on the groups.

A major advantage of this approach is that you can follow large numbers of stocks while having to make far fewer analyses than if you were analyzing each one separately. It also assures that all stock purchases that are made occur when they have group sponsorship. You will never buck the trend.

As an example, Exhibit 11.13 shows the utility group, with a buy for the group given at the point marked, based on the three-step rule on a weighted moving average. Once a buy signal is given, the trading strategy requires the strongest stock (or stocks if you wish to buy more than one) to be purchased. How do you find the stock that is the strongest? As we have

EXHIBIT 11.12   Technical Analysis of Horizontal Line Formations

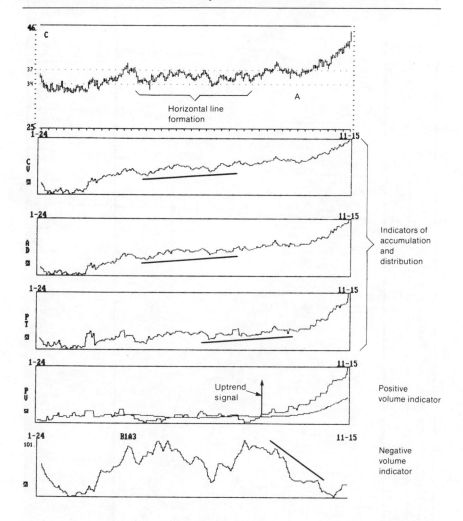

seen in other parts of this book, there are a number of alternative measures.

One approach is to rank the stocks based on their action index value as given in the View Trend report (see Chapter Four for details). Another method is to make a full technical analysis of each stock and choose the one that looks the best in a technical sense. Still another is to use the relative strength charting feature of the Dow Jones Market Analyzer PLUS to

EXHIBIT 11.13 Custom Utility Index with Simple Buy Point

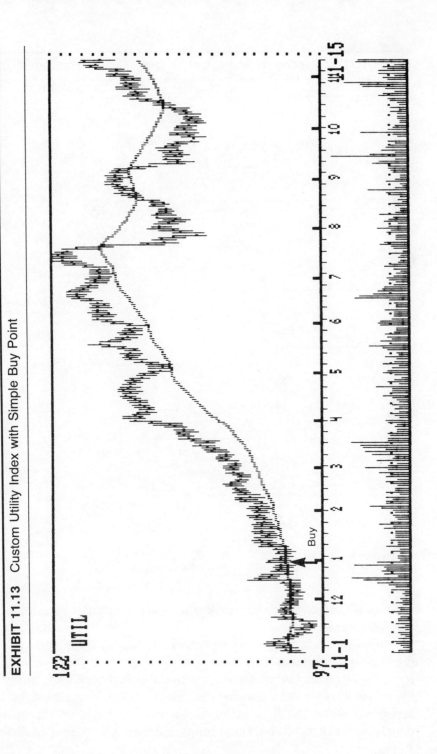

EXHIBIT 11.14   Relative Strength Determination of Strongest Stock

---

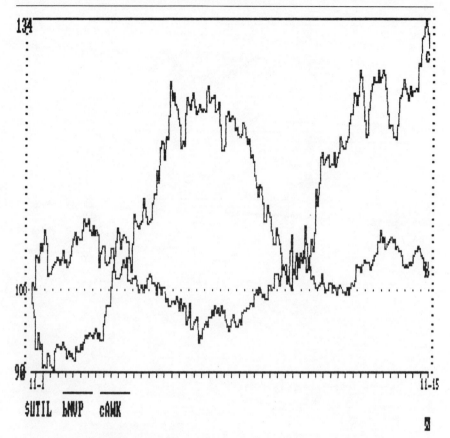

SUTIL LNUP cANK

make comparisons between the stocks. This approach will be illustrated here.

If you have more than four stocks in your group, you may
want to compare them in subgroups, as the screen can get clut-
tered with too many stocks charted at once. (A color monitor is
very helpful!) The procedure is to use the group index as a base,
then use the components of the index to plot against it. Plotting
the component stocks in subgroups will allow you to eliminate
those acting most poorly until you get down to a few that you
can plot together on one chart. Exhibit 11.14 shows a relative
strength chart of the two best stocks in the group. At the point
of the buy signal, the strongest-acting stock is the one marked
C, so it is chosen for purchase.

EXHIBIT 11.15   Price Top Determination

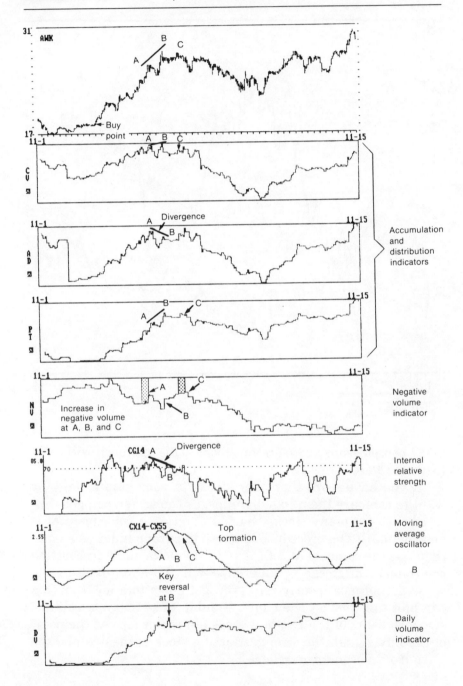

Accumulation and distribution indicators

Negative volume indicator

Internal relative strength

Moving average oscillator

B

Daily volume indicator

Exhibit 11.15 shows the point of purchase of the stock. The exhibit also shows a number of indicators plotted below the price chart for the purpose of demonstrating the identification of a selling point.

The first three indicators are used to attempt to find divergencies that would indicate stock distribution. The second of the three shows a major divergence from Peak A to Peak B, and to show divergencies from B to C. After a long move downward, the negative volume indicator shows increases up to A, to B, and to C. The internal relative strength indicator shows a major drop from A to B, indicating an end to the trends. The moving average oscillator, which had moved up nicely past the A point, has shown a definite rounded top at Points B and C. Finally, the daily volume indicator shows Point B to be a key reversal point.

In looking at the bulk of the evidence, there appears to be little reason for the intermediate-term trader to sell before Point B. By the time Point C is reached, the evidence of a top formation is overwhelming, and the stock is sold.

Alternative III: Stock Group Switching

This trading method substitutes your chosen groups for the mutual funds used in the specialty fund switch strategy described in Chapter Nine. You essentially create your own minimutual funds and switch them using the same switching rules as used with the mutual funds. The difference is that instead of buying the entire group, you choose only two or three of the strongest stocks in the group for purchase. This approach has the potential for providing much more action, one way or another, than using mutual funds. It also permits the use of groups that are not represented by funds. As an example, automobile manufacturers can be a group in this system, while they could not be represented by a mutual fund owing to their small numbers.

The measure of strength used to choose specific stocks for purchase can be obtained from ranking the stocks using the Action Index in the Trend Report program. Another option is to make comparisons on the basis of relative strength, with the strongest chosen for purchase. Exhibit 9.10 details the required procedures.

EXHIBIT 11.16 *Barron's* Weekly Group Averages

BARRON'S GROUP STOCK AVERAGES

1986 High-a	Low-a		May 15	May 8	% change
1,371.92	1,099.97	Aircraft manufacturing	1,277.92	1,321.25	− 3.28
349.82	252.56	Air transport	325.45	337.00	− 3.43
191.66	133.91	Automobiles	157.86	166.25	− 5.04
364.41	297.31	Automobile equipment	326.37	342.60	− 4.77
486.71	360.59	Banks	449.18	462.84	− 2.95
490.59	343.02	Bldg material, equipment	481.27	490.08	− 1.80
674.15	493.60	Chemicals	651.63	647.60	+ .62
42.06	37.88	Closed-end invest	41.57	41.89	− .75
4,452.66	3,349.94	Drugs	4,229.69	4,316.37	− 2.01
1,357.14	1,147.35	Electrical equipment	1,264.78	1,307.88	− 3.29
446.49	359.85	Farm equipment	431.41	436.70	− 1.21
1,147.03	863.11	Foods and beverages	1,121.64	1,097.75	+ 2.18
594.44	484.64	Gold mining	L 480.88	490.41	− 1.94
707.56	620.29	Grocery chains	H 733.35	675.63	+ 8.54
596.72	538.49	Installment financing	L 523.10	540.18	− 3.16
2,208.32	1,778.22	Insurance	1,908.48	1,948.36	− 2.05
2,149.06	1,629.57	Liquor	2,030.55	2,075.86	− 2.18
234.07	157.95	Machine tools	204.74	224.08	− 8.63
197.79	162.04	Machinery (heavy)	183.92	176.74	+ 4.06
2,164.28	1,444.23	Motion pictures	1,984.24	2,027.78	− 2.15
207.85	173.92	Non-ferrous metals	177.78	175.85	+ 1.10
5,640.94	5,204.08	Office equipment	L 5,195.86	5,326.35	− 2.45
809.43	698.44	Oil	806.11	809.43	− .41
776.04	556.90	Packing	754.39	776.04	− 2.79
607.67	478.99	Paper	571.34	579.94	− 1.48
330.83	288.79	Railroad equipment	326.75	326.79	− .01
1,604.46	1,256.48	Retail merchandise	H 1,635.94	1,604.46	+ 1.96
569.10	461.61	Rubber	486.37	501.75	− 3.07
152.16	125.19	Steel and iron	L 119.68	125.19	− 4.40
328.64	271.48	Television	H 332.05	319.79	+ 3.83
515.87	383.03	Textiles	484.29	492.92	− 1.75
628.52	465.19	Tobacco	595.24	618.14	− 3.70
1855.90	1502.29	Dow-Jones Industrials	1774.68	1786.21	− .65
830.84	686.97	Dow-Jones Transportation	776.50	783.00	− .83
193.73	169.47	Dow-Jones Utilities	182.34	183.73	− .76
724.19	602.83	Dow-Jones Composite	689.43	694.36	− .71

a-1986 highs and lows through preceding week ended Thursday. In this table daily closings for trading week ended last Friday used in the range for the Dow Jones Averages. H-New high. L-New low.

Some Final Thoughts on Trading

The methods discussed in this chapter apply equally well to short sales as to the long trades used as examples. It is simply a matter of looking for the weak groups and weak stocks within these groups to find short sale candidates. The basic implementation procedures remain the same.

To increase the chances of making a profit, you should pare your commission expenses by dealing in 100-share lots and using a discount broker. Another reason for using a discount broker is that you will not have to explain anything when a trade is made. Successful trading requires a considerable amount of discipline that becomes difficult to maintain if you feel that you have to convince your full-service broker of the merits of each decision. Unless you can find a technically oriented full-service broker who understands what you are doing and can help you with the strategy, stay with a discount firm.

If you are an intermediate-term trader using weekly data for making your decisions, ready-made group averages are available. Exhibit 11.16 shows the group data that are available each week in *Barron's*. It is quite a simple task to manually enter, once each week, the group averages that you are interested in maintaining.

Another source of weekly industry group data is the Warner Computer Services online database service which has weekly data on over 100 industry groups, with historical data going back to 1977.

Daily industry group data can be obtained from *Investor's Daily* for 196 groups. Along with industry group index values, this source provides earnings per share and relative strength ranking, as well as sales growth rates for all groups.

To summarize and reemphasize the trading philosophy discussed in this chapter, the following generalizations are offered.

1. Concentrate your efforts on a manageable number of stocks and get to know their behavior well.
2. Trade only stocks that have group sponsorship. Either the market, an individual industry group, or both should support the trade.
3. Develop a probabilistic attitude toward the trades you

make, knowing in advance that many of them will not work out.

4. Develop your own rules for selling at the time a purchase is made. The management of losses must be part of your rule system.

5. Think defensively by limiting the amount of money used in this strategy to a *small fraction* of your total investments.

6. Assess your personal feelings about trading. A major benefit of a trading strategy is the excitement it creates. If your psychological reaction is nervousness and worry instead of enjoyment, you should consider a different strategy.

SELECTED REFERENCES

APPEL, GERALD. *Winning Stock Market Systems*. Great Neck, N.Y.: Signalert Corp., 1974.

DAHL, CURTISS. "Moving Averages Approach to Profits in the Stock Market." In *The New Encyclopedia of Stock Market Techniques,* ed. Michael L. Burke, Larchmont, N.Y.: Investor's Intelligence, 1985.

DIAMOND, WILLIAM. *Bulls, Bears and Massacres*. Belmont, Calif.: Wadsworth Publishing, 1982.

PRING, MARTIN. *Technical Analysis Explained*. New York: McGraw-Hill, 1985.

SCHULTZ, HARRY D., and SAMSON COSLOW, eds. *A Treasury of Wall Street Wisdom*. Palisades Park, N.J.: Investor's Press, 1966.

WEINSTEIN, STAN. "Reading the Charts." *Wealth,* Summer 1984, pp. 64–66.

CHAPTER TWELVE

Investing in Unattractive Stocks

Prejudice has long been part of the human condition, with the more common adverse judgments based on religion, skin color, sex, and place of origin. Besides these obvious prejudices, other more subtle biases operate on a day-to-day basis to influence feelings and behavior. One of the more powerful of these is our perception of attractiveness and unattractiveness. In general, perceptions of attractiveness lead to an overvaluation of an entity, while perceptions of unattractiveness lead to an undervaluation. Our treatment of the extreme case, ugliness, certainly ranks as one of our greatest (but least mentioned) prejudices.

This prejudice affects behavior in many ways. On a social basis, many examples can be found. Differential treatment is often shown to children based on how cute they are or are not thought to be; physically attractive young women receive much more attention from men than those considered homely; and good-looking men often have greater success in the dating game. In the workplace, the employee perceived to be attractive is often given the benefit of the doubt in hiring and promotion decisions over equals whose appearance is thought to be unattractive.

How does this affect the stock market? Stocks, like people, can be viewed in similar terms, and similar value-distorting prejudices apply. Unattractiveness of stocks may result in an undervaluation by the human-based supply and demand pricing mechanism.

Unattractive stocks can be placed into two major categories.

The first consists of companies with chronic, serious troubles of a "crisis" nature that result in deficit earnings and may affect the structure (or possibly the existence) of the organization. The second category consists of companies with temporary (or potential) problems that may affect earnings but most likely will not affect the asset structure or survivability of the firm.

Chronically Troubled Companies. Examples of companies in the first category include those with *multiperiod deficit earnings.* Often there will be news stories and investment reports expressing concern for the future viability of these companies in their current form; this leads investors to shun them. *Close brushes with disaster* are another reason for unattractiveness. Companies in default on their bank loans that go through a renegotiation process is one example. Another is the sale of assets in an effort to stem the flow of red ink. Finally, *bankruptcies*, either actual or potential, also may tend to color the company "ugly."

Temporarily Troubled Companies. There are many reasons why stock in these companies may be regarded as unattractive. A stock may have a *blemish*, an actual, although temporary, problem that will not significantly impact long-term operations. A strike in one division of a company or the unexpected death of the chief executive officer are examples of blemishes. The downgrading of a stock from a "buy" to a "hold" by a large brokerage house is another example. Still others include industrial accidents and lawsuits. Although dramatic in nature, they are often (but not always) handled without major long-term disruption in the ongoing business or the structure of the firm. There also may be an *association with ugliness* that produces a halo or guilt-by-association effect leading to a negative view of the stock. A company that belongs to an out-of-favor industry group or that does business with a foreign government held in low regard by the investment community are examples. *A temporary decline in earnings* is another potential cause. A change in product line, start-up problems in the production area, shortages of raw materials, or a foreign currency devaluation may all lead to a temporary decline in earnings and a psychological aversion by investors.

EXHIBIT 12.1 Procedure for Investing in Chronically Troubled
Companies

Procedure	*Comments*
Screen for candidates	
Is the stock down by 80 percent or more and having deficit earnings?	Monthly based chart books are an excellent source.
Is the company in Chapter 11 bankruptcy proceedings?	//MEDGEN .I/BCY
Monitor	
Do the fundamentals indicate that the company will be likely to survive?	Monitoring must be an ongoing effort over many months.
	Fundamental and technical evidence must be maintained.
Time	
Is all the bad news out? Any potential triggers? Clear technical signals?	An incremental buy policy is an alternative.

In most cases, the income statement has greater impact on
views of attractiveness and unattractiveness than does the balance sheet. More specifically, the impact of events on current
and future earnings tend to dominate the views of most investors. This fixation on changes in real or potential earnings provides wide swings in stock prices and special opportunities for
profit.

Investing on the basis of company troubles is the riskiest of
all the approaches in this book. It is not recommended unless
you have the funds to risk, the time to keep up with your positions, and the discipline to limit your losses.

INVESTING IN CHRONICALLY
TROUBLED COMPANIES

Exhibit 12.1 provides an overview of the procedure for investing in these unattractive stocks. The strategy is a combination of fundamental and technical analysis, and requires a considerable amount of judgment.

The basic idea is to invest in a company after all the bad
news is out, investors have given up on it, and the stock price
has shown evidence of having made a bottom. If the company
survives and its fortunes change for the better, it will again at-

tract the attention of mainstream investors and the price will be bid up.

It is frequently the case that when a turnaround comes, earnings will increase dramatically. This is because losing operations have likely been shut down during the crisis period and the huge losses that have accrued are used to shelter future income from taxes. Exhibit 12.2 shows two examples of stocks that emerged from periods of earnings deficits, then recovered to post enormous percentage gains. As you can well imagine, for each such winner, there are many more for which there are no charts to show, because they are no longer in business.

As the procedure detailed in Exhibit 12.1 shows, you will first need to find candidates for analysis. Fortunately there are a number of good sources. Chart books having monthly plots of prices over a 5- to 10-year period can be very effective for screening purposes. For these deeply troubled companies, you are looking for chart patterns that show a decline in price of 80 percent or more from the high in combination with current or recent deficit earnings. The easiest chart books to use are those that have the earnings plotted along with the price or given in a table below the price chart.

Dow Jones News/Retrieval is another good source for finding deeply distressed, unattractive companies. Information on bankruptcies, for example, is available from //DJNEWS .I/BCY. The stories are from 90 seconds to 90 days old, and you can quickly scan the headlines to find information you might be interested in. Using the EZ terminal option on the Dow Jones Market Analyzer PLUS allows you to save any of the stories on disk so you can read them offline at your leisure. Exhibit 12.3 shows an example of what the bankruptcy headlines look like and how they are accessed.

The Wall Street Journal is another place to look. Most investors read the *Journal* anyway; it's just necessary to change the orientation from being in tune with the good and interesting news to tuning in to the kind of bad news associated with these awful stocks.

You may be surprised to find that your screening effort provides you with many candidates. In good times or bad there is never a shortage of companies in crisis, so your search will always bear fruit.

EXHIBIT 12.2 Companies Having Deficit Earnings Followed by a Turnaround

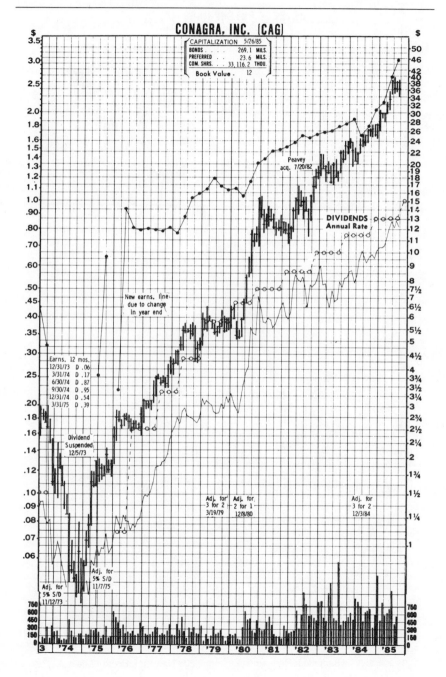

CONAGRA, INC. (CAG)

CAPITALIZATION 5/26/85
BONDS . . . . 269.1 MILS.
PREFERRED . . 23.6 MILS.
COM. SHRS. . . 33,116.2 THOU.
Book Value - 12

Peavey acq. 7/20/82

DIVIDENDS Annual Rate

New earns. line due to change in year end

Earns. 12 mos.
12/31/73 D .06
3/31/74 D .17
6/30/74 D .87
9/30/74 D .95
12/31/74 D .54
3/31/75 D .39

Dividend Suspended 12/5/73

Adj. for 3 for 2 3/19/79

Adj. for 2 for 1 12/8/80

Adj. for 3 for 2 12/3/84

Adj. for 5% S/D 11/7/75

Adj. for 5% S/D 11/12/73

EXHIBIT 12.2 (*concluded*)

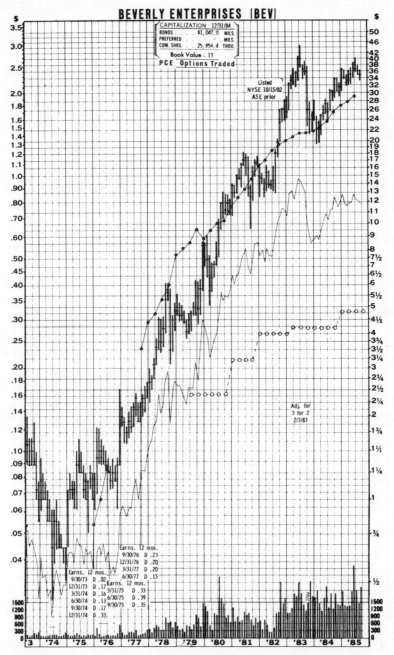

Charts courtesy of Securities Research Company, 208 Newbury, Boston Mass. 02116.

EXHIBIT 12.3 Bankruptcy Headlines

```
 N   I/BCY        21/21
AH 08/14 DEVELOPER FILES UNDER
  (WJ) CHAPTER 11 OF BANKRUPTCY CODE
AG 08/14 LIABILITIES AT HUNTS' FIRM
  (WJ) TOP ASSETS BY $24 MILLION
AF 08/13 JAPAN'S SANKO STEAMSHIP CO.
  (WJ) FACES PRESSURE TO SEEK RELIEF
AE 08/12 AMERICAN MEDI-DENT FILES
  (DJ) REORGANIZATION PLAN
AD 08/09 VIABLE RESOURCES SETTLES
  (DJ) DISPUTE WITH GATX LEASING
AC 08/08 OMNIDENTIX SYSTEMS SELLS
  (DW) TWO-THIRDS OF STOCK TO FIRM
AB 08/08 UPI MANAGEMENT, CREDITORS
  (DW) AGREE TO SET DEADLINE FOR SALE
AA 08/08 APPALACHIAN OIL MOVES TO
  (DW) DISMISS CHAPTER 11 PETITION
```

After EZ terminal
log-on:

From the set of troubled companies that you have identified you next must determine which are the likely survivors. This is a very difficult task that will require a combination of fundamental analysis and luck. What should you look for? The following fundamental factors offer a starting point.

1. Earnings. For these companies, earnings will likely be on a deficit basis. You will want to look at past earnings to develop a benchmark figure for making assessments of future possibilities. Earnings estimates are also important. //EARN from Dow Jones News/Retrieval will provide an idea of what the professional forecasters think. In general, the wider the range of earnings estimates, the more uncertainty there is about the stock and the greater is the chance that the current price of the stock will not reflect its "true" value. Remember, many investors fixate on earnings per share, so a poor showing here may overly distort perceptions of the stock, creating opportunities for you.

2. Sales and the Price-to-Sales Ratio.   Comparing current sales figures and the stock's current price-to-sales ratio with past years provides valuable information. Price-to-sales ratios tend to be more consistent from year to year than price-to-earnings ratios. If the sales base is there despite deficit earnings, a rapid turnaround may be possible.

3. Book Value.   The firm's book value also offers potentially important information. If the company should be liquidated, the book value represents the worth of each share of stock, as stated by the company's accountants. The current per share prices of many truly ugly stocks will be below their book values, sometimes by 50 percent or more.

Unfortunately, you may have a problem using this figure for making a definitive analysis. Book value as stated often does not represent the market value, should there be an actual liquidation. Some companies carry their assets on their books at values far above the market value they would receive if they had to sell them. Basic industries that have obsolete factory equipment, for example, fall into this category. Other companies have real estate holdings on their books at values far below market, making the book value figure look worse than it really is. In short, book value can be an excellent measure of the basic worth of the company, but only if assets are valued correctly. For most of us, determining this value is difficult. In many cases the company accountants themselves do not know the market value of the assets, so you, too, will likely have trouble discerning it. The book value figure should be used only to provide a rough idea of what the company is worth. Buy or sell decisions should never be made on this data alone.

4. Current Assets.   Substantial current assets, relative to total assets and current liabilities, are a positive sign that the firm may be able to "weather the storm."

5. Debt.   When business is good, a high percentage of debt can have a very favorable impact on the firm's earnings. During bad times, the opposite is true. To get a feeling for a firm's debt load, you must compare the debt-to-equity ratio to the industry average for the stock. High fixed costs from massive debt combined with rapidly falling sales can quickly force a company into liquidation.

6. New Stock.   If the company is in reorganization, it is important for you to know how many new shares of stock will be issued as part of the restructuring plan. The more the shares, the more the earnings will be diluted as the company makes a comeback.

7. Trigger Mechanism.   A very positive development is to have an identifiable change or event that may trigger an increase in the favorable perception of the stock. A new product, a government guaranteed loan, emergence from bankruptcy, sale of an unprofitable division, change of name, or a change in management are all examples of these trigger mechanisms.

After evaluating a number of distressed companies, you will keep those that look most promising for monitoring on a continuing basis. The most effective way of doing this is to establish and maintain a price and text history on each stock, and to keep it current.

To succeed with this high-risk strategy you must not be in a hurry to buy. In most cases it will take months of watching and waiting before the proper moment comes to take action. With these stocks it is important never to underestimate the extent to which bad can become worse and unattractiveness can turn to abject ugliness. Absolute price levels mean very little. A $60 stock may look like a bargain at $10, but this price may just be a pause on the way down to 1/2. Your task is to get to know all you can about the company until the bad news has been rung out and the stock begins acting well on a technical basis.

One of the safest ways to play this high-risk strategy is to track a stock for the purpose of gathering information, from the time it initially becomes interesting (down at least 80 percent from the high with deficit earnings, or from a bankruptcy situation) until the company has restructured itself and the price appears to have bottomed over a number of months. Keeping up with the price and volume activity along with news on the company during this high-risk period is necessary to allow the stock's "personality" to become known to you. Having no monetary commitment in the stock will permit you to see more objectively the fundamental and technical developments as they occur. You will get to know, for example, how the price action reacts to good and bad company news and how its performance relates to the market as a whole. Moreover, you will gain an overall sense of what is normal and what is unusual about the price performance of the stock. You will develop knowledge-based feelings about the company from this ongoing monitoring that could never be attained from an occasional "snapshot" of the stock's fundamental and technical history.

Determining buy and sell points for these stocks is difficult. Each situation is unique and the stocks often do not act well, in a technical sense. The patient approach advocated here will greatly increase the odds of successful timing.

Your essential technical analysis goal for these stocks is identifying the long-term bottom of the price slide. Technical indicators most useful for this task are (1) the accumulation / distribution indicators, (2) the positive volume indicator, (3) the internal relative strength measure, (4) the moving average trend identifier, and (5) the daily volume indicator. As we learned from Part Two of this book, these indicators "test" the data in order to assess the current status of the situation, so an informed opinion can be developed concerning future possibilities. The following examples will demonstrate how the monitoring and technical analysis are accomplished.

AM International: A Bankruptcy Example

Formerly Addressograph-Multigraph, this company filed for bankruptcy in April 1982 after sustaining large earnings deficits. From a high of 32 7/8 in 1978 the stock sank to under $1 a share. While the company was in bankruptcy, some operations were discontinued and management began to turn the company around. In 1983 the company posted positive earnings, and the company appeared to be a survivor with reasonably good long-term prospects. A trigger mechanism to aid in removing the cloak of ugliness from the stock was its emergence from Chapter 11 bankruptcy in July 1984. Exhibit 12.4 shows the stock's price behavior from the time that it came out of bankruptcy.

EXHIBIT 12.4   AM International: Technical Analysis

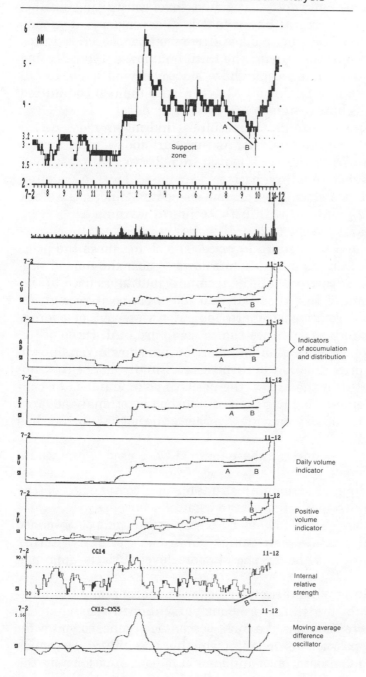

There are two approaches to timing the purchase of a stock coming out of bankruptcy. The first involves waiting until a clear low-risk technical buy signal is given, even if it means missing a significant price move. The second approach requires incremental purchases, with the initial purchase (typically one half of the total planned purchase amount) being made in advance of the out-of-bankruptcy trigger, with the rest committed after clear technical signals are given.

The exhibit contains the technical indicators most useful for making a bottom analysis. As the chart shows, after a relatively quiet period, the stock moved from 2½ to 5⅞ in less than two months, before falling back to near the $3 level. As is often the case, when a stock like this one sheds its ugliness, the stock moves rapidly upward with little technical warning.

The clear low-risk technical signal came after the correction from the rapid run-up in price. The chart shows the price falling back from its initial thrust down to near the zone of support. As the price drops, all the technical indicators used to signify a bottom of this type fall into line with positive signals. The internal relative strength indicator rises out of overextended territory as the price continues to drop. All three of the indicators of accumulation and distribution show divergence to the falling price, another bullish signal. Finally, at the first up-day marked with the arrow, the positive volume indicator confirms that an uptrend has been established by strongly advancing above its 50-day moving average. The signal to buy has been given.

If the incremental purchase method were used, a buy would have been made prior to emergence from bankruptcy based on the improving fundamental situation and knowledge of the Chapter 11 "trigger" that was to come.

Stop losses should always be placed at the time of purchase to preserve capital when things go wrong. For AM International, a stop just below the support level (2½) is appropriate.

The selling of bankruptcy stocks is usually related to long-term fundamentals. As previously mentioned, these stocks have the potential to make huge percentage gains, so you want to be in a position to benefit from this possibility. The stock should be monitored on a fundamental basis. As long as the fundamentals look good for the company the stock should be held.

Omnicare, Inc.: A Nonbankruptcy Distressed Company Example

The second type of stock that can be regarded as chronically troubled is one that has deficit annual earnings but is not currently in bankruptcy. Omnicare, Inc. is an example of a stock having these characteristics. The monthly based chart shown in Exhibit 12.5 indicates how the fortunes of the company changed, with the price dropping from a high of near 50 to a low of about 6 in a two-year period.

Having dropped by more than 80 percent, the stock becomes an interesting one for monitoring. To keep current on the company, both technical data (price and volume) and fundamental information need to be assessed on a continuing basis. While the technical data are easily available from a single source (Dow Jones Quotes), the fundamental information requires more effort to obtain.

Besides keeping the company in mind when you read your usual financial publications, at least once each week, the //DJNEWS database should be accessed for possible news stories. On a monthly basis, //MEDGEN and //SP should be accessed for fundamental information and //EARN and //INVEST for professional opinions on the earnings and future operations of the company. Saving all data to text disk will provide a historical record of the firm's plight. Appendix 12A provides a sampling of the type of information these databases provide.

The data for Omnicare shows a deeply troubled company with good prospects for survival. Although earnings for the last 12 months show a deficit of 0.03 (S&P data) the company is currently in the black. All earnings estimates are positive for the next year (S&P, EARN, and INVESTEXT), and the company is restructuring and cutting costs to aid in remaining profitable (DJNEWS and INVESTEXT). Revenues have remained reasonably strong throughout the troubled period (S&P), although sales of losing divisions will cut future sales figures significantly (INVESTEXT). The sales of these divisions will reduce the debt burden and will free up funds for

EXHIBIT 12.5 Monthly Price History, Omnicare, Inc.

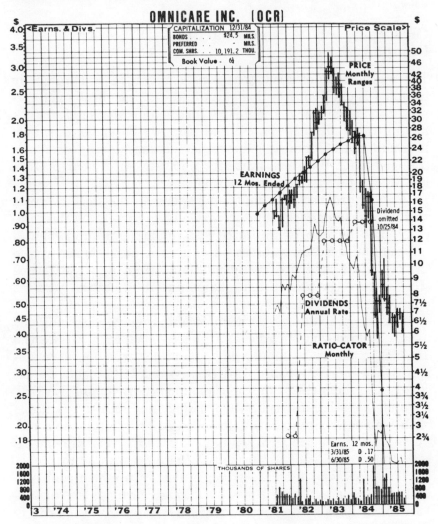

Chart courtesy of Securities Research Company, 208 Newbury, Boston Mass. 02116.

making acquisitions (INVESTEXT). The book value as stated by S&P is about equal to the current selling price of the stock. In short, the fundamental picture does not at all look hopeless, and possible acquisitions combined with continued positive earnings may be a trigger to change the stock's image.

The procedure used for possible purchase determination is to keep tracking the stock until fundamentals improve to the point of indicating that a turnaround may be near *and* technical indicators provide a bottom-formation buy signal. As with bankruptcies, patience combined with dedicated monitoring and analysis is the key to success.

For making an ongoing technical analysis of the stock, you should program your disk for Auto Run to chart the indicators you find useful for assessing the technical status of the stock. The Auto Run procedure will enable you to make a quick assessment each time you update your data disk.

Exhibit 12.6 shows Omnicare's price history with a minimum complement of indicators useful for bottom determination. A study of the indicators shows no clear purchase point, so monitoring should continue.

As we have seen before, stocks that move in a sideways pattern often break out quickly to the upside or downside, sometimes without technical warning. As an aid to determining whether a move in price is large enough to be considered a breakout from the line pattern, the percentage change approach (discussed in Chapter Three) can be useful.

Using past price history as a guide, upper and lower limits are developed to establish an envelope about the smoothed price. Exhibit 12.7 shows how this is done. If the price breaks upward through the limit and technical indicators confirm the move as it is occurring, a purchase can be made.

INVESTING IN TEMPORARY UNATTRACTIVENESS

Distressed companies of a less troubled nature also offer opportunities for profit. Strategies involve finding short- or intermediate-term price bottoms on stocks that have been driven down to a level that is either technically unsustainable or fundamentally undervalued. The implementation procedure, provided in Exhibit 12.8, involves screening for the right stocks, monitoring and timing purchases.

The Wall Street Journal is probably the best source for finding companies with temporary problems. The "Heard on the Street" column often provides good information for using this

EXHIBIT 12.6 Omnicare, Inc.: Technical Analysis

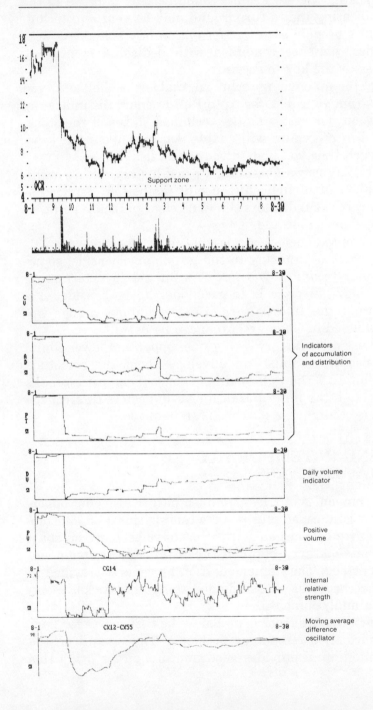

EXHIBIT 12.7   Percentage Change Envelope for Omnicare, Inc.

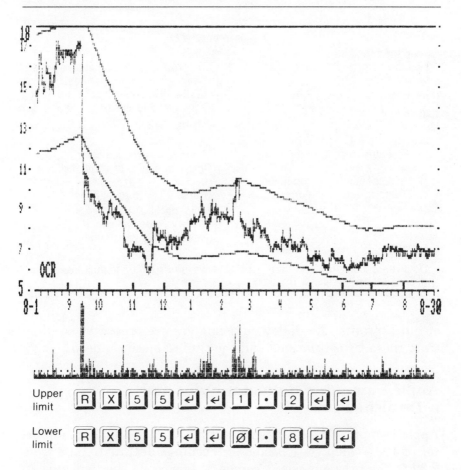

strategy, along with the "What's News" (Business and Finance) column on the first page. Dow Jones News/Retrieval (//DJNEWS) is another source. Chart books are typically less useful for this form of unattractiveness because it is difficult to tease out the difference between fluctuations due to unattractiveness and price movements from more permanent causes.

Like the chronically distressed companies in the previous section, the analysis of these stocks is very situation specific. The approach taken is either to buy at a price that makes the stock temporarily undervalued for an intermediate-term gain or to buy into a technical overextension in price for an attempt

---

EXHIBIT 12.8   Procedure for Investing in Temporarily
Unattractive Stocks

Procedure	Comments
Screen for candidates	Sources
Has the company's image been tarnished?	*The Wall Street Journal Investor's Daily,* Financial Magazines,
Does it look like a temporary problem?	//DJNEWS. (Chart books are not very useful for these stocks.)
Monitor	Controlled decline
Has the stock bottomed?	A/D indicators.
-Repeated decline to the same level.	Positive volume indicator.
	Internal relative strength. Difference
-Multiple month line formation.	oscillator.
-End to a rapid price drop.	Percent up, Percent down.
	"Panic" decline
	Daily volume indicator.
	Internal relative strength.
Time purchases	
Do divergences exist? A return from overextension? Indicator breakout?	Always use a stop to limit losses.

---

at quick profits. The following examples are presented to illustrate these two situations and the timing methods used.

Apple Computer: Softening Sales and a Tarnished Image

Apple Computer's earnings problems began in the fourth quarter of 1983 when they posted an earnings decline to 0.08 from 0.32 in the previous year's comparable period. The firm saw an improving situation the following year with earnings posting a strong rebound in the fourth quarter. However, in fiscal 1985 the entire computer industry fell on hard times, and Apple's earnings again suffered. During this troubled period, Apple closed manufacturing plants and laid off employees, further tarnishing its image but reducing its cost structure.

In 1985, a widely publicized management shake-up resulted in the resignation of the chairman and cofounder of the company, Stephen Jobs. The company's "dirty laundry" was allowed to hang in the open, rendering the company even more unattractive. From the beginning of the firm's earnings problems to their management difficulties, the stock dropped in price from over $60 to under $15 a share.

Despite all of these problems, the company was a going concern with numerous potential trigger mechanisms that could operate to improve the company's image and possibly propel the stock higher. The firm had over $300 million in cash with no long-term debt, making an acquisition a possibility. A new product could also provide a trigger along with improved earnings. If a bottom could be identified by technical analysis, the stock appeared to be worth buying.

Exhibit 12.9 shows the technical indicators used to identify the bottom. Their interpretation is similar to that in other examples in this chapter. The arrow in the price chart indicates a favorable buy point.

You may notice that the exhibit omits the accumulation/ distribution (AD) indicator and the daily volume indicator (DV), typically used in bottom determination. This is because Apple is traded over-the-counter, and only bid and asked prices are available. The two indicators mentioned require high, low, and close data for proper construction, so they are not appropriate for use on this or other over-the-counter issues.

When should a stock with this form of unattractiveness be sold? These stocks tend to be intermediate-term plays rather than long-run holds, although each situation has to be addressed on its own merits.

Toys "R" Us: An Example of a Blemish

In the last week of 1984, Toys "R" Us, Inc. announced that sales for the eight-week period that ended December 24 were up by 17 percent from the year before, but on a per store basis, sales were up only by 3 percent. The cause for the less than expected result was electronics sales, down by 47 percent from the year earlier (see Exhibit 12.10). On this news the stock plummeted, dropping by over *22 percent in one day*.

Unattractiveness of this kind, where the bad news that emerges is a decrease in positive expectations rather than an actual decline in earnings, frequently provides an opportunity for profit.

Rapid sell-offs in light of a blemish can often be timed for a

EXHIBIT 12.9 Apple Corporation: Technical Analysis

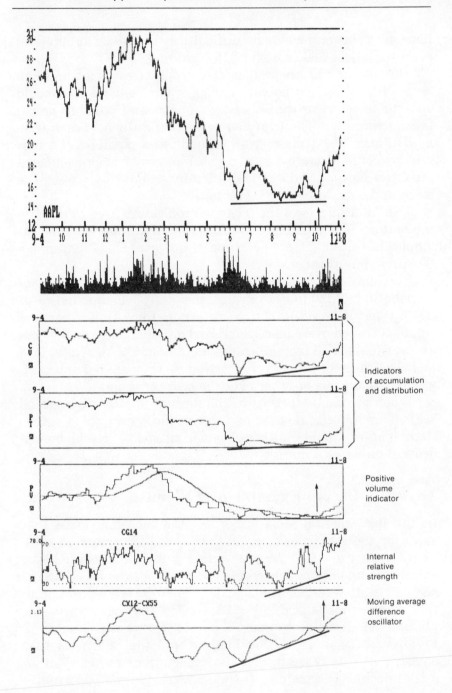

EXHIBIT 12.10 News about Toys "R" Us

4 THE WALL STREET JOURNAL
Friday, December 28, 1984

Toys 'R' Us Stock Plunges on News Of Holiday Sales

Big Drop in Electronics Area Hurt Results; Shares Fall $7.125 in Active Trading

By TOM BAKER
Staff Reporter of THE WALL STREET JOURNAL

ROCHELLE PARK, N.J.—Toys "R" Us Inc. said a big drop in electronics sales hurt its results for the Christmas selling season, and the toy maker's shares promptly tumbled $7.125 in active New York Stock Exchange trading.

The company, one of the first retailers to report for the holiday period, said sales for the eight weeks ended Dec. 24 rose 17% to $726 million from $621 million in the year-earlier period. But on a comparable-store basis, sales grew only 3%. In the past year, the retailer has added 41 toy and other stores for a current total of 216.

Norman Ricken, president and chief operating officer, said lower prices and reduced consumer spending halved sales of electronic products, with the volume falling to 9% of total sales. On a same-store basis, he said, electronics sales fell 47%. One analyst noted that the retailer has been "moving away" from electronics sales but said: "This was worse than expected."

After the announcement, Wall Street analysts began lowering their Toys "R" Us earnings estimates for fiscal 1985, ending Jan. 31, and the stock plunged to $40.25 in Big Board composite trading. It was the most active issue with volume of 2.5 million shares.

The Toys "R" Us news also dragged down other toy makers' stocks. Tonka Corp. fell $3, to $41.50, and Mattel Inc. dropped 50 cents, to $10.875, on the Big Board. On the American Stock Exchange, Hasbro Bradley Inc. fell $5.25 to $56.

Petrie Stores Corp., which holds 25% of Toys "R" Us, fell $2.50 to $33.25 on the New York exchange.

Daniel D. Barry, an analyst at Kidder, Peabody & Co., cut his Toys "R" Us earnings-per-share estimate for the year to $1.95 from $2.30 and lowered his fiscal 1986 projection to $2.55 from $2.90.

Sales of home computers were "down somewhat" while video games were "way off," Mr. Ricken said. Such products accounted for 18% of total sales in both the 1982 and 1983 Christmas seasons, he said.

Part of the weakness was attributed by Mr. Ricken to lower sale prices after manufacturers cut their prices. He added that last year's results were helped by increased volume as Texas Instruments Inc. ended production of home computers and dumped inventory on the market.

A Morgan Stanley & Co. analyst, Walter F. Loeb, said the Texas Instruments "closeouts had people standing in line." He said he continued to recommend Toys "R" Us stock, but he cut his per-share earnings estimates to $1.95 for fiscal 1985 and to $2.50 for fiscal 1986.

"In general," Mr. Ricken said, "the holiday retailing environment was characterized by a slowdown in consumer spending, combined with a highly promotional atmosphere."

Christmas sales were a record for the company, though "they were below our aggressive sales plan," Mr. Ricken said. He noted that sales of traditional toys continued strong. On a same-store basis, he said, sales of traditional toys climbed 14.6% from a year earlier.

Fiscal 1985 "will be another year of record sales and earnings for the company," but he declined to provide a profit estimate. For the first 11 months of fiscal 1985, total sales grew 28% to $1.59 billion.

A year earlier, total sales rose 26% in the Christmas selling season and 25% for the 11 months.

In fiscal 1984, ended Jan. 29, Toys "R" Us net income increased 44% to $92.3 million, or $1.62 a share, on a sales gain of 27% to $1.32 billion.

The company said that it opened 29 toy stores in the past year and that it plans to open an additional 40 to 45 toy stores in the coming year.

The Kids "R" Us operations "made substantial progress," Mr. Ricken said, and an additional 15 of the children's clothing stores will be opened next year, bringing the total to 25.

Sales rose 17 percent, the stock dropped over 22 percent in one day

EXHIBIT 12.11 Toys "R" Us: Technical Analysis

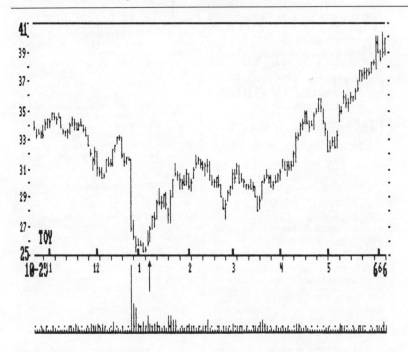

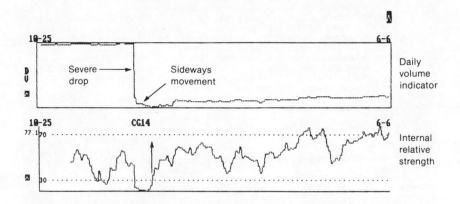

quick turnaround by using the daily volume indicator and the internal strength measure in combination. This is a high-risk strategy, so it should be attempted only with a very small portion of your capital during periods when the market is not in a prolonged decline.

EXHIBIT 12.12   Questions to Ask Yourself Before Purchasing
Stock in an Unattractive Company

Chronically troubled companies
   Have you monitored the company over a period of months?
   Have fundamentals stabilized?
   Do you have evidence of survivability?
   Is there a potential trigger mechanism?
   Has the price stabilized to a bottoming formation?
   Is there a technical indication of a price rise?
   Are you planning to use a small percentage of your investment capital?
   Have you chosen a selling price in the event that the purchase does not work
      out as planned?
Temporarily troubled companies
   Are you confident the tarnished image is based on temporary problems, or
      is it just the start of a long period of bad news?
   Is there a potential trigger mechanism?
   Is there evidence of a technical price bottom?
   Has the price begun to rise?
   Are you planning to use a small percentage of your investment capital?
   Have you chosen a selling price in the event that the purchase does not work
      out as planned?

Exhibit 12.11 shows the technical interpretation of the indicators with the buy point marked with an arrow. When the
price dropped on high volume and closed near the low for the
day, the daily volume indicator made a major move to the
downside and the internal relative strength indicator plunged
into overextended territory. After a few days, the total volume
dropped to normal levels and the daily volume indicator began
to move sideways, indicating that the panic condition had
played itself out. At the point marked by the arrow on the price
chart, the price reversed direction to the upside, volume increased, and the internal relative strength indicator broke up
through the overextended threshold, giving a buy signal.

SOME FINAL THOUGHTS ON INVESTING IN
UNATTRACTIVE STOCKS

Beginners in the stock market often find investing in unattractive stocks to be an attractive strategy because it operates in
harmony with the "buy low-sell high" philosophy that is so
easy to believe in. A few successful early trades made during a

bull market period may lead the investor to think it is an easy way to make money. In fact, investing in troubled companies is one of the most difficult ways to make money on a consistent basis and can result in devastating losses if precautions are not taken. As an aid in preventing a major loss in capital, Exhibit 12.12 offers a set of questions that should be asked and answered before making a purchase.

APPENDIX 12A: OMNICARE DATA

Omnicare S & P Fundamental Data

(S&P) 10/17/85   (OCR)   PAGE 1 OF 1
Omnicare, Inc.:: SUMMARY

Offers health care services to U.S.
hospitals, mainly thru management of
hospital pharmacies... sells medical
equipment & supplies... Lower hospital
occupancy rates and loss of 12
contracts with Amer. Medical Int'l hurt
1st 9 mos. '85 sales... but profit
comparisons should benefit from cost
controls, lower interest expense...
About 25% owned by Chemed.

(S&P) 10/17/85   (OCR)   PAGE 1 OF 1
Omnicare, Inc.

Outlook: '85 EPS expected at $0.40 vs.
'84's $0.26... $0.23 quarterly dividend
suspended in Oct. '84.

(S&P) 10/17/85   (OCR)   PAGE 1 OF 1
Omnicare, Inc.:: LINES

1984	Revs.	Profits
Hospital services...	48%	118%
Equipment/supplies...	52%	-18%

Tel.# 513-762-6666

(S&P) 11/08/85   (OCR)   PAGE 1 OF 1
Omnicare, Inc.

-------- EARNINGS PER SHARE --------

9 Mo Sep	.25
...Prev. Yr.	.54
Last 12 Mos	(.03)
P/E	n/m
5 Yr. Growth %	-60

(S&P) 11/08/85   (OCR)   PAGE 1 OF 1
Omnicare, Inc.

-------- DIVIDENDS PER SHARE --------

Rate	.....%
Yield	....%
Last Div.	.230
Ex-Date	08/17
PayDate	09/10/84

Omnicare S & P *(concluded)*

------ FINANCIAL OVERVIEW ------
------ FISCAL YEAR HISTORY ------

Fiscal Year Dec	EPS	Revenue	Net Income	Book Value Per Share
84	.26	211.8	2.6	6.31
83	1.69	200.0	17.6	7.47
82	1.46	202.7	15.2	6.95
81	1.21f	176.3	12.1	5.98

(Revenue and net income in millions)

------ MARKET ACTION ------

1984-85 Range	
High	10.50
Low	5.50

Average Daily Volume	24600
Beta	
Institutional Holdings	60%
Primary Exchange	NYSE

------ MARKET ACTION ------
------ CALENDAR YEAR HISTORY ------

Yr	High	Low	PE Range		Div
84	31.87	5.75	n/m	22.1	.69
83	49.50	27.75	29.3	16.4	.80
82	32.33	15.33	22.1	10.5	.44
81	17.00	13.00	14.0	10.7	.05

3-for-2, '83.

------ FINANCIAL OVERVIEW ------
------ BALANCE SHEET ------

Current Ratio	3.51
Long Term Debt	17.50
Shares	10.19
Report of	06/30/85

(Long term debt and Shares in millions)

Omnicare INVESTEXT Data

```
INVESTEXT  3/04/85      OCR                    PAGE   1 OF  1

Omnicare Inc. - Company Report
SMITH BARNEY, HARRIS UPHAM & CO., INC.
Hyman, L.R.

OMNICARE INC. (OCR - NYSE)

Price (3/1/85)                  7 7/8
52-Week Price Range          28-5 3/4
Dividend/Yield           (a) NONE
Shares (million)             10.2
S&P 500 (3/1/85)            183.45
EPS 1986E                   $0.60
EPS 1985E                   $0.35
EPS 1984A                   $0.26
Price/1985E                 22.5x
1985 P/E Relative to S&P 500  2.3x

(a) Dividend of $0.92 has been indefinitely suspended.
(-) Previous estimates were $0.50 for 1985 and $0.70 for 1986.
```

Outlook for 1985

     The sale of HPI should be concluded by late May so that HPI's
first quarter results will be included in Omnicare's earnings. Although
both Greene & Kellogg, and Inspiron are losing money at this time,
Greene & Kellogg should make money the rest of the year, while Inspiron
is expected to reach breakeven in the third quarter. Veratex is
continuing to meet both sales and earnings projections. The closure of
Inspiron's plant is likely to have a positive effect on that division's
margins. Even when sales were strong, the plant was significantly
underutilized, and operating costs swelled further when production
volumes began to decline. As a replacement, manufacturing operations
for respiratory disposable products have been established in Mexico
where low labor rates should improve Inspiron's standard costs. The
remaining services in the Hospital Services group, Labtronics,
MedCharge, and respiratory therapy, are growing at 20%-30% rates. By
paying off its debt, Omnicare should reduce this year's interest
expense by one-half compared to 1984. All totalled, earnings in 1985
could increase to $0.35 from $0.26, a 35% gain.
     The effect of HPI's sale on Omnicare's balance sheet will be to

     * ANALYST'S OPINION: NEUTRAL. The company is actively pursuing
acquisitions to reinvest the money received from the sale of HPI. We
would view these as critical indicators of the company's new long-term
strategy.

     * HPI Health Care Services, accounting for 44% of 1984 revenues,
was sold to Hospital Corporation of American for $35 million in cash.
The remaining businesses are still in a turnaround mode.

Omnicare Earnings Estimates

```
OMNICARE  INC
--FISCAL  YEAR  ENDS    12/85

EARNINGS  PER  SHARE  ESTIMATES
--MEAN      0.48
--HIGH      0.65
--LOW       0.35
NUMBER  OF  ANALYSTS    6
P/E  RATIO  (ESTIMATED  EPS)    12.63
PAST  EARN  PR  SH  ESTIMATES  (MEAN)
--WEEK  AGO      0.48
--13  WEEKS  AGO    0.50
--26  WEEKS  AGO    0.52
--------------------------------------
PRESS  RETURN  FOR  NEXT  PAGE




OMNICARE  INC
--FISCAL  YEAR  ENDS    12/86

EARNINGS  PER  SHARE  ESTIMATES
--MEAN      0.53
--HIGH      0.60
--LOW       0.45
NUMBER  OF  ANALYSTS    5
P/E  RATIO  (ESTIMATED  EPS)    11.32
PAST  EARN  PR  SH  ESTIMATES  (MEAN)
--WEEK  AGO      0.53
--13  WEEKS  AGO    0.54
--26  WEEKS  AGO    0.54
```

Omnicare Media General Fundamental Data

```
OMNICARE INC
-FUNDMNTL DATA- 11/08/85    (553)
REVENUE              (1)
-LAST 12 MOS $198 MIL
-LAST FISCAL YEAR $212 MIL
-PCT CHANGE LAST QTR -2.2%
-PCT CHANGE YR TO DATE -8.0%
EARNGS 12MOS -$0.4N MIL
EARNINGS PER SHARE
-LAST 12 MONTHS -$0.03
-LAST FISCAL YEAR $0.26
-PCT CHANGE LAST QTR      NE
-PCT CHANGE FY TO DATE -53.7%
-PCT CHANGE LAST 12MOS -100.0%
-FIVE YR GROWTH RATE      NC


DIVIDENDS            (2)
-CURRENT RATE $0.00
-CURRENT RATE YIELD 0.0%
-5 YR GROWTH RATE 0.0%
-PAYOUT LAST FY 0%
-PAYOUT LAST 5 YEARS      NE
-LAST X-DVD DATE 02-17-83
RATIOS
-PROFIT MARGIN 17.8%
-RETURN ON COMMON EQUITY      NE
-RETURN ON TOTAL ASSETS      NE
-REVENUE TO ASSETS 107%
-DEBT TO EQUITY -382%
-INTEREST COVERAGE 0.0X
-CURRENT RATIO 1.5


SHAREHOLDINGS        (3)
-MARKET VALUE $48 MIL
-LTST SHR OUTSTND 20,052,000
-INSIDER NET TRADING 0
-SHORT INTEREST RATIO 0.5 DYS
-FISCAL YEAR ENDS 12 MOS
```

Omnicare Dow Jones News

```
N   OCR          01/01 AB   1/2
/OCR                        /TNM        /
    11/06 OMNICARE INC. SELLS HOSPITAL
(DJ) SALES DIVISION FOR CASH, NOTES
    CINCINNATI -DJ- OMNICARE INC. SAID
IT HAS SOLD ITS HOSPITAL SALES DIVISION
TO NORTHWEST MEDICAL SPECIALTIES INC.
EFFECTIVE SEPT. 1   1985.
    IT DIDN'T DISCLOSE A PRICE BUT SAID
THE AMOUNT INCLUDED CASH AND NOTES.
    THE COMPANY SAID THE HOSPITAL SALES
DIVISION IS BEING SOLD AT AN AFTER-TAX
LOSS OF ABOUT $500 000   OR ROUGHLY THE
ESTIMATED OPERATING LOSS THAT THIS
BUSINESS WOULD HAVE INCURRED FOR THE
REMAINDER OF 1985.   AS A RESULT   THE
COMPANY SAID THE SALE OF THE DIVISION
WILL HAVE LITTLE IMPACT ON ITS RESULTS
FOR THE FOURTH QUARTER AND FULL YEAR.
    THE HOSPITAL SALES DIVISION
DISTRIBUTES HOSPITAL RESPIRATORY
EQUIPMENT AND RELATED DISPOSABLE
```

SELECTED REFERENCES

BAND, RICHARD. *Contrary Investing.* New York: McGraw-Hill, 1985.

BOLAND, JOHN. "Troubled Companies." *Sylvia Portor's Personal Finance*, October 1985, pp. 64–69.

GRACE, WILLIAM. *The Phoenix Approach.* New York: Bantam Books, 1984.

LADERMAN, JEFFREY. "A Fund Manager Who Favors the Out-of-Favor." *Business Week*, October 29, 1984, p. 95.

MORGENSON, GRETCHEN. "Hidden Values in High-Tech Rejects." *Money*, May 1984, pp. 151–54.